EMBODIED COGNITION

Embodied cognition often challenges standard cognitive science. In this outstanding introduction, Lawrence Shapiro sets out the central themes and debates surrounding embodied cognition, explaining and assessing the work of many of the key figures in the field, including George Lakoff, Alva Noë, Andy Clark, and Arthur Glenberg.

Beginning with an outline of the theoretical and methodological commitments of standard cognitive science, Shapiro then examines philosophical and empirical arguments surrounding the traditional perspective. He introduces topics such as dynamic systems theory, ecological psychology, robotics, and connectionism, before addressing core issues in philosophy of mind such as mental representation and extended cognition.

Including helpful chapter summaries and annotated further reading at the end of each chapter, *Embodied Cognition* is essential reading for all students of philosophy of mind, psychology, and cognitive science.

Lawrence Shapiro is Professor in the Department of Philosophy at the University of Wisconsin—Madison, USA. His research currently focuses on the issues and debates around embodied cognition. He is editor (with Brie Gertler) of *Arguing About the Mind* (2007), also available from Routledge.

New Problems of Philosophy
Series Editor: José Luis Bermúdez

The *New Problems of Philosophy* series provides accessible and engaging surveys of the most important problems in contemporary philosophy. Each book examines either a topic or theme that has emerged on the philosophical landscape in recent years, or a longstanding problem refreshed in light of recent work in philosophy and related disciplines. Clearly explaining the nature of the problem at hand and assessing attempts to answer it, books in the series are excellent starting points for undergraduate and graduate students wishing to study a single topic in depth. They will also be essential reading for professional philosophers. Additional features include chapter summaries, further reading and a glossary of technical terms.

Also available:

Fiction and Fictionalism
R.M. Sainsbury

Analyticity
Cory Juhl and Eric Loomis

Physicalism
Daniel Stoljar

Noncognitivism in Ethics
Mark Schroeder

Moral Epistemology
Aaron Zimmerman

Forthcoming:

Self Knowledge
Brie Gertler

Semantic Externalism
Jesper Kallestrup

Perceptual Consciousness
Adam Pautz

Consequentialism
Julia Driver

Philosophy of Images
John Kulvicki

Folk Psychology
Ian Ravenscroft

Praise for *Embodied Cognition*

"*Embodied Cognition* provides a balanced and comprehensive introduction to the embodied cognition movement, but also much more. Shapiro is careful to sift empirical results from broader philosophical claims, and the concise, simple arguments for cognition's embodiment that he articulates will help advanced students and researchers assess the diverse literature on this hot topic in cognitive science."
Robert A. Wilson, *University of Alberta, Canada*

"*Embodied Cognition* is the first of its kind—a beautifully lucid and even-handed introduction to the many questions and issues that define the field of embodied cognition. Psychologists, neuroscientists, computer scientists, and philosophers should jump on this book. It promises to set the terms of debate in this exciting new enterprise for years to come."
Elliott Sober, *University of Wisconsin—Madison, USA*

"Embodied Cognition is sweeping the planet and Larry Shapiro has just written the first comprehensive treatment of this exciting and new research program. This book is now and for years to come will be unquestionably the best way for students and researchers alike to gain access to and learn to evaluate this exciting, new research paradigm in cognitive science."
Fred Adams, *University of Delaware, USA*

"A must read for those who support the embodied program, those who question it, and those who are just trying to figure out what the heck it is. It's definitely on the reading list for my course in embodied cognition."
Arthur Glenberg, *Arizona State University, USA*

"*Embodied Cognition* is an outstanding introduction to this increasingly important topic in cognitive science. Written in a clear and lively style, with a critical approach, it is a strong contender for the most useful introductory text on any topic in all of cognitive science, and a genuine contribution to the scientific and philosophical literature on embodied cognition."
Kenneth Aizawa, *Centenary College of Louisiana, USA*

For my daughters
Thalia and Sophia,
comedy and wisdom.

EMBODIED COGNITION

Lawrence Shapiro

LONDON AND NEW YORK

First published 2011
by Routledge
2 Park Square, Milton Park, Abingdon, Oxon OX14 4RN

Simultaneously published in the USA and Canada
by Routledge
711 Third Avenue, New York, NY 10017, USA

Routledge is an imprint of the Taylor & Francis Group, an informa business

Typeset in Joanna and Scala Sans by
Bookcraft Ltd, Stroud, Gloucestershire

British Library Cataloguing in Publication Data
A catalogue record for this book is available from the British Library

Library of Congress Cataloging in Publication Data
Shapiro, Lawrence A.
Embodied cognition / by Lawrence Shapiro.
p. cm. — (New problems of philosophy)
Includes bibliographical references (p.) and index.
1. Philosophy of mind. 2. Cognitive science. 3. Cognition. I. Title.
BD418.3.S47 2010
121—dc22

2010008572

ISBN 10: 0-415-77341-5 (hbk)
ISBN 10: 0-415-77342-3 (pbk)
ISBN 10: 0-203-85066-1 (ebk)

ISBN 13: 978-0-415-77341-6 (hbk)
ISBN 13: 978-0-415-77342-3 (pbk)
ISBN 13: 978-0-203-85066-4 (ebk)

Printed and bound in the United States of America by
Edwards Brothers Malloy on sustainably sourced paper

CONTENTS

List of illustrations   xi

Acknowledgments   xiii

Introduction: Toward an Understanding of Embodied Cognition   1

Chapter 1 Standard Cognitive Science   **7**

1.1   Introduction   7

1.2   Newell and Simon's General Problem Solver   7

1.3   Descriptive Frameworks   9

1.4   Back to General Problem Solver   12

1.5   Sternberg's Analysis of Memory Scanning   14

1.6   The Computational Vision Program   20

1.7   The Solipsistic View   26

1.8   Summary   27

1.9   Suggested Reading   27

Chapter 2 Challenging Standard Cognitive Science   **28**

2.1   Introduction   28

2.2   Gibson's Ecological Theory of Perception   29

2.2.1 Structure in Light   30

2.2.2   The Brain's Role in Vision   35
2.3   Hatfield's Noncognitive Computationalism   37
2.4   The Connectionist Challenge   41
2.5   Summary   48
2.6   Suggested Reading   50

Chapter 3 Conceptions of Embodiment   **51**
3.1   Introduction   51
3.2   Varela, Thompson, and Rosch: World Building   52
3.3   Thelen: Representation *Lite*   56
3.4   Clark: Thinking with the Body   61
3.5   Summary   67
3.6   Suggested Reading   69

Chapter 4 Embodied Cognition: The Conceptualization Hypothesis   **70**
4.1   Conceptualization   70
4.2   Linguistic Determinism   71
4.2.1   The Linguistic Determination of Time Conceptions   72
4.2.2   Sex With Syntax   74
4.3   Concepts and Conceptions   76
4.4   Testing Hypotheses   79
4.5   The Embodiment of Color   81
4.6   Embodiment and Metaphor   86
4.6.1   Putting Lakoff and Johnson's Conceptualization Thesis to the Test 89
4.6.2   Second-Generation Cognitive Science   91
4.7   The Symbol Grounding Problem   95
4.8   The Indexical Hypothesis   98
4.8.1   Perceptual Symbols   98
4.8.2   Affordances   100
4.8.3   Meshing   101
4.8.4   Experimental Evidence for the Indexical Hypothesis:
        The Action-Sentence Compatibility Effect   102
4.9   Assessing the Indexical Hypothesis   104
4.9.1   Meaningfulness in Amodal Representation   104
4.9.2   Sensibility Judgments   106
4.9.3   Standard Cognitive Science and the Action-Sentence
        Compatibility Effect   107
4.10   The Body in the Brain   108

4.11   Summary   112
4.12   Suggested Reading   113

Chapter 5 Embodied Cognition: The Replacement Hypothesis   114

5.1   Replacement   114
5.2   Dynamical Systems   116
5.3   Van Gelder's Dynamical Hypothesis   118
5.4   Explaining Watt's Centrifugal Governor   119
5.5   The Dynamics of Cognition   124
5.6   Categorical Perception from a Dynamical Perspective   127
5.7   Do Dynamical Explanations Explain?   133
5.8   Replacement and Robotics   137
5.9   The Case for Representational Skepticism   141
5.9.1   Are There Representations in the Centrifugal Governor?   144
5.9.2   The Argument for Representational Skepticism   149
5.9.3   The "They're Not Representations!" Argument against
        Representations   154
5.10   Summary   156
5.11   Suggested Reading   157

Chapter 6 Embodied Cognition: The Constitution Hypothesis   158

6.1   Constitution   158
6.2   A Quick Refutation of Constitution? The Argument from
        Envatment   161
6.3   Sensorimotor Theories of Perceptual Experience   164
6.4   Constituents and Causes   170
6.5   More Than Just a Gesture?   173
6.6   Coupling and Constitution   175
6.7   Extending Cognition Further   178
6.8   The Coupling-Constitution Fallacy   179
6.9   A Parity Argument for Constitution   182
6.10   Against Parity – Meeting The Marks of the Cognitive   184
6.10.1 Mark I: Intrinsic Content   186
6.10.2 Mark II: Causal Processes   189
6.11   Extended v. Embedded Cognition   193
6.12   Whose Action is it Anyway?   197
6.13   Summary   199
6.14   Suggested Reading   200

Chapter 7 Concluding Thoughts   **201**

7.1   Back to the Decision Tree   201

7.2   Conceptualization and Standard Cognitive Science   202

7.3   Replacement and Standard Cognitive Science   206

7.4   Constitution and Standard Cognitive Science   208

7.5   The Final(?) Score   210

Glossary   211
Notes   221
References   227
Index   235

ILLUSTRATIONS

Figures

1.1 The steps by which GPS transforms L1 into Lo set beside the reasoning of a human subject   13

1.2 The mean reaction time for searches that yield a negative response will have the same slope for both exhaustive and self-terminating searches because the test stimulus must, in both cases, be compared to all items on the memorized list.   17

1.3 The mean reaction time (RT) for positive and negative responses increases linearly with the size of the positive set and the time for positive and negative responses follows the same slope.   17

1.4 Programs for both exhaustive and self-terminating searches   18

1.5 An infinite number of distinct shapes can project the same image on the retina   20

1.6 The pencil will appear to the left of the doorknob when the left eye is closed   21

1.7 With just one object, there is no difficulty finding the point on the right retina that matches point 1 on the left retina   23

1.8 The correct matches of three objects labeled with the same
     numbers on each retina   23
1.9 Empty circles show false targets that are consistent with various
     mappings of points on the left retina with points on the right retina   24
2.1 The ambient optic array is defined as the light at a point of
     convergence in this case the eyes of the seated observer   31
2.2 As the observer stands and moves forward, the ambient optic
     array is transformed into a new array   32
2.3 The table on the left and the structure on the right project identical
     shapes on the retina of the observer   33
2.4 A connectionist net with an input layer consisting of seven nodes,
     a hidden layer with four nodes, and an output layer of two nodes   44
4.1 Examples of a horizontal and a vertical spatial prime   73
5.1 Watt's centrifugal governor   121
5.2 The environment, body, and nervous system are each dynamical
     systems and are in continuous interaction   125
5.3 As the agent moves back and forth, it must try to center itself
     beneath the falling circle, but avoid the falling diamond   128
5.4 Catch performance and avoidance performance as a function of
     the initial position of the falling object   129
5.5 Control systems   140
6.1 The line of sight shifting from a straight line to a point above it;
     and the retina depicted as a flat surface   166
6.2 Self-portrait of Rob Wilson in which the computational process
     of multiplying two numbers involves constituents within the
     head and both within and outside the head   192

Plate

5.1A–C   Steady-state horizontal velocity fields   *This colour plate appears
                                                          between pp. 146 and 147*

Every effort has been made to trace copyright holders but this may not have been possible in all cases. Any omissions brought to the attention of the publisher will be remedied in future editions.

ACKNOWLEDGMENTS

Many people have helped me with this project – so many that I'm sure to forget to acknowledge some of you and for that I apologize. For commenting on chunks or entire drafts of earlier manuscripts I'm grateful to: Fred Adams, Ken Aizawa, Randy Beer, Andy Clark, Juan Comesaña, Malcolm Forster, Brie Gertler, Art Glenberg, Chuck Kalish, Vanessa Simmering, Elliott Sober, and Peter Vranas. This book began while I was a resident at the Centre for the Foundations of Science, at the University of Sydney, and I'm grateful to Mark Colyvan for making this possible and to members of the philosophy department there for making me feel so welcome. Thanks also to José Bermúdez for recruiting me for this project, and to Tony Bruce and Adam Johnson of Routledge for seeing it through. Also a great help in preparing the manuscript were Sarah Mabley, Nick Morgan, and Judith Oppenheimer. Finally, I'm grateful to the University of Wisconsin for providing me with research assistance during the summers in which I researched and wrote the manuscript.

Madison, Wisconsin
January 2010

INTRODUCTION

TOWARD AN UNDERSTANDING OF
EMBODIED COGNITION

Embodied cognition is often presented as an alternative or challenger or "next step in the evolution of" standard cognitive science. The aim of this book, broadly, is to introduce and develop the central themes of embodied cognition. A secondary goal is to build on this discussion so as to assess more accurately the relationship between embodied cognition and standard cognitive science.[1] Those not familiar with standard cognitive science are unlikely to appreciate the significance of this goal, but significant it is. At stake in the debate between proponents of embodied cognition and standard cognitive science are nothing less than profound and entrenched ideas about what we are — about what it means to be a thinking thing. Simply put, whether minds are as standard cognitive science describes them, or are instead embodied in ways yet to be explicated, *matters* to our understanding of who and what we are.

Fortunately, despite the weightiness of these issues, the road toward their resolution wends its way past interesting and remarkable attractions. Among these attractions are philosophical theories of mind, logical questions concerning the validity of arguments, methodological issues regarding hypothesis testing, and scientific research spanning areas of psychology, robotics, and dynamical systems theory. The case for embodied cognition has drawn on behavioral curiosities, such as the use of hand gestures when solving problems in spatial reasoning; engineering marvels like robotic creatures that navigate through cluttered environments, collecting soda cans for recycling; the discovery of neurons that fire not only when subjects initiate their own actions, but also in response to their observing others performing the same actions; psychological experiments that show how certain bodily motions can help or hinder performance on cognitive tasks; and flights of fancy such as spherical beings living in weightless environments. The sheer variety of evidence for embodied cognition makes an evaluation of its prospects especially fascinating, but also sometimes frustrating.

One sort of challenge arises when trying to direct these disparate sources of support toward a single, unified theory of embodied cognition. In fact, I think that an effort to cover all the evidence under a single umbrella is not likely to succeed. But I also think that this is not presently a major cause for concern. Embodied cognition, at this stage in its very brief history, is better considered a *research program* than a well-defined theory. The motivation for this distinction becomes clear when contrasting embodied cognition to standard cognitive science.

The domain of standard cognitive science is fairly clearly circumscribed (perception, memory, attention, language, problem solving, learning). Its ontological commitments, that is, its commitments to various theoretical entities, are overt: cognition involves algorithmic processes upon symbolic representations. Furthermore, cognitive scientists employ standardized methodological practices for revealing features of these algorithmic processes and representations, such as reaction time experiments, recall tasks, dishabituation paradigms, and so on. Moreover, these ontological commitments, methodological practices, and subject matters serve to constrain each other, helping to clarify even more precisely the nature of cognitive science. If, for instance, language learning were to turn out to be inexplicable in terms of rules and representations, this would be something of a catastrophe for cognitive science. The result would force cognitive science to reconsider its subject matter, or to re-examine its ontological commitments, or to question its methodological tools.[2] On the other hand, the fact that a phenomenon is best understood in terms of algorithms and representations, or reveals itself readily to time-tested methodological practices, is good reason to include it within the domain of cognitive science.

As a *research program*, embodied cognition exhibits much greater latitude in subject matter, ontological commitment, and methodology than does standard cognitive science. The domain of embodied cognition certainly overlaps that of cognitive science, but seems also to include phenomena that might hold little interest for a cognitive scientist (e.g. the development of stepping behavior in infants (Thelen and Smith 1994)). In pace with this greater diversity in subject matter are more roughly defined theoretical commitments and fewer uniform methodological practices. In sum, the ties between subject matter, ontological commitments, and methodology are, within embodied cognition, longer and looser than they are within standard cognitive science. Yet, this state of affairs is no reason to dismiss or disparage embodied cognition. Today's research program may be tomorrow's reigning theory. However, embodied cognition's status as a research program does invite special caution when considering claims that it might replace or supersede standard cognitive science.

A profitable way to investigate embodied cognition, and the one I shall take, involves concentration on those several themes that appear to be prominent in the body of work that is often seen as illustrative of embodied cognition. This strategy has the advantage of postponing hard questions about "the" subject matter, ontological commitments, and methods of embodied cognition until more is understood about the particular interests and goals that embodied cognition theorists often pursue. This approach might show embodied cognition to be poorly unified, suggesting that the embodied cognition label should be abandoned in favor of several labels that reflect more accurately the distinct projects that have (misleadingly) been clumped together under a single title. Alternatively, it might show that, in fact, there are some overarching commitments that bring tighter unity to the various bodies of work within embodied cognition that seem thematically only loosely related.

Naturally, depending on how matters end up, embodied cognition's challenge to standard cognitive science can also take several directions. If embodied cognition in fact comprises several enterprises that are better distinguished, then the result may be that some of these pose genuine challenges to cognitive science whereas others do not. Perhaps some of the various research projects are better conceived as welcome accessories, in some sense, to standard cognitive science, or as non-competing alternative means of investigating cognitive phenomena. On the other hand, if embodied cognition indeed amounts to a nicely unified area of research, its relationship to cognitive science is likely to be easier to evaluate because one would need to compare just two disciplines rather than what might have turned out to be several or many disciplines. This comparison, ideally, would reveal whether embodied cognition and cognitive science are offering competing explanations of the same phenomena, are targeting different *explananda* altogether, or, perhaps most happily, are extending different but compatible viewpoints from which to understand the mind.

Three Themes of Embodiment

Although, as I have mentioned, the sea of topics that receives discussion within the field of embodied cognition is vast, there are three general themes that tend to float to its surface.[3] I will present these themes now, but will have much more to say about them in later chapters when considering the weight of evidence and argument in support of each. In drawing attention to these three themes, I mean only to imply that they are very prominent in the embodied cognition literature. Others might wish to emphasize additional themes,[4] but I do believe that failure to attend to the three I have selected would result in an incomplete and probably inaccurate description of embodied cognition. Furthermore, in distinguishing three themes, I do not intend to imply that they are incompatible. Some work in embodied cognition might support more than one. However, when this is the case, often one theme receives stronger support than another. This is a reason to insist on a separation of these themes, even if in fact some experimental results or engineering successes or biological discoveries lend support to all three at once.

The themes, in no particular order of importance, are these:

1   CONCEPTUALIZATION: The properties of an organism's body limit or constrain the concepts an organism can acquire. That is, the concepts on which an organism relies to understand its surrounding world depend on the kind of body that it has, so that were organisms to differ with respect to their bodies, they would differ as well in how they understand the world.

2   REPLACEMENT: An organism's body in interaction with its environment replaces the need for representational processes thought to have been at the core of cognition. Thus, cognition does not depend on algorithmic processes over symbolic representations. It can take place in systems that do not include representational states, and can be explained without appeal to computational processes or representational states.

3   CONSTITUTION: The body or world plays a constitutive rather than merely causal role in cognitive processing. To illustrate this distinction in a different context, consider constitutive versus causal roles of oxygen. Oxygen is a *constituent* of water, because water consists in atoms of oxygen conjoined with atoms of hydrogen. On the other hand, oxygen might be a *cause* of an explosion, because without the presence of oxygen, the fuse would not

have ignited. Likewise, according to the Constitution claim, the body or world is a constituent of, and not merely a causal influence on, cognition.

Clarifying and motivating these themes requires a fair amount of work, but if I am right that these themes capture the direction of much of the work in embodied cognition, then this is work that serves the promised goal of developing an understanding of embodied cognition. It is also work that will facilitate an explication and evaluation of embodied cognition's claim to usurp standard cognitive science.

However, before diving into the business of discussing Conceptualization, Replacement, and Constitution, an account of the nature of standard cognitive science, as well as a sense of what a challenge to standard cognitive science might look like, will be tremendously useful. This is because embodied cognition is without question a reaction to standard cognitive science, and thus one good way to approach embodied cognition is in light of an appreciation of the science against which it is moving. But what I have been calling standard cognitive science has faced other challenges. Among the more prominent are those from the ecological school of psychology that owes its creation mainly to J. J. Gibson, and connectionism, which came into its own in the late 1980s. A discussion of both ecological psychology and connectionism will serve two goals. First, it will provide an example of how a challenge to cognitive science might proceed. Just as importantly, it will provide an underpinning to the three themes around which I will organize discussion of embodied cognition, for both Gibson's theory of perception as well as features of connectionism have inspired many of the research projects in which embodied cognition theorists engage.

A Meta-Theme

One final word is in order before embarking on the project I have described above. Although the point is already fairly explicit in comments I have made so far, it is worth highlighting. Throughout the following presentation of embodied cognition, we should never lose sight of the need to understand exactly what embodied cognition is trying to explain. A decision tree is useful for displaying the issues at hand. The most basic question at the root of the tree is this:

Do embodied cognition and standard cognitive science have the same subject matter?

From there, the tree proceeds as follows.

> If yes: Do they offer competing explanations of this subject matter?
> If yes: Scientists should adopt the better explanation.
> If no: The explanations are redundant or complementary in some sense, and scientists should feel free to pursue either.
> If no: Are the distinct subject matters worth pursuing?
> If yes: All is well – embodied cognition and standard cognitive science both have their uses.
> If no: Either embodied cognition or standard cognitive science should be abandoned.

According to this tree, the two main branches lead to similar possibilities: either embodied cognition and standard cognitive science are both worthwhile pursuits or only one of them is. That is, regardless of whether embodied cognition and standard cognitive science share a subject matter, it can turn out that embodied cognition and standard cognitive science are both valuable or that only one of them is. The interesting questions, then, and the ones that will motivate many of the discussions to follow, are why embodied cognition and standard cognitive science are both worthwhile – is it because they offer different perspectives on the same subject matter, or is it because they shed light on different subject matters – or why one of embodied cognition and standard cognitive science should be eliminated – is it because one offers a better explanation of a shared subject matter, or is it because the subject matter of one is, for some reason, not worthy of investigation?

In this introductory chapter I have tried to motivate and set some ground rules for an investigation of embodied cognition. The project I propose to undertake requires familiarity with what I have been calling standard cognitive science. The business of the next chapter is to supply this background.

Suggested Reading

Shapiro, L. (2007). "The Embodied Cognition Research Programme," *Philosophy Compass* 2: 338–46.

Shapiro, L. (forthcoming). "Embodied Cognition," in E. Margolis, R. Samuels, and S. Stich (eds.) *Oxford Handbook of Philosophy and Cognitive Science* (Oxford: Oxford University Press).

1

STANDARD COGNITIVE SCIENCE

1.1 Introduction

What I shall be calling standard cognitive science has roots in a number of disciplines, including computer science, psychology, linguistics, and philosophy. Because my interest is less in tracing the history and development of standard cognitive science than in providing an idea of its theoretical and methodological commitments,[1] I propose to introduce some important ideas within standard cognitive science through discussion of several exemplary research projects. These projects are (i) Allen Newell and Herbert Simon's General Problem Solver; (ii) Saul Sternberg's work on memory recall; and (iii) computational analyses of perception. Despite the diverging explanatory targets of these three enterprises, they are remarkably similar in how they conceive of the *process* of cognition and in their commitments to how cognition should be studied.[2]

1.2 Newell and Simon's General Problem Solver

In the early 1960s, Newell and Simon created a computer program they called *General Problem Solver* (GPS),[3] the purpose of which was not only to solve logic problems, but to solve them in the same way that a human being would (1961; 1976). That is, the program was intended to replicate the internal thought processes that a human being undertakes when solving a logic problem. As such, just as Newell and Simon claim, GPS is a theory of human thinking (1961: 2016). Examination of some of the details of GPS thus provides us with a picture of what the mind looks like, for a cognitive scientist.

Because the purpose of GPS was to replicate the stages involved in human problem solving abilities, its assessment required that the problem solving procedure it used be tested against the problem solving procedures that human beings use. Thus, Newell and Simon asked human subjects to "think out loud" while solving logic problems. For instance, a subject was shown a logical expression, such as

(1) R & (~P ⊃ Q)

and was asked to transform this expression into

(2) (Q ∨ P) & R.

The subject was also provided with various transformational rules of the sort that would be familiar to anyone with a background in simple sentential logic. No interpretation was offered for the logical expressions. Subjects merely had to identify the rules that would transform one syntactical object into another and then apply them.

Obviously, transformations of expressions like (1) into others like (2) are a simple matter for any suitably programmed general purpose computer. As Newell and Simon describe, a computer

> is a symbol-manipulating device, and the symbols it manipulates may represent numbers, words, or even nonnumerical, nonverbal patterns. The computer has quite general capacities for reading symbols or patterns presented by input devices, storing symbols in memory, copying symbols from one memory location to another, erasing symbols, comparing symbols for identity, detecting specific differences between their patterns, and behaving in a manner conditional on the results of its processes.
>
> (1961: 2012)

The hypothesis that motivates GPS as a theory of human thinking is that thought processes are just like those processes that take place within a computer:

We can postulate that the processes going on inside the subject's skin – involving sensory organs, neural tissue, and muscular movements controlled by the neural signals – are also symbol-manipulating processes; that is, patterns in various encodings can be detected, recorded, transmitted, stored, copied, and so on, by the mechanisms of this system.

(1961: 2012)

Finally, given that human thought processes are computational, i.e. involve the manipulation of symbols, GPS provides a model of human cognition just in case the kinds of computations it uses to solve a problem are similar to the computations that take place in a human brain, where these latter computations become visible through Newell and Simon's "thinking out loud" experimental protocol.

1.3 Descriptive Frameworks

Before proceeding further with discussion of GPS, it is worth pausing to consider Newell and Simon's claim that there are symbols and symbolic operations within the brain. In one sense, this must seem obviously false. If one could peer into a brain as it is solving a logic problem, nowhere would one see letters and connectives, or symbols of any sort. What, then, does it mean to say that human thought is symbolic, or that the processes that take place in a human brain are analogous to those that occur in a computer?

One quick way to defuse this worry is to point out that as hard as it is to find symbols in the brain, finding them in a computer is no easier. Open up a computer and you are no more likely to find letters, numerals, and other symbols than you are when you dissect a brain. But, of course, computers are symbol processors par excellence. So, where are the symbols?

The way out of this mystery requires the recognition that the world and its contents lend themselves to different kinds of descriptions which, despite their differences, may nevertheless be consistent with each other. For instance, the coffee mug sitting dangerously close to my keyboard is a collection of molecules. But it is also a mass of ceramic. And, of course, it is also a coffee mug. It is also my coffee mug. All of these descriptions are true of the object on my desk, and the truth of one description does not exclude the truth of the others. Precisely why the various descriptions of my mug "fit," why they are each true of it, turns out to be a difficult issue. Part of the explanation will involve chemical facts, another part facts from materials science, still other parts of the explanation will depend on facts about, perhaps, the individuation of artifacts and the social contracts that justify certain property rights.

Although obvious on reflection, the idea that items in the world can be described in distinct but compatible ways opens the door to the possibility that neurons, or their activities, can be symbolic. Whether they are symbolic, i.e. whether the description of them as being symbolic is true, depends on whether they meet the criteria for something's being a symbol. The question, "What makes a part of the brain a symbol?" is, in effect, like the question, "What makes this mass of ceramic a coffee mug?" Some masses of ceramic are not coffee mugs (e.g., the ones to which power lines are attached), but some are. And, while perhaps there may be no certain answer to the coffee mug question in all cases, often enough we have sufficient grasp of the meaning of "coffee mug" to say of a mass of ceramic that it is or is not a coffee mug. If the ceramic is shaped cylindrically, is closed on the bottom and open on top, is impermeable, has a handle, is within a certain range of sizes, then this is usually a good enough reason to describe the ceramic object as a coffee mug.

Now consider the sorts of things that are properly described as symbols. Words are symbols, as are numerals, but why are they symbols? The answer to this question has little to do with the physical material out of which words and numerals are constructed. Words and numerals can be scratches of graphite on paper, illuminated pixels on a computer monitor, or light bulbs on a billboard. The conditions for being a symbol do not, apparently, mandate that symbols be made of any particular stuff, but instead focus on *functional* criteria, on criteria about what symbols must do. Among the relevant conditions seem to be these. First, symbols can "stand for" or represent things. The words "lamb" and "αρνι'" are both symbols, and both happen to represent the same wooly object. Similarly, the numeral "12" represents the number 12, as does "XII." And while "X" can represent the number 10, when found on a map it can represent the location of a treasure chest. A band of gold, when worn on a finger, can also be a symbol, representing, as it often does, devotion.

In addition to having a representational function, sometimes symbols can be combined with others in accordance with various rules, such that new symbols result.[4] The words "Mary," "had," "a," "little," and "lamb" can be combined, according to rules of English grammar, to form the sentence "Mary had a little lamb," which represents the state of affairs of Mary having a little lamb. The rules that permit the combination of those symbols to form that sentence also prohibit the combination that results in "Mary a lamb little had." Similarly, rules of arithmetic permit the construction "12 + 45 = 57" but do not allow "= 12 45 + 57." These obvious points suffice to illustrate a feature of some symbols: they may be combined according to rules that dictate which operations upon them are "legal."[5]

The fact that some symbols display combinatorial properties is especially important for understanding standard cognitive science, for the idea that thinking involves operations on words in a "language of thought" (Fodor 1975) has become mainstream. On this view, thoughts are sentences in an internal language, and reasoning involves combining and manipulating the components of these sentences, just as one might do when performing syllogisms in a natural language. As we shall see in the next chapter, some critics of standard cognitive science have sought to undermine the idea that ⌈cognition relies on linguistic structures.⌉

The combinatorial power of symbols, as well as their capacity to represent or stand for objects apart from themselves, are, of course, not intrinsic features of the symbols on their own. Scratches of graphite on paper or sequences of on- and off-currents in a computer gain these capacities in virtue of some sort of controller — a human agent, perhaps, or, in a computer, a central processing unit (CPU). A series of on- and off-currents becomes a string of symbols because the CPU treats it as such — combining and transforming members of the series according to a rule-prescribed grammar, which in turn may be encoded in electrical current that the CPU has been designed to read.[6]

A final point about symbols, and one that will loom larger in the context of some theories of embodied cognition, is that their relation to their content — to what they represent — is often arbitrary. The word "lamb" represents lamb, but not because the word and the animal are similar. The word is neither white, nor fluffy, nor best when grilled on a spit and served with lemon. Likewise, the particular assignments of numerals to numbers that is present today was by no means inevitable (Romans represented numbers with different symbols than those we use). The numeral "6" might as well have been used to represent 5 as it was to represent 6. Of course, this point about the arbitrary connection between symbols and their contents raises a hard question about how one thing can come to be about something it does not resemble, but we needn't wade into those troubled waters for the purposes at hand.[7]

We have available now enough pieces to make sense of Newell and Simon's speculation that⌈the human brain is, like a computer, a symbol-manipulating device.⌉The elements of the brain are, under one description, neurons, but, if they behave in a certain way, they might also be symbols. And, Newell and Simon suppose, (some) neurons do behave in such a way that a description of them as symbols is true. Neurons, singly or in a group, represent – they stand for things in the world in virtue of processes that begin with the stimulation of the body's sensory organs. Presumably neurons that code for one concept can be combined with neurons coding for different concepts so that these neurons together form some new concept. The fact that neurons do not resemble what they stand for does not speak against their representational capacity. The word "lamb," recall, looks nothing like a lamb, and this should be enough to ease doubts about the possibility that neurons might represent.

1.4 Back to General Problem Solver

Newell and Simon believe that GPS simulates the activity that goes on in the brains of human beings when they solve logic problems. We saw above that the presence of symbolic processes in the brain is a theoretical possibility. If neurons have the functional characteristics of symbols, this justifies treating them as symbols. But what is the evidence that human beings solve logic problems in the same way that GPS does? Let's return to the logic problem that Newell and Simon asked a subject to solve. The subject was asked to transform

(1) R & (~P ⊃ Q)

into

(2) (Q ∨ P) & R.

To perform this task, the subject was provided with a collection of transformation rules, and the experimenter would write on a blackboard the results of the application of the rule that the subject chose. Because the subject would talk through his reasoning, the steps the subject takes in solving the problem could be compared to the algorithm GPS used to solve the same problem. Figure 1.1 presents a sample of Newell and Simon's data.

Comparing the computer trace with the subject's protocol, Newell and Simon thought, made possible an assessment of the accuracy of GPS as a model of human reasoning. And although they were quick to acknowledge that different subjects might solve the problem in different ways, and that there were some uncertainties in the procedure by which human language was matched against the computer trace, in general, they thought, "the

Computer Trace	Protocol of Subject
Lo (Q ∨ P) & R	I'm looking at the idea of
L1 R & (~P ⊃ Q)	reversing these two things now.
GOAL 1 TRANSFORM L1 INTO Lo	*Thinking about reversing what?*
GOAL 2 CHANGE POSITION IN L1	
GOAL 3 APPLY R1 TO L1 [A&B→B&A]	The R's ... then I'd have a
PRODUCES L2 (~P ⊃ Q) & R	similar group at the beginning
	but that seems to be ... I could
GOAL 4 TRANSFORM L2 INTO Lo	easily leave something like that
GOAL 5 CHANGE POSITION IN LEFT L2	'til the end, except then I'll ...
GOAL 6 APPLY R2 TO LEFT L2	
[A ⊃ B → ~B ⊃ ~A]	*Applying what rule?*
PRODUCES L3 (~Q ⊃ P) & R	
	Applying, ... for instance, 2.

Figure 1.1 The steps by which GPS transforms L1 into Lo set beside the reasoning of a human subject. Formulae in brackets are the rules of transformation. Italicized sentences are the experimenter's questions to the subject. From Newell and Simon (1961: 2015).

evidence suggested that GPS provides a rather good approximation to an information-processing theory of certain kinds of thinking and problem-solving behavior. The processes of thinking can no longer be regarded as completely mysterious" (1961: 2016).[8]

Naturally, the success of GPS as a theory of human problem solving depends heavily on the kind of problem the subject is asked to solve. As Newell and Simon note, transforming one logical formula into another requires a *means-end analysis*. In such an analysis, a starting position is well defined, as is a goal position toward which subjects are asked to move. Moreover, there are determinate rules that guide the steps the subject can take in moving from the starting position to the goal. Other tasks that reveal their solutions to means-end analyses include games like chess, checkers, and the Tower of Hanoi puzzle. Furthermore, in addition to problems in logic, problems in geometry and computer programming might also be represented in terms of an initial state, a goal state, and a collection of determinate rules that decide a path from the former to the latter. If GPS removes some of the mystery involved in human thinking, as Newell and Simon suggest, then programs for playing chess and checkers, proving geometric theorems, and designing algorithms all promise to remove even greater portions of this mystery (1961: 2016). On the other hand, one might wonder how useful GPS might be as a guide to *all* of cognition, given the very constrained nature of problems to which means-end analyses are suited.

For the purpose of distilling from this discussion of GPS some of the main theoretical commitments of cognitive science, the points to highlight are these. First, the cognitive scientist is interested in describing the "inner workings" of the mind. This marks a swing from behaviorist psychology, which was largely content to leave unopened the black box inside of which are the mechanisms that translate stimulus into response. Cognitive science is focused precisely on these mechanisms. Second, these mechanisms, cognitive scientists assume, are computational. That is to say they involve operations over symbols, where these symbols are entities with a representational content and an arbitrary connection[9] to that which they represent. The goal of cognitive science is to describe the programs that determine the behavior of the mind's computational mechanisms. Finally, the domain of cognitive science will include those tasks an organism performs by use of a means-end analysis, because such tasks open themselves readily to a computational solution.

1.5 Sternberg's Analysis of Memory Scanning

Once one conceives of mental processes as computational – as consisting of operations over symbolic representations – certain questions about how the mind works, and particular approaches to its investigation, become quite natural. This is not to say that similar questions or methods did not exist prior to the computational turn that marked the advent of standard cognitive science, but surely the rise of the computer in the 1950s and 1960s brought with it a fresh vocabulary and an assemblage of computationally inspired ideas that influenced and encouraged a way of doing psychology. Sternberg's work on memory scanning in the late 1960s is a splendid illustration of this point.

Consider the following task. A subject is asked to memorize a list of numerals, where this list might contain from one to six members. The subject is then exposed to a single numeral and asked whether the numeral appears in the list that she has memorized. If the subject judges that the numeral is among those on the list, she pulls a lever to indicate a positive response. If the subject does not remember the numeral as being among those on the list, she pulls a different lever to indicate a negative response.

Although this task is limited to the recall of numerals, it is plausible that the same processes of memory retrieval are operative in less artificial domains. For instance, perhaps your routine is to jot down a list of items to purchase before going to your grocery store, only to find, once you arrive there, that you have left the list on the kitchen table (this is my routine). Fortunately, there were only six items on the list and you are pretty sure you remember them all. As you cruise the aisles, you pick up the products whose names you wrote on the list. To be sure, there are differences in this task and the one Sternberg designed. Rather than being exposed to a test stimulus and then judging whether it is on the list, you have to actively seek the items on the list. Nevertheless, the task does require the retrieval of information, and the basic structure of the task does seem quite similar. For instance, you may even end up standing in front of the corn meal in the baking aisle and asking yourself "Did I need corn meal?" In answering this question, you might find yourself mentally scanning your shopping list.

But now suppose you wanted to write a computer program for performing Sternberg's retrieval task. There are two search algorithms you might consider. The first, *exhaustive search*, requires that you compare the test stimulus to each item on the memorized list before rendering the judgment that the stimulus is or is not a member of the list. The second search strategy, *self-terminating search*, requires that the test stimulus be compared with each item on the memorized list until a positive match is made, at which point the search terminates.

The exhaustive search strategy appears to be less efficient. To return to the shopping analogy, what would be the point, once having picked up the corn meal, of going through a mental rehearsal of the rest of the items on the list if corn meal was the second item to pop into your head? Once you retrieve the information that corn meal is something you wish to purchase, why bother asking whether the item in your hand is also chicken stock, or parmesan cheese, and so on?

Still, the appearance of inefficiency, although an argument against programming a computer with an exhaustive search strategy of retrieval, is no argument that human memory retrieval is self-terminating rather than exhaustive. Discovering which search strategy human memory scanning employs was the focus of Sternberg's groundbreaking investigations.

Sternberg reasoned that both search strategies require a fixed amount of processing time independent of the number of items on the list that subjects were asked to memorize. For example, regardless of whether there are two or six items on the list that a subject has memorized, the task of deciding whether the test stimulus is a member of the list requires that the subject first identify the test stimulus (e.g. identify the stimulus as a "4" or as an "8"), and also that the subject formulate a response (positive or negative) and decide on the appropriate action (pulling one lever or the other). Importantly, all mental operations take some amount of time to perform, but the identification of the test stimulus, and the performance of a response will take the same amount of time, regardless of differences in the size of the list that the subject must encode and whether the search is exhaustive or self-terminating.

The next assumption Sternberg made concerned the effect that list size has on the time required for a subject to complete the retrieval task. The subject's *reaction time* is the amount of time that elapses from the moment that the subject is exposed to the test stimulus until the moment that the subject pulls a response lever. Because both exhaustive and self-terminating search strategies assume that the searching process is serial, i.e. that a comparison between the test stimulus and the items in memory proceeds consecutively, then an exhaustive search and a self-terminating search should take the *same* amount of time, for a given list size, if the test stimulus is *not* a member of the memorized list. For instance, if the subject has memorized the list {2, 5, 3, 8} and then is exposed to the test stimulus {4}, the subject must compare the test stimulus to every member of the list before being in position to render a negative judgment. Thus, test stimuli that are not in the memorized list fail to distinguish between exhaustive and self-terminating searches.

Crucially, however, subjects' reaction times will differ depending on whether they use an exhaustive or self-terminating search when the test stimulus *does* match a member of the memorized list. Reaction time for an exhaustive search, on a given list size, will remain the same for positive and negative results because in both cases the test stimulus must be compared to every member of the list. A positive response resulting from a self-terminating search, however, will take on average only half the time that an exhaustive search requires. This is because, on average, a self-terminating search will end at the middle of the memorized list, for a given list size. Thus, subjects' reaction time for positive responses *does* provide evidence for distinguishing exhaustive from self-terminating search strategies. Figure 1.2 presents graphical representations of the differences in reaction time that each search strategy predicts.

The data Sternberg actually collected are presented in Figure 1.3.

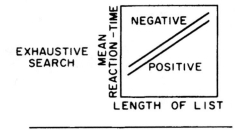

EXHAUSTIVE SEARCH

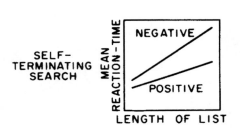

SELF-TERMINATING SEARCH

Figure 1.2
The mean reaction time for searches that yield a negative response will have the same slope for both exhaustive and self-terminating searches because the test stimulus must, in both cases, be compared to all items on the memorized list. The slope of the reaction time for positive responses will be half the slope of the time for negative responses because, on average, a self-terminating search will yield a match by the time it reaches the midpoint of the memorized list. From Sternberg (1969: 427).

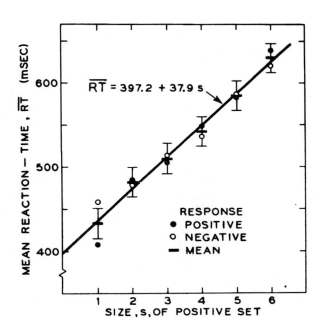

Figure 1.3 The mean reaction time (RT) for positive and negative responses increases linearly with the size of the positive set and the time for positive and negative responses follows the same slope. The slope intercepts the y-axis at approximately 400msec, which is the time required to identify the test stimulus and organize a response. From Sternberg (1969: 426).

These data show, as expected, that response times are longer depending on the number of digits the subject was asked to memorize. But, remarkably, they also show that the curve fitting positive responses has the same slope as the curve fitting negative responses. This evidence favors the hypothesis that subjects conducted an exhaustive search, comparing the test stimulus against each member of the memorized set regardless of whether a match is discovered prior to reaching the end of the set.

Sternberg's work is notable for a number of reasons. First, like Newell and Simon's hope for GPS, Sternberg's experimental design is intended to yield information about the "program" that underlies a cognitive task. Indeed, it is not difficult to describe a program for each of the alternative search strategies that Sternberg considers. Figure 1.4 does just this.

In assuming that something like one of the programs below explains human memory retrieval, Sternberg's conception of cognition shares much with Newell and Simon's. Item recognition is described in a manner that permits a means-end analysis of its operations. There is a determinate

Exhaustive Search Program	*Self-terminating Search Program*
TASK: IDENTIFY WHETHER TEST STIMULUS (TS) IS MEMBER OF POSITIVE SET (PS)	TASK: IDENTIFY WHETHER TEST STIMULUS (TS) IS MEMBER OF POSITIVE SET (PS)
GOAL 1: COMPARE TS TO FIRST MEMBER OF PS. GOTO GOAL 2.	GOAL 1: COMPARE TS TO FIRST MEMBER OF PS. GOTO GOAL 2.
GOAL 2: IF MATCH IS POSITIVE THEN PRODUCE "P" AND GO TO GOAL 3. IF MATCH IS NEGATIVE THEN GO TO GOAL 3.	GOAL 2: IF MATCH IS POSITIVE THEN POSITIVE RESPONSE. HALT. IF MATCH IS NEGATIVE THEN GO TO GOAL 3.
GOAL 3: COMPARE TS TO NEXT MEMBER OF PS. GO TO GOAL 2. IF NO MORE MEMBERS THEN GO TO GOAL 4.	GOAL 3: COMPARE TS TO NEXT MEMBER OF PS THEN GO TO GOAL 2.
GOAL 4: IF P THEN POSITIVE RESPONSE. IF NO P THEN NEGATIVE RESPONSE. HALT.	

Figure 1.4 Programs for both exhaustive and self-terminating searches.

starting point – exposure to the test stimulus – and a determinate ending point – a positive or negative response. Thought involves the manipulation of symbols, where, in this case, the symbols represent items that the subject has memorized, as well as a test stimulus. Symbols must be stored in something like a data buffer, just as they would be in a computer, and item-recognition requires that the symbol which represents the test stimulus be compared to the symbols stored in the memory buffer.

The experimental methodology Sternberg uses to uncover the mind's programs is perhaps more reliable than the method of "thinking out loud" on which Newell and Simon depend. There are doubtless many layers of cognition that intervene between the unconscious processes involved in problem solving and the verbalization of thought that Newell and Simon used as evidence for the veracity of GPS. In as much as this is true, support wanes for the claim that GPS reveals something of the "mysteries" of thinking processes or, at any rate, of the mysteries of thinking processes that take place unconsciously.

In contrast, Sternberg's reaction time measure does apparently reflect unconscious cognitive processing. The measure shows that comparison of the test stimulus with items of the memorized set takes approximately 38msec per item. This is quite fast. So fast, Sternberg claims, that "the scanning process seems not to have any obvious correlate in conscious experience. Subjects generally say either that they engage in a self-terminating search, or that they know immediately, with no search at all, whether the test stimulus is contained in the memorized list" (1969: 428). This comment raises another problem with Newell and Simon's procedure. Apparently subjects' conscious reports can in fact misrepresent the unconscious processes that occur in cognitive activity. Whereas Sternberg's subjects might claim to have engaged in a self-terminating search (or no search at all!), the reaction time measurements tell a different story. Given this inconsistency between the subjects' reports and the experimental data, there is further reason to doubt that the reports on which Newell and Simon rely accurately reflect the unconscious processes that humans use when solving logic problems.

In sum, although the methods that Newell and Simon and Sternberg use to reveal the nature of human thought differ, they share a commitment to the idea that cognitive processes are computational processes. A cognitive task can be made the subject of a means-end analysis, broken into regimented stages, and solved through the application of determinate procedures to symbolic representations.

1.6 The Computational Vision Program

So far we have seen examples of standard cognitive science in the areas of problem solving and memory recall. An examination of how a cognitive scientist approaches the study of vision will round out our discussion of standard cognitive science. Cognitive scientists conceive of the visual system as a special kind of problem solver. The question vision theory addresses is this: how does stimulation on the retina become a perception of the world? Cognitive scientists also emphasize the apparent fact that the patterns of stimulation on the retina do not carry enough information on their own to determine a unique visual perception. The visual system must therefore embellish visual inputs, make assumptions, and draw inferences in order to yield a correct solution, i.e. an accurate description of the visual scene. Richard Gregory, a vision scientist whose work pre-dates but anticipates much of the current work in computational vision, makes this point nicely: "Perceptions are constructed, by complex brain processes, from fleeting fragmentary scraps of data signaled by the senses" (1972: 707). Research in computational vision consists mainly in describing the problems that vision must solve and in devising algorithms that suffice to transform "fleeting fragmentary scraps of data" into our rich visual world.[10]

To have a better sense of the magnitude of vision's task, consider Figure 1.5.

The retina is a concave surface, like the inside of a contact lens, and so the pattern of light projecting onto it is roughly two-dimensional. Figure 1.5 illustrates that surfaces differing in size and shape can project identical patterns of light in two dimensions. Somehow, the visual system

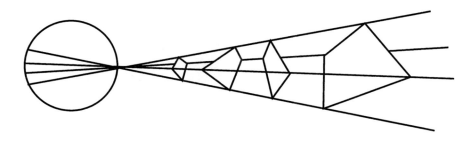

Figure 1.5 An infinite number of distinct shapes can project the same image on the retina.

must identify which one of an infinite number of possible surfaces is the actual cause of a given retinal image. And, whereas the laws of optics make possible a computation of the two-dimensional image that a given surface will produce on the retina, the inverse calculation – from image to external surface – is impossible. Vision, in a sense, must do the impossible. It must do *inverse* optics.

Yet, of course, vision is largely successful. The task of vision becomes tractable, computational vision theorists argue, because certain facts about the world can be exploited to reduce the number of possible visual descriptions of the world from many to one.[11] By building into their algorithms rules that represent these real-world constraints, the nut of inverse optics might be cracked. Marr and Poggio's work on stereo vision is a paradigm in this respect. When a pair of eyes fixate on a nearby object, the object will reflect light to a point on each retina. However, often the positions of these points on the two retinas are not the same. If it were possible to lay the left retina atop the right, you would find that the elements of the image on the left retina do not all rest on top of the same elements of the image on the right retina.[12] This fact is easy enough to confirm (Figure 1.6).

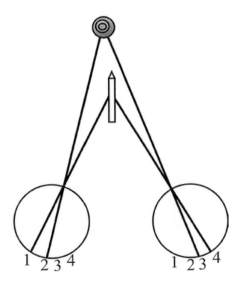

Figure 1.6 The pencil will appear to the left of the doorknob when the left eye is closed, and to the right when the right eye is closed. Both the pencil and the doorknob project to different points on the two retinas. The distance between corresponding image points on the two retinal images (e.g., between 1 and 4 and 2 and 3) is the degree of disparity.

If you hold a pencil at arm's length between you and a more distant object, perhaps a doorknob, and alternately close one eye and then the other, you will notice that if the pencil appears to the left of the doorknob when viewing it through the right eye, it may appear to the right of the doorknob when viewing it through the left eye. This shows that the location of the image of the pencil relative to the image of the doorknob is not in the same position on each retina. In Figure 1.6, points 1–4 on the left and right retinas mark corresponding locations. Thus, the pencil appears at location 1 on the left retina, but at a different location (4) on the right; the doorknob appears at location 2 on the left but at 3 on the right. The distance between corresponding points on the two images is called the degree of disparity.[13] Because the distance between points 1 and 4 is greater than the distance between points 2 and 3, the image of the pencil has a greater degree of disparity than the image of the doorknob.

That disparity information can be used to compute relative depth is well known. The calculation is actually quite simple, relying on some basic trigonometry and requiring nothing more than information about the degree of disparity (measured in either radians or arc seconds), the distance between the eyes, and the angle of the lines of sight. However, *recovering the necessary information for the calculation is not at all simple. The problem is that the visual system must be able to match the points of an image on one retina with points of the image on the other retina in order to identify the precise degree of disparity. Thus, imagining the pattern of light on each retina to be like a picture, the visual system must be able to determine for each point on picture 1, which point on picture 2 is its match.

To understand why this task is far from trivial, consider first the simplest case of matching. Figure 1.7 shows a visual scene comprising just a single object. There is no difficulty finding which point on the right retina matches point 1 on the left retina, for there is only one contender. In Figure 1.8, there are now three objects, each projecting points on the left and right retinas.

Given the relative distances of the objects, the correct matches are those shown: point 1 on the left with point 1 on the right, 2 with 2, and 3 with 3. But do not let the obviousness of these matches lead you to believe that they are the only possible ones. Indeed, point 2 on the left retina might as well be matched with point 1 on the right, and point 3 on the left might just as well be matched with point 2 on the right. As Figure 1.9 illustrates, there are, in addition to the three correct matchings, six incorrect matchings (1–2; 1–3; 2–1; 2–3; 3–1; 3–2) that all lead to what Marr and Poggio (1976) describe as *false targets*.

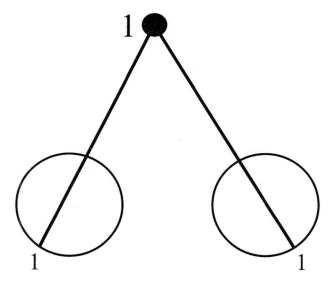

Figure 1.7 With just one object, there is no difficulty finding the point on the right retina that matches point 1 on the left retina (note, "1" represents the object, not a location on the retina).

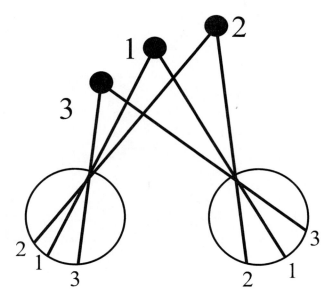

Figure 1.8 The correct matches of three objects labeled with the same numbers on each retina.

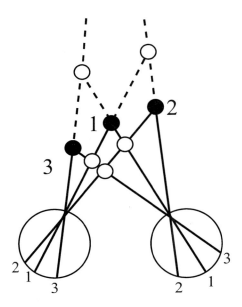

Figure 1.9 Empty circles show false targets that are consistent with various mappings of points on the left retina with points on the right retina. There is a sixth false target not drawn in the figure but which would fall at the intersection of the topmost dashed lines.

The problem, as the figure shows, is that wherever lines of sight intersect, there is a possible object (remember, the visual system does not yet "know" the distance of the objects, so it cannot know where to "end" a line of sight). Each possible object accounts for each possible match (1 with 1, 1 with 2, 1 with 3, 2 with 1, and so on). The visual system needs to figure out which of the n^2 possible objects are the n actual objects responsible for the images on the retinas. Within the larger context of developing a computational theory of visual processes, the detection of corresponding points on the two retinal images is treated as a kind of "sub-routine" that must be performed as an early step toward the goal of visual perception. The stages are as follows: first detect corresponding points, then compute disparity, then compute depth.

In response to this problem of identifying corresponding points on each retinal image, Marr and Poggio (1976) developed an algorithm that made use of two assumptions about the physical world that were then implemented as rules within the algorithm. The first assumption was that each point on a retinal image corresponds to exactly one point in the physical world. Because this is true, each point on the left retina must correspond to exactly one point on the right retina, yielding the first rule:

(R1) Uniqueness: there is just one disparity value for each point on a retinal image.

The second assumption was that surfaces in the world tend to be cohesive rather than diffuse (i.e., more like solids than clouds) and are generally smooth, so that points on a surface near to each other tend to lie along the same plane (i.e., surfaces are more likely to have smooth discontinuities than they are to be like a tire tread). From this assumption the second rule follows:

(R2) Continuity: disparity will typically vary smoothly.

Together, these rules constrain the space of possible solutions, preventing errant matches and zeroing in on the correct ones.

The details of the algorithm are complicated,[14] but familiarity with them is not necessary for present purposes. The salient points are these. Computational theories of vision constitute a dominant approach to explaining vision in standard cognitive science. Like the other examples of cognitive science we have seen, vision is conceived as involving a series of stages, each of which involves procedures with well-defined initial and end states. While we have been examining just one such procedure, the derivation of depth from disparity, vision researchers have taken a computational approach to a range of other visual processes. As Rosenfeld, a computer vision scientist, describes: "A variety of techniques have been developed for inferring surface orientation information from an image; they are known as 'shape from X' techniques, because they infer the shape of the surface ... from various clues ... that can be extracted from the image" (1988: 865). Some of these techniques compute shape from information about shading, or shape from motion, or shape from texture. In each case, information on the retina marks the starting point, assumptions about the world are encoded as rules that constrain the set of possible solutions,[15] and then an algorithm is devised that takes as input a symbolic representation of features on the retina[16] and produces as output a symbolic description of the physical world. As with problem solving and memory scanning, the guiding idea is that vision is a computational task, involving the collection and algorithmic processing of information.

1.7 The Solipsistic View

A final aspect of standard cognitive science, related to its computational commitments, is important to highlight before closing this chapter. When using a computer, you strike keys or insert devices into USB drives that provide input to various programs – word processors, spread sheets, graphics editors, and so on. These programs perform various operations on the inputs, eventually displaying the results as outputs that you are free to use as you choose. The computational processes in this description of events take place in the temporal space between the receipt of inputs and the display of outputs. All the "action," so to speak, begins and ends where the computational processes touch the world. The cause of the inputs and the effect on the world that the outputs produce are, from this perspective, irrelevant for purposes of understanding the computational processes taking place in the space between input and output. Who is typing on the keyboard, the truth of what he or she is typing, and what this person does with the resulting outputs simply makes no difference to how the program works or to how one should go about describing how the program works. This is the sense in which computational processes are solipsistic: give them their inputs and the rest of the world makes no further difference to them.

But insofar as cognitive processes are computational, many cognitive scientists endorse a similarly solipsistic attitude toward cognition (e.g. Fodor 1980; Stich 1983; Segal 1989; Egan 1991; 1992). They tend to draw the boundaries of *cognition* at the same place that a computer scientist might draw the boundaries of *computation* – at the points of interface with the world. Holyoak, for instance, asserts that "[t]he central focus of psychology concerns the information processing that intervenes between sensory inputs and motoric outputs" (1999: xxxix). And Hurley describes this same idea more vividly, drawing from it the solipsistic consequence:

> If perception is input from the world to the mind and action is output from the mind to the world, then the mind as distinct from the world is what the input is to and the output is from. So, despite the web of causal relations between organisms and environments, we suppose the mind must be in a separate place, within some boundary that sets it apart from the world.[17]
>
> (1998: 1–2)

Simply put, cognition is computation, computation operates over symbols, symbols begin with inputs to the brain and end with outputs from the brain, and so it is in the brain alone that cognition takes place and it is with the brain alone that cognitive science need concern itself.

This solipsistic perspective often reflects itself in the methods and controls cognitive psychologists use when collecting data. Unlike cognitive ethologists, who emphasize the importance of studying their non-human subjects in ecologically valid settings, i.e. environments of the sort that the subjects normally inhabit – cognitive psychologists will typically exert efforts to insulate their subjects from their normal environments. The hope is that in a carefully controlled laboratory setting it becomes possible to discover precisely which features of the world are encoded for use in a particular cognitive task, and what effect these features have on cognitive performance. Rather than roaming a noisy and distraction-laden environment, subjects are thus often seated in front of a computer monitor, focusing their attention on a very deliberately constructed set of stimuli, performing a task for which they may have received special training or instruction. They are, in a sense, passive recipients of stimulation that has been especially designed to elicit information about cognitive algorithms located exclusively in their brains. Embodied cognition, we shall see, resists the idea that cognition is solipsistic, and so rejects the idea that subjects are passive receivers of stimulation.

1.8 Summary

An examination of some paradigm work in standard cognitive science reveals commitments to a computational theory of mind, according to which mental processes proceed algorithmically, operating on symbolic representations. Cognitive tasks have determinate starting and ending points. Because cognition begins with an input to the brain and ends with an output from the brain, cognitive science can limit its investigations to processes within the head, without regard for the world outside the organism.

1.9 Suggested Reading

Dawson, M. (1998). *Understanding Cognitive Science* (Malden: Blackwell Publishers, Inc.).

Fodor, J. (1980). "Methodological Solipsism as a Research Strategy in Cognitive Psychology," *Behavioral and Brain Sciences* 3: 63–73.

Haugeland, J. (ed.) (1981). *Mind Design*, 1st ed. (Cambridge: MIT Press).

Pinker, S. (1997). *How the Mind Works* (New York: W. W. Norton & Company, Inc.).

Von Eckardt, B. (1995). *What is Cognitive Science?* (Cambridge: MIT Press).

2

CHALLENGING STANDARD COGNITIVE SCIENCE

2.1 Introduction

In the previous chapter we examined some work that exemplifies what I have been calling *standard cognitive science*. From this we extracted a few ideas and methods that are, in a loose sense, defining features of cognitive science. I say "loose sense" because I do not believe that there are necessary and sufficient conditions that a body of research must meet for it to count as cognitive science. Nevertheless, cognitive science, no less than other sciences like physics or biology, has a roughly circumscribed subject matter that it approaches from a fairly distinctive perspective by way of methods that are specially designed to shed light on its problem space. We saw that cognitive scientists typically view cognitive processes as computational. Commensurate with this view is the idea that cognition consists in the manipulation of symbols, where these manipulations often involve the application of rules for the purpose of deriving conclusions that go beyond the information contained in the input stream. Because cognitive operations begin with the receipt of symbolic inputs and end with the production of symbolically encoded outputs, the subject matter of cognitive science lays nestled between the peripheral shells of sensory organs and motor systems, making possible an investigation of cognition that needn't concern itself with understanding the cognizer's environment nor with examining the interactions between the two.

Given this assemblage of commitments, there might be several ways to go about challenging or questioning cognitive science. In this chapter I will consider two prominent approaches to cognition that are explicit in their antagonism toward the computational ideas that form the core of standard cognitive science. The reason to do this is twofold. First, because embodied cognition is often presented as an alternative to cognitive science, and, just as often, as *superior* in a number of ways, an examination of how an alternative to cognitive science might look and how a challenge to cognitive science might proceed will prove beneficial. The second reason to consider challenges to standard cognitive science is more bound to the particular two rivals we will be studying: J. J. Gibson's ecological theory of perception and connectionist accounts of cognition. Embodied cognition, as we shall see in the coming chapters, has incorporated rather extensively a variety of insights emerging from research in both ecological psychology and connectionism. Taking time now to develop an understanding of Gibson's work as well as some basic principles of connectionism will pay dividends later when we turn our attention more directly toward embodied cognition.

2.2 Gibson's Ecological Theory of Perception

The quickest route to Gibson's theory of perception is to see it as a repudiation of the idea that the visual system confronts an inverse optics problem. Recall that cognitivist theories of perception suppose the stimuli for perception to be impoverished. Because the retinal image underdetermines the shape of the surface that causes it, shape information must be derived from the sum of retinal information together with various assumptions about the structure of the world. In the discussion of stereo vision, we saw that the computation of relative depth from disparity information required assumptions about the uniqueness of the location of objects and the tendency of objects to be cohesive and their surfaces smooth. Without the addition of these assumptions, information on the retinal image is insufficient to determine facts about relative depth. In these cases and others, perception is conceived as an inferential process – reconstructing a whole body from a bare skeleton.

Gibson denies the inadequacy of perceptual inputs. Of course, it can be demonstrated mathematically that an infinite number of differently shaped surfaces can produce a single retinal image (see Figure 1.5). Hence, Gibson cannot be denying that the retinal image is by itself insufficient to provide knowledge of one's visual surroundings. Instead, Gibson denies that the retinal image is the proper starting point for vision. Rather, the inputs to vision are various *invariant* features of structured light, and these features can be relied on to specify unambiguously their sources. Gibson takes his research to show

> that the available stimulation surrounding an organism has structure, both simultaneous and successive, and that this structure depends on sources in the outer environment ... The brain is relieved of the necessity of constructing such information by *any* process ... Instead of postulating that the brain constructs information from the input of a sensory nerve, we can suppose that the centers of the nervous system, including the brain, resonate to information.
>
> (1966: 267)

There are two ideas in this passage that require careful attention. The first concerns what it means to say that the stimulation around an organism is structured; the second has to do with the idea that the brain doesn't need to process sensory stimuli in order to obtain information, but need only *resonate* to the information already within the stimulation.

2.2.1 *Structure in Light*

Most of the light that enters our eyes, unless we are looking at stars or the moon, is either diffused light in the atmosphere above us or light reflected from the surfaces of objects surrounding us. Diffused light has very little structure. Its intensity might change as one shifts one's eyes from the center of the sky to the horizon, but this variation must count as a minor bit of structure when compared to the structure present in reflected light. Different surfaces, depending on their textures and colors, will reflect different kinds of light. Consider, for instance, the light reflected from a recently plowed field. In the morning sun, the shadowed troughs will reflect less light than the exposed crests. This difference in the intensity of the reflected light creates structure that in turn reveals something about its source – the light will contain the information that the surface is not smooth but is instead corrugated. In contrast, light reflected from the surface of a still pond will have a very different structure – a structure characteristic of smooth and flat surfaces.

Now imagine that you are sitting in a chair in the middle of a room. Light from the surfaces around you converges on your eyes. This light will have a structure corresponding to discontinuities in the room's surfaces. Gibson calls the light present as a result of diffusion and reflection as it converges on a point of observation, the *ambient optic array*. The ambient optic array will have structure as a result of the arrangement of surfaces surrounding the point of observation. The orientation of surfaces, their color, texture, relationships to each other, and other facts will create angular pyramids of light, the boundaries of which correspond (typically) to the edges of surfaces. Figure 2.1 illustrates an ambient optic array.

Surface properties determine the boundaries of the pyramids of light in the array. The top and bottom of the window, for instance, will reflect light of an intensity that differs from the intensity of the light reflected from the tree outside the window. Similarly, the light reflecting from the tabletop differs in quality from the light the floor reflects, creating discontinuities in the light that reaches the observer's eyes.

Now consider what happens to the ambient optic array when the observer stands up and takes a step forward. Figure 2.2 shows how the observer's motion transforms the array.

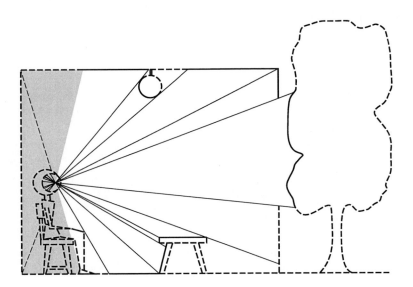

Figure 2.1 The ambient optic array is defined as the light at a point of convergence, in this case the eyes of the seated observer. The optic array has a structure determined by the layout of reflecting surfaces. The dark area represents features of the array not currently available to the observer. From Gibson (1979: 71).

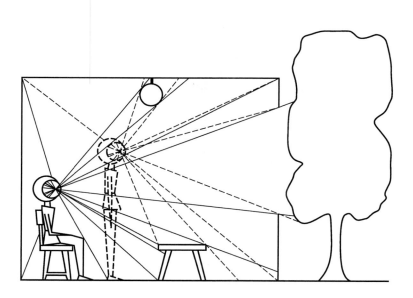

Figure 2.2 As the observer stands and moves forward, the ambient optic array is transformed into a new array. The boundaries defining the original angular pyramids (represented with solid lines) change in a regular and lawful way. From Gibson (1979: 72).

The observer's motion causes the faces of some surfaces, for instance the tabletop, to present themselves at different angles, reshaping the pyramids of light they reflect. Other surfaces, previously occluded, such as the floor behind the table, will reveal themselves for the first time; while some surfaces, like those on the table's legs, disappear from view.

Gibson uses the term "invariant" to describe features of the ambient optic array that remain constant through transformation. Consider again the tabletop in Figures 2.1 and 2.2. As the observer stands and moves forward, the trapezoidal shape that the tabletop projects on her retina changes. However, "although the changing angles and proportions of the set of trapezoidal projections are a fact, the unchanging relations among the four angles and the invariant proportions over the set are another fact, equally important, and they uniquely specify the rectangular surface" (1979: 74). Invariants, such as the relations among angles and proportions between edges are, in a sense, landmarks in an otherwise changing cityscape. As long as you can keep the Parthenon in view, you can orient yourself in the bustle of Athenian streets. Similarly, despite the significant transformations taking place in the optic array as the observer moves about, frozen in the light will be an invariant structure that "tells you" what is present in the surrounding environment. "The changes come from the locomotion, and the nonchanges come from the rigid layout of environmental surfaces" (Gibson 1979: 73).

More can be said about the structure of the ambient optic array. Looking again at Figure 2.1, one might imagine the possibility of designing a room that would create an identical optic array at the point of observation despite the presence of a different arrangement of surfaces. This would not be very difficult and is in fact the sort of "trick" that perceptual psychologists have long enjoyed playing on their subjects. Figure 2.3 shows the table that appears in Figures 2.1 and 2.2 next to a different structure that would project an identical shape on the observer's retina.

Thus, by replacing every surface in the room with one that creates the same boundaries defining the original angular pyramids, it is possible to invent countless different surroundings that, to the stationary observer, are indiscernible.

This possibility is an instance of the problem described in the previous chapter as *inverse optics*. The retinal image underdetermines the actual layout of surfaces in the environment. Although the shape of a surface determines a single projection on the retina, a projection on the retina does not determine the shape of the surface that causes it. This, recall, was a motivation for conceiving of perception as involving inferential processes. What comes to the eye does not, on its own, specify what is in the world, and so the visual system must rely on various assumptions in order to "get things right;" in order to derive correct conclusions about distal causes of the retinal image.

Gibson, however, denies that the visual system confronts an underdetermination problem. To be sure, if an observer were bound to a chair, unable to stand up or move his head, then worries about underdetermination might well arise.[1] But, Gibson says, the fact that observers are mobile makes all the

Figure 2.3 The table on the left and the structure on the right project identical shapes on the retina of the observer.

difference: "There could be a family of optically equivalent rooms for the seated man; there could be another family of optically equivalent rooms for the standing man; but there could only be that particular rectangular room for the particular motion perspective obtained when he stands up" (Gibson 1966: 199).[2] In standing, the flow of transformation from one optical array (that available to the seated figure) to another (that present to the standing figure) provides a rich source of information about surrounding surfaces. As the figure stands, the edges of occluding surfaces will "wipe" against the surfaces they occlude, corners will produce distinctive discontinuities in the pattern of flow, and so on. The angular pyramids of light reflected from the two objects in Figure 2.3, for instance, will undergo different transformations as the observer stands up. The edges of the objects will reveal and hide different parts of the room. Hence, if one conceives of the stimulus for vision as extended in time, rather than as a series of snapshots, the idea that the visual system must infer the structure of the distal layout from an ambiguous proximate stimulus loses its motivation. That anything but the table top can generate the shifting assemblage of images that project into the eyes of the moving observer is implausible.

Insofar as Gibson is correct that there is invariant structure in the light converging on an observer's eyes, the task of understanding vision becomes, in part, the task of identifying the invariants that light contains and learning what these invariants specify in the organism's environment. Much of Gibson's research was occupied with discovering and describing these invariants. For instance, among the many invariants he discusses are horizon cuts. An object in front of the horizon will have some proportion above the horizon and some below. This ratio of above-to-below is invariant for all objects of the same height, regardless of their distance from the observer. Thus, information about relative object size is specified directly in the light – there is no need for computations involving values for distances and angles. Gibson also noted that as an observer moves, the optic array will flow in characteristic directions and speeds. As one moves forward, the point dead ahead remains stable, but the world surrounding this point appears to smear, with points along the edge of vision smearing at the highest rate. Thus, in order to stay on course, one need only keep the point of zero flow on the desired destination (Goldstein 1981: 192). The ground texture in the environment is also a rich source of information. When texture is evenly distributed, as it might be on a grass-covered field or pebble-strewn beach, areas equal in size will contain equal numbers of texture units; objects that are the same size will cover the same number of texture units with their bases (Goldstein 1981: 192). The discovery of these invariants, as well as many others, constitutes, for Gibson, a description of the inputs for vision. In contrast to the meager inputs that provide a basis for computational vision, the stimuli reaching the eyes of Gibson's subjects are infused with a bounty of information, rendering unnecessary the additional assumptions that appear in computational descriptions of visual processes.

2.2.2 *The Brain's Role in Vision*

Gibson's remarks about the brain's role in vision requires further discussion. We saw above that Gibson speaks of the brain and nervous system as "resonating" to information, but this is hardly illuminating. In order to understand and assess Gibson's references to "resonating," we need first to become clear about the job Gibson takes the brain to have in vision. Following that, we will be in a better position to see how the brain does what Gibson thinks it must do.

As will become clearer in this section, Gibson's theory of vision not only resists the traditional cognitivist's belief that the stimuli for vision are impoverished, but it also denies the solipsistic conception of cognition that is at least implicit in the standard methodological practices of cognitive scientists. Visual processes are not exclusively located in the nervous system. A complete characterization of the processes going on in the brain when light hits a subject's eyes would not, for Gibson, suffice to explain vision. Vision is an extended process, involving bodies, motions, and interactions; thus, the methodological solipsist who finds nothing disagreeable in the idea of partitioning the subject's brain from the rest of the world would, if Gibson's view is accepted, be focused on just a small piece of a much larger visual system.[3]

If information arrived to an observer like a parcel in the mail, then perhaps there would be something to the idea that vision could begin with the retinal image — observers need just sit patiently, waiting for the world to come to them. However, on Gibson's view, information does not typically come to you, but instead must be actively hunted. Perceptual systems include the various organs and actions that do this hunting:

> Each perceptual system orients itself in appropriate ways for the pickup of environmental information, and depends on the general orienting system of the whole body. Head movements, ear movements, hand movements, nose and mouth movements, and eye movements are part and parcel of

the perceptual systems they serve ... They serve to explore the information available in sound, mechanical contact, chemical contact, and light.

(Gibson 1966: 58)

We saw in the previous section that the invariants appearing in the optic array – the relationship between the corners of a surface, the relative depth of surfaces, the point of zero flow in the direction one is headed – emerge *as* invariant only in the context of change. Invariants such as these are what the visual system is designed to detect, and it can do so only through activity. If the components of the visual system are those parts and actions that are necessary for collecting visual inputs, then the visual system must include things like the head, the body, and the activities of these parts.

Moreover, because the stimulation that the visual system explores is already rich with information, the brain, Gibson believes, needn't process this information any further: "the function of the brain when looped with its perceptual organs is not to decode signals, nor to interpret messages, nor to accept images. These old analogies no longer apply. The function of the brain is not even to *organize* the sensory input or to *process* the data, in modern terminology" (Gibson 1966: 5). In his effort to replace these old analogies, Gibson hits on the idea of "resonating." Unfortunately, as analogies go, *resonating* has hardly the precision or fecundity of the computational analogies that Gibson wishes to displace.

Gibson expands only slightly on the idea of resonating:

[t]he "resonating" or "tuning" of a system suggests the analogy of a radio receiver. This model is inadequate because there would have to be a little man to twiddle the knobs. A perceiver is a *self-tuning* system. What makes it resonate to the interesting broadcasts that are available instead of to all the trash that fills the air? The answer might be that the pickup of information is *reinforcing*.

(1966: 271)

How should we make sense of this description of resonating? Consider first the radio receiver. As you turn the tuner knob, seeking your favorite radio station, the broadcast will contain static as you approach the correct frequency, will clarify as you hit it, and will then become noisy again as you move past it. In order to ensure that you have the clearest reception, you might wiggle the knob back and forth over the correct frequency. The instances of clearest reception reinforce your movements, so that your tuning motions become ever finer until they settle on the precise radio frequency you seek.

Now, what would it be for a system to be *self-tuning*? Gibson suggests that the accommodation mechanisms in the eye, i.e. the mechanisms that shape the lens in order to focus light on the retina, are self-tuning. The ocular system focuses "automatically," without requiring anyone to "tune in" the proper lens shape to maximize the clarity of the retinal image. Somehow, the clarity of the image reinforces particular adjustments to the lens, so that when the image loses its sharpness, the lens makes the appropriate corrections. There needn't be anything magical behind such corrections. As we will see in later chapters, certain dynamical systems are capable of self-correction so as to maintain a desired level of performance. For instance, a Watt's governor automatically controls an engine's speed by closing a valve when the engine exceeds the desired speed and then re-opening the valve when the speed drops below the desired rate. Even a device as simple as a thermostat is able to maintain an approximately constant temperature without having a "little man" inside to make the necessary adjustments. Devices such as these might usefully be thought of as tending toward a desired state, much as a marble will roll to the lowest point on a slanted floor.

To "pick up" information in light, on this way of conceiving matters, is to be designed in such a way that the information will naturally attract an appropriate response from the visual system. Just as the marble will roll to the lowest point, and the Watt's governor is drawn toward the correct engine speed, and the thermostat is attracted to the proper temperature, the visual system homes in on the information in the light. Whether this talk of being "drawn toward" or "attracted to" or "homing in on" illuminates any further Gibson's metaphor of resonating, or whether this is a case of one cloudy metaphor merely being replaced others, is a hard question. However, even if the metaphor cannot be made more precise, one might still find in it the seed of a challenge to the computationalism that pervades standard cognitive science. This, clearly, is the perspective that the philosopher Gary Hatfield has taken towards Gibson's work, and in the next section we will see how Hatfield develops this idea into a more fully grown challenge.

2.3 Hatfield's Noncognitive Computationalism

Motivating Hatfield's interest in Gibson's theory of perception is a desire to understand more clearly the extent to which cognitive science is committed to the rules and symbols conception of cognition that I introduced in the previous chapter. Gibson's detractors (e.g. Fodor and Pylyshyn 1981) portray ecological psychology as merely a form of dressed-up behaviorism. An antagonism toward explanations of psychological processes that make reference to unobservable, internal, mental states is a keystone of behaviorism. Psychology, for a behaviorist, is the study of how an organism comes to pair stimuli with responses, where a description of an organism's history of reinforcement with particular pairings exhausts an answer to this question. Why does the organism respond to stimulus X with behavior Y? Because, the behaviorist asserts, Y responses to X have been reinforced in the past.

An obvious rejoinder to this conception of psychology is to note that this explanation of an organism's behavior leaves unanswered a variety of different kinds of question: What processes internal to the organism account for the tendency to do Y in response to X? Why does the organism do Y rather than Z? How does the organism identify Xs? How does the organism learn to do Y in response to X? These questions, the cognitivist is confident, require an explanation in terms of computational processes operating in a medium of symbolic thought. Gibson, in contrast, eschews the need for such processes, claiming instead that an organism can respond directly, can *resonate*, to informationally rich stimulation. And, although Gibson does not avail himself of many of the methodological tools or vocabulary of the behaviorist school, he does share with behaviorists a hostility toward explanations that posit representations, mental images, and other internal states. Not surprisingly, the same questions that haunt the behaviorist also fall hard on Gibson: What are the mechanisms by which information is picked up? How does an organism organize its response? How does an organism learn to make use of information?

To see more clearly the gap in Gibson's account of perception, consider again his explanation of perception of object height. Two objects of the same height will be cut by the horizon in the same proportions. Thus, a telephone pole fifty meters from an observer will have the same fraction of its total height above the horizon as a telephone pole one hundred meters from the observer. An observer can use this invariant property to judge the poles to be the same size despite the fact that the retinal image of the nearer pole is twice the size of the image of the more distant pole. But, although Gibson is undeniably correct that horizon cuts carry information about object size, he gives no indication as to how an observer recognizes and uses this information. Notice that the same information is present to any observer – human being, squirrel, robin, dog – but this does not mean that all observers are capable of recognizing and using this information.

One might reasonably ask how this invariant is detected, and once detected, how it is assimilated in judgments of size. The suggestion that observers simply resonate to such information begins to show signs of anemia when one asks why some observers resonate while others do not; why adults may while infants may not. If resonating is to be more than an empty phrase, one should be able to describe the mechanisms it involves. The cognitivist bets that these mechanisms are computational in nature.

Notice that this controversy stands, regardless of the richness of stimulation. True, cognitivists tend to believe that the stimulus affecting an organism is impoverished and thus in need of amplification through inferential processes, whereas the Gibsonian denies the former point and thus rejects the latter. But stipulating that Gibson is correct about the nature of stimulation does nothing to allay the present objection. The question how an organism detects and organizes its response to information remains whether stimulation is impoverished or flush (Hatfield 2009: 57). Accordingly, the dispute between the cognitivist and the Gibsonian is more centrally a contest over how best to characterize the workings of the perceptual mechanisms.

But while the cognitivist might be correct in noting a deficiency in Gibson's explanation of perceptual abilities, and might further be correct that a fuller account of perception demands a description of computations by which information is gathered and processed, Hatfield is suspicious of the assumption that these computations must have the form of inferences and must take place over a domain of symbols. Gibson's resistance to mediating psychological processes is misplaced, on Hatfield's view, but his opposition to the depiction of these processes as inferential, and to the need for an internal medium of symbolic representations, is coherent and, perhaps, prescient.

The line Hatfield seeks to walk is between, on the one hand, Gibson's view that there are no psychological processes involved in the detection and use of stimulus information, and the cognitivist's insistence that cognition consists first in the symbolic encoding of information and then proceeds by inferential steps involving the application of various rules and representations in the course of computing a solution (recall, e.g., Richard Gregory's comment in §1.6 about the "construction" of perceptions). Hatfield calls the position he stakes out "noncognitive computationalism." The position is noncognitive in its rejection of the cognitivist's insistence that psychological processes be construed as inferential; but it is computational in retaining the idea that psychological processes are best described as performing computations and as containing representational states.

A useful approach to Hatfield's noncognitive computationalism is by way of an example he discusses. Consider a spring scale with a pan into which weights of different magnitudes might be placed. The scale can be used as an adding machine: placing weights of 100g and 200g on the pan will cause the scale's needle to point to the sum of these two weights. The calculation the scale performs, however, is ill-conceived as an inference, or as taking place over a domain of symbolic representations. Attributions of inferential operations involving rules and symbolic representations make sense only within a broader framework of computational commitments. For instance, rules must be stored somewhere, and the typical place would be a buffer of some sort. Something must be in charge of identifying strings of symbols and applying the correct rules to them. This job is usually assigned to a central processing unit (CPU). Inferential processes involve routines and sub-routines, which in turn often include means for testing outputs of still other sub-routines. The algorithms that the CPU oversees operate on discrete symbols, the identities of which are determined by their syntactic proper-ties. Within this broader complex of concepts, the cognitivist's computa-tional loyalties take form.

The spring scale, quite plausibly, is not a suitable target of this sort of computational description. There is nothing in the scale corresponding to a CPU, there is no buffer that serves as a temporary storage house for rules and partial solutions, there are no strings of symbols that might be concate-nated or disjoined in response to the demands of rule-guided routines. Any attempt to impose a traditional computational description upon the spring scale will surely meet with resistance. Like trying to shove a square peg through a round hole, the description simply does not fit the device.

However, computational systems might be conceived in other ways. Consider that the spring scale is, in a legitimate sense, computing a sum. The result of placing weights of 100g and 200g upon its pan is an output of "300g." There is nothing metaphorical in a description of the scale as adding, and indeed, if one had the need, one might use the scale as an adding machine. However, granting Hatfield's argument that the spring scale is not a computational device in the cognitivist's sense, he must next defend the idea that there is a level of description at which the device might properly be conceived as more than simply a physical mechanism. The reason for this emerges from reflection once more on the charge that Gibson's theory of perception is ultimately behaviorist in character.

Gibson's critics, recall, accuse him of neglecting the very phenomena that are of distinctive interest to psychology. Whereas behaviorists were largely content to leave uninvestigated the processes occurring within the skull of the subject, the cognitivist sees the activities within the brain as the very subject matter of psychology. However, this is not to say that cognitive psychology is neuroscience. Although neuroscience might serve as a constraint on psychological hypotheses, cognitive science operates at a level of abstraction above the neural nuts and bolts of the brain – just as computer scientists might focus their energy on understanding algorithmic processes without attending to facts about the hardware on which these algorithms run. The ontological and methodological commitments of cognitivism are distinct from, and not suited to, an examination of brain hardware. The psychological level, as the cognitivist sees it, is the level at which mental activity, such as the recall of ordered items, or the derivation of depth information from binocular disparity, is analyzed in terms of representations, rules, inferences, and symbols. Gibson's theory, insofar as it never attempts to peer into the "black box" of the cranium, has no use for the cognitivist's conceptual tool kit, and this is one reason for critics' dismissive attitude toward Gibson (e.g. Fodor and Pylyshyn 1981).

But, Hatfield observes, insisting that psychological investigation include within its domain activities like information detection and processing is one thing; asserting that computational accounts of the sort cognitivists offer to explain these activities are the "the only game in town" (Fodor 1975) is quite another. As the adding device shows, computing devices needn't depend on internal symbol systems, needn't explicitly represent rules, and needn't act upon programs that, in effect, infer solutions from a series of inputs. Hatfield's goal is to make compelling the suggestion that psychological operations might usefully be conceived as computational, representational, and yet nonsymbolic and non-inferential. While the example of the spring scale adder takes us some way toward Hatfield's objective, the conception of psychology that Hatfield envisions has a much fuller expression in the work of the connectionists. Thus, to see more clearly how a challenge to cognitivism might proceed, we need to examine with some care connectionist theories of mental processes.

2.4 The Connectionist Challenge

When cognitivists claim that psychological processes are computational, and that the brain is to computer hardware as the mind is to software, one might wonder where in the brain this computer exists and where mental programs are stored. Perhaps you have installed additional RAM in your home computer, or have replaced broken components. If so, you may have taken the opportunity to look at the computer's motherboard and noticed a variety of circuits, cards, wires, processors, and so on. Some of these things are read-only memory, others controllers for video and sound devices, and one is the CPU. Although you might not have been able to identify these various components, they were certainly identifiable *as* components, and the idea that you were looking at the internal workings of a computer would have struck you as relatively unsurprising. In contrast, if you were to look at a photograph or functional magnetic resonance image of a brain, the idea that this thing is a computer might seem quite remarkable. Where are the components? How are they connected to each other? Increased magnification would only add to the mystery. At some level of magnification, the brain would appear as a mass of cells each with hundreds or thousands of tendrils reaching out to touch each other. How is one to carve components from such a mess?

As I noted in the previous chapter (§1.3), the idea that the brain is a computer requires a leap of abstraction. Justification for this leap comes in the form of explanatory and predictive utility. If conceiving of the brain as a computer yields insights into its operation, and allows us to predict how it will perform in particular circumstances, this is evidence that the brain *is* a computer. There is no reason to belittle this judgment as a mere case of "as if-ing." The brain would be no less a computer as the device on your desktop which is, after all, "nothing more" than a collection of silicon and plastic when examined under a high level of magnification.

On the other hand, if the psychological capacities of the brain might be understood without attributing to the brain the architectural features of a standard desktop computer (this architecture was originally designed by the Hungarian genius John von Neumann and consequently bears his name), then the motivation for conceiving of the brain as a computer wears thin. Moreover, if the brain is *better* conceived as something other than a computer, then so much the worse for the computational theory of mind.

As connectionists see matters, the brain appears to be less like a von Neumann-style computer than it does a connectionist computer. This view of things is in part no accident: Connectionist machines were inspired by the vast connectivity that the brain's billions of neurons exhibit, and so it is hardly a shock to be told that brains resemble connectionist computers more so than they do von Neumann computers. Of course, physical resemblance cannot be the whole story. As we just observed, if the brain *is* a computer, this is because of how it functions, not because it has readily identifiable components with labels like "ROM," "DRAM," and "CPU." However, connectionists also declare that brains *behave* more like connectionist networks than they do von Neumann computers.

In defense of this assertion, connectionists note, first, that brain function is not "brittle" in the way that a standard computer's functioning is. If you have ever tried to construct a web page using HTML code then you have a sense of this brittleness. Misplacing a single semicolon, or failing to insert a closing parenthesis, or typing a "b" instead of an "l," can have devastating effects on the web page. Programs typically work or they don't, and the difference between working and not can often depend on the presence of a single character. But brains typically do not behave in this all-or-nothing manner. Damage to a brain might degrade a psychological capacity without rendering it useless, or might have no noticeable effect at all. Connectionist computers exhibit similar robustness – the loss of some connections might make no difference to the computer's capacities, or might only attenuate these capacities.

Second, von Neumann computers operate serially – one operation at a time. This fact imposes a severe constraint on the speed these computers can achieve. Consider how this constraint might manifest itself in a brain. If the basic processing unit of the brain – a neuron – requires 1–3msec to transmit a signal, and if psychological abilities (such as recognition, categorization, response organization, and so on) can unfold in as little as a few hundred milliseconds, then the brain must be capable of producing these abilities in no more than a few hundred steps.[4] This is remarkable, for simulations of these abilities on standard computers often require many thousands of steps. Connectionist machines avoid this speed constraint by conducting many operations simultaneously, so that in the time a standard computer takes to perform a hundred operations, a connectionist machine can perform many times that.

The secret to these connectionist successes lies in the features of connectionist architecture. Typically, a connectionist machine consists in three layers of nodes (Figure 2.4). The nodes in the bottom or input layer represent stimulus variables. Depending on the stimulus a node represents, the node will have a particular level of internal activity. This level of activity determines the strength of the signal the node then transmits to the nodes in the hidden layer. But, because the connections between layers are weighted, the signals that reach the hidden layer may be strengthened or weakened, kept positive or made negative. In short, the weightings of the connections between the input and hidden layers make the signals that reach the

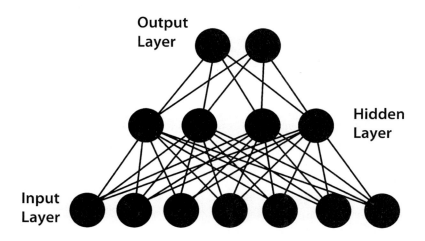

Figure 2.4 A connectionist net with an input layer consisting of seven nodes, a hidden layer with four nodes, and an output layer of two nodes.

hidden layer a complex function of the signals that left the nodes in the input layer.

The sum of the values of the signals that reach each hidden unit then determines the internal activity of that node, which in turn determines the strength of the signal it proceeds to send to the output nodes. As with the connections between nodes in the input and hidden layers, the connections between hidden layer nodes and output nodes are weighted, so that the signals that reach the output nodes are a complex function of the signals that leave the hidden nodes. The level of activity the output nodes assume as a result of the signals they receive from the hidden layer determines their final value – a solution to the computational task at hand.

Michael Dawson (1998) describes a connectionist network that he and colleagues designed to analyze brain images for indications of Alzheimer's disease. The images were created with SPECT (single photon emission computed tomography) and appeared inadequate for the purpose of identifying mild cases of the disease. Dawson, et al. wondered whether the fault lay not in the images but in the subsequent analysis of the images. They designed a connectionist net with fourteen input layer nodes, each of which represented the number of photons detected in a distinct brain region. These nodes were connected to fifteen nodes in a hidden layer, which in turn were connected to two output layer nodes. The network was trained using sample data from known cases, thus allowing Dawson and his colleagues to modify the connection weights between layers until the network produced correct diagnoses. In the end, the results were very satisfying. The network was able to distinguish diseased brains from healthy brains even in those cases where the Alzheimer's disease was in its early stages. This showed that the SPECT images were not, after all, deficient. They contained all the information necessary to identify mild cases of Alzheimer's disease.

Dawson's description of the processes taking place in the network is worth quoting in full, for it brings into relief the contrast between connectionist and classical computations:

> First, an input was presented to the network, which was accomplished by setting the internal activations of all 14 input units to values that represented a single subject's data. Second, signals traveled from all of the input units through the first layer connections, where they were scaled. Third, all 15 hidden units computed their net input, and on the basis of this net input adopted an internal level of activity. Fourth, signals traveled from all of the hidden units through the second layer of connections, where they were scaled. Finally, the two output units computed their net input, and adopted an internal level of activation, which was interpreted as the network's response to the presented stimulus.
>
> (Dawson 1998: 48)

Let's now consider how networks of the sort Dawson describes fulfill Hatfield's vision of mechanisms that are at once computational and representational, without also involving inferential operations on a domain of discrete symbols.

First, the network is clearly performing computations. The activation of each unit in the hidden layer is a function of the activation of the input layer nodes, modulated by the weighting function contained in the connections between the nodes. This talk of functions is to be understood quite literally: the activation values of the input nodes compose a domain, and the values that the hidden layer nodes acquire form a range. Similarly, the activation values for the units in the hidden layer then form the domain for a function whose range is the activation values that the output layer nodes assume. However, despite the ease with which the network may be described as computing functions, there is no obvious need to conceive of the network as availing itself of rules of inference, of testing hypotheses, of making assumptions, and so on. The idea that that there is somewhere in the network an algorithm that dictates the manipulation of symbols also seems out of place.

Instead, the operation of the network seems much closer in spirit to the spring scale I described earlier than it does to a von Neumann-style computer. Just as the tension of the spring does the work of adding the weights of the items in the pan, the connections between layers, because of the way they modulate the signals that pass through them, simply bring about the level of activation in the layers to which they are connected. Indeed, one might imagine the connections as something like wires, which, depending on the metal composing them, dampen or amplify the signals they carry. Describing the connections in this way seems more natural – less forced – than describing them as performing rule-guided inferences on symbolic constructions.

Similarly, there appears to be a natural way of understanding the networks as containing representations that does not require that there is somewhere instantiated in the network an internal symbol system. Rather than seeing the internal activity of the input layer units representing features of the stimulus symbolically, it would seem to make more sense to see them as representing in the same way that a mercury thermometer represents temperature. The ambient temperature causes the mercury column to reach a certain height; this height then "stands for" the temperature of the room. This conception of representation is unproblematic and widespread, and yet does not depend on the existence of a body of syntactically defined symbols for its coherence.

On this model, the level of activity in the input nodes stands for some dimension of the stimulus as a result, perhaps, of a simple causal response to the stimulus, just as the height of the mercury column is a response to ambient temperature.[5] Alternatively, on Hatfield's view, representational content might derive not from causal relationships, but from the teleological functions of the devices in question. The height of the mercury column represents temperature because that is its role in a device that has the function of representing temperature. Likewise, Hatfield would argue, states of biological systems, such as the visual system, represent what they do as a result of the role they play in a system that has evolved to represent visual information.[6]

In the present context a detailed defense of any particular analysis of representation is less important than the tenability of a conception of representation that (i) does not require the resources of a symbol system, and (ii) might fit well with the representational aspirations of connectionist networks. The suggestions above for understanding representation in a manner free of symbolist trappings seem adequate for these purposes. The units in the input layer stand for features of the stimulus; those in the hidden layer stand for dimensions of the stimulus that are extracted after application of the weighting functions in the connections between the layers; the units in the output layer represent the outcome of still further processing, yielding, for instance, a verdict on the presence of Alzheimer's disease. What's more, the connection weights on which the network settles might be said to represent the network's knowledge, in the sense that when the weights are adjusted so, the network is capable of making the discriminations it has been trained to make.

Insofar as this characterization of connectionist computation is correct, there is available an alternative to the rules and representation approach to computation that has predominated in cognitive science. Whereas the standard scientist conceives of representations as akin to words in a language of thought, and of cognition as consisting in operations on language-like structures, connectionists conceive of representations as patterns of activity, and of cognition as a process in which a network of connections settles into a particular state depending on the input it has received and the connection weightings it has, through training, acquired. What's more, the tasks for which connectionist nets have been devised reflect long-standing areas of interest among cognitive scientists. Nets have been designed that transform present tense English into past tense, that categorize objects, that transform written language into speech, and so on. Connectionist successes in these domains have at least strained and, just as plausibly, put the lie to the standard scientist's mantra that standard computationalism is the only game in town.

Of course, standard cognitive scientists have not sat idly by as connectionists encroach on their territory. Jerry Fodor and Zenon Pylyshyn (1988) have been especially ferocious in their criticisms of connectionism. They argue that because representations within a connectionist net are distributed across patterns of activity, they are unsuited to decomposition into components, and thus cannot accommodate linguistic structures. Insofar as connectionist nets are unable to model linguistic structures, they will fail as a model of thought, for thought, according to many standard scientists, takes place in an internal language. On the other hand, if connectionist nets can model linguistic structures, they must be relegated to the status of mere implementations of psychological processes, where it falls to the theories and methods of standard cognitive science to understand these processes.

In response, connectionists have sought to show how linguistic structures can appear in connectionist nets. David Chalmers, for instance, designed a connectionist network that transforms sentences in the active voice into sentences in the passive voice and does so, he claims, without ever resorting to discrete, symbolic, representations (Chalmers 1990). Moreover, Chalmers argues that his network is not simply an implementation of a classical computational system, because there is never a step in the connectionist processing that decomposes the sentences into their constituent parts, as would have to occur if the sentences were represented in the network as concatenations of linguistic symbols (Chalmers 1993).

The debate between connectionists and so-called classicists continues, and we will see some of its epicycles in chapter 5 when we examine dynamical systems approaches to cognition. In the present context, connectionism is significant for the starkly distinct portrait of cognition it offers to that of standard cognitive science. Ultimately, connectionism's success depends on how much of cognition it is able to explain without having to avail itself of a language-like conceptual apparatus.

2.5 Summary

This chapter has focused on some ideas that, more or less explicitly, might be taken to challenge the orthodox conception of cognitive science. In closing this chapter, I would like to pull together the various strands of thought we have examined and point them in the direction of embodied cognition. Doing so will make the road ahead that much easier to travel.

The assumptions of standard cognitive science that are most vulnerable to the challenges we have examined are the following. First, the stimuli for psychological processes are impoverished. They are "short" on the information that is necessary for an organism to interact successfully with its environment. Consequently, the second assumption cognitive scientists make is that psychological processes must make inferences, educated guesses, about the world on the basis of incomplete information. These inferences might deploy assumptions about the environment in order to extract correct conclusions from the data. Third, the inferential processes characteristic of psychology are best conceived as involving algorithmic operations over a domain of symbolic representations. Cognition proceeds by encoding stimuli into symbolic form, manipulating these symbols in accord with the rules of a mental algorithm, and then producing a new string of symbols that represents the conclusion of the algorithmic process. Fourth and finally, because the goal of psychology is a description of mental algorithms, and because these algorithms are realized in the brain, psychological investigations can limit themselves to processes within the brain.

We can now see how all of these assumptions might be questioned. First, whether the inputs to psychological processes are meager depends on how one defines the inputs. We saw that the problem of inverse optics exists when one conceives of visual inputs as snapshots of the surrounding world. In contrast, a different picture emerges when one conceives of inputs as temporally extended and arising through active exploration of the environment. Whereas a snapshot of the world is consistent with innumerable possible sources, a continuous sequence of snapshots of the sort that results from motion through the world will narrow down the number of possible sources.

The idea that an organism's actions can reveal invariant features within the stimuli it confronts indicates a response to the fourth point above. Standard cognitive scientists see the brain as the complete organ of cognition because they take cognition to consist in the algorithmic processes that mediate between a symbolically encoded stimulus and a symbolically encoded response. But the possibility that an organism's interactions with the environment can suffice to extract invariants from stimuli suggests an alternative conception of the locus of cognition. The assumption that the brain functions as an inference engine beings to look misguided. Still correct is the idea that cognition involves "intelligent" responses to stimuli, but because the detection of stimuli requires active exploration of the environment, the organs and processes of cognition extend beyond the brain to include those parts of the body that are involved in the activities by which information about the environment is collected. The brain, on this view, is better conceived as a controller and organizer of activities that result in the extraction of information than as a computer for processing this information.[7]

So far these reactions to standard cognitive science follow closely Gibson's conception of psychology. However, we saw that Gibson's description of psychology leaves unaddressed fundamental questions about how information is picked up and used. We might add another complaint at this point, viz. that Gibson's focus is on perception, and the extent to which Gibsonian ideas might apply to areas of cognition not involved in perception – problem solving, language, memory, and so on – is at best unclear. Might the idea of cognition as computation retain its hold in these domains? Hatfield's noncognitive computationalism becomes relevant at this point. Granting the limitations in Gibson's program, the leap to a view of computation-alism that adopts the language of rules, symbolic representations, inference, and hypothesis testing may still appear unwarranted. Hatfield articulates a conception of computation that leaves behind the accouterments of the traditional framework, and weds it to a conception of representation that rejects the need for a symbolic language of thought. Hatfield's ideas find support in the advent of connectionism, which provides a framework for understanding a form of computation to which the vocabulary of inference is poorly suited, and in which representations exist outside a medium of discrete symbolic expressions.

Most fundamentally, the conceptual tools that Gibson, Hatfield, and connectionist research bring to the study of cognition plow a ground of new possibilities into which an embodied approach to cognition might take root. No longer must we equate psychological processes with symbolic computations within the confines of the brain. Recognition that interactions between the body and the world enhance the quality of stimuli available for psychological processing, and that processing needn't take place over a domain of neurally realized symbolic representations, invites a re-thinking of the body's place in psychology. How might the body contribute or constrain our psychological capacities? Might the body be a constituent in psychological processes? What might be retained from standard cognitive science, and what should be jettisoned in favor of new ideas?

2.6 Suggested Reading

Dawson, M. (2004). *Minds and Machines: Connectionism and Psychological Modeling* (Malden: Blackwell).

Gibson, J. J. (1966). *The Senses Considered as Perceptual Systems* (Prospect Heights: Waveland Press, Inc.).

Hatfield, G. (2009). *Perception and Cognition* (New York: Oxford University Press), Chs. 2–3.

Ramsey, W., Stich, S., and Rumelhart, D. (eds.) (1991). *Philosophy and Connectionist Theory* (Hillsdale: Lawrence Erlbaum Associates).

Rowlands, M. (1995). "Against Methodological Solipsism: The Ecological Approach," *Philosophical Psychology* 8: 5–24.

3

CONCEPTIONS OF EMBODIMENT

3.1 Introduction

In this chapter we will scrutinize various attempts to define what it means for cognition to be embodied. Claims about the meaning of embodiment, we shall see, are far from uniform in the commitments they entail. More troubling still is that the claims often step far beyond the evidence or argument made in their support. Questions also arise concerning whether, and if so how, the assorted views on embodiment we shall examine mark a real departure from standard cognitive science. This chapter will be partly expository, but also critical, for there is much to criticize in many of the recent efforts to characterize embodiment. However, from the tangle of conceptions we will consider, we shall be able to pull a few straight threads that will lead the way toward a clearer grasp of the issues involved. The accounts of embodiment I will present in this chapter are drawn from some of the most prominent and widely cited sources in the field, and so represent something as close to a common background as is possible. This fact makes all the more surprising the remarkable multiplicity of ideas that have been hailed in the name of embodied cognition.

3.2 Varela, Thompson, and Rosch: World Building

Within embodied cognition, Varela, Thompson, and Rosch's The Embodied Mind (1991) is often regarded as an urtext. Many of its themes – disillusionment with cognitive science's allegiance to computationalism, sympathy for Gibsonian and connectionist approaches to cognition, suspicion that the concept of representation has been overplayed in explanations of cognition, confidence that perception and cognition must be linked to action – have ascended to the status of dogma within embodied cognition. Other themes, such as the rejection of a "pre-given" world, and the value of incorporating Buddhist doctrine into a science of mind, have failed to garner much of a following. Notable also is the background of its authors. Varela (who died in 2001) was a biologist and neuroscientist, Thompson is a philosopher, and Rosch a cognitive psychologist. The central arguments of the book reflect this diversity in specialization, drawing as they do on neuroscience, evolutionary theory, theories of categorization, and the phenomenological tradition within philosophy.

Varela, Thompson, and Rosch (VTR) reject the traditional view of cognition as computation over representations, choosing instead to conceive of cognition as "embodied action" (1991: 172).

> By using the term *embodied* we mean to highlight two points: first, that cognition depends upon the kinds of experience that come from having a body with various sensorimotor capacities, and second, that these individual sensorimotor capacities are themselves embedded in a more encompassing biological, psychological, and cultural context. By using the term *action* we mean to emphasize once again that sensory and motor processes, perception and action, are fundamentally inseparable in lived cognition
>
> (1991: 173, note omitted)

Clearly, these comments require some elaboration. Let's begin with the claim that cognition depends upon a particular kind of experience, viz. the kind that comes from a body's sensorimotor capacities. The sensorimotor capacities of which VTR speak seem to be capacities to interact successfully with one's environment, where successful interaction will involve a tight loop between perception and motion. As an organism moves through its environment, its motion will produce opportunities for new perceptions while at the same time erasing old ones. In turn, the perception of new features will reveal opportunities for new activities. Thus motion influences perception, which in turn influences future motion, which then determines new perceptions, and so on.

In order to understand the significance of the body in this perception-action cycle, consider two organisms with very different bodies. Perhaps one is twice the size of the other, or the first walks vertically whereas the second is on all fours. The perceptual systems of the organisms may well differ too. Perhaps the first has its sensory organs facing forward whereas the other has sensory organs that provide it with a 270° view of the world. The first may be able to detect portions of the electromagnetic spectrum that the second cannot. As a result of these differences in bodies and perceptual systems, the sensorimotor capacities of the two organisms will differ. As the first organism moves, its perceptual system will confront features of the world that will not be apparent to the second organism, even supposing that the two organisms move from the same initial location to the same new location. Similarly, the second organism will perceive portions of the world that remain hidden from the first organism. Given the differences in what the organisms perceive, there may well also be differences in the actions the organisms choose to take, which in turn lead to further differences in perception, and then action, and so on.

The idea of a perception-action loop, in which the contents of perception are determined (in part) by the actions an organism takes, and the actions an organism takes are guided by its perceptions of the world, seems to capture the meaning of the final part of the passage from VTR that I quoted above. "Perception and action," they say, "are fundamentally inseparable in lived cognition." They are inseparable in the sense that they determine each other. Perception leads to action, leads to perception, and so on.

Left to understand is the middle portion of the passage. Why is it important that an organism's sensorimotor capacities are "embedded in a more encompassing biological, psychological, and cultural context?" Unfortunately, answering this question is not so easy, although VTR do make other comments that are suggestive. Here's one attempt at an answer. VTR oppose the approach to cognition that receives clearest expression in the computational vision program that we examined in chapter 2. With its efforts to "recover" information about the world from representations of some its properties – e.g. shape from shading, shape from motion, etc. – computational vision adopts what VTR call the chicken position:

Chicken Position: The world out there has pregiven properties. These exist prior to the image that is cast on the cognitive system, whose task is to recover them appropriately (whether through symbols or global subsymbolic states).

(1991: 172)

VTR wish to reject the chicken position, but to do so without having to fall into what they call the *egg position*:

Egg Position: The cognitive system projects its own world, and the apparent reality of this world is merely a reflection of internal laws of the system.

(1991: 172)

As VTR see these two options, the first is a statement of realism and the second of idealism. The chicken position commits one to belief in a world that is independent of any sensory awareness of it. It is a world that organisms come to know only by their representations of it. The egg position expresses idealism. It denies a reality external to the mind of the cognizer.

VTR intend the concept of *embodied action* as a middle ground between the realism of the chicken and the idealism of the egg. They believe that because cognition depends on sensorimotor capacities, which in turn reflect the nature of an organism's perceptual and bodily properties, the idea of a pregiven world is unsustainable. The world becomes "perceiver-dependent" (1991: 173). On the other hand, VTR wish also to reject the idealist view that the world is only apparent – a construction emerging from cognitive activity. The suggestion that sensorimotor capacities are "embedded" in a shared biological, psychological, and cultural context becomes significant in this context. Presumably, because we share common perceptual and bodily equipment with our conspecifics, we can expect that we share as well a conception of the world. Our joint evolutionary and cultural history constrains how we conceive the world, and thus moderates the subjectivism implicit in the egg position.

Enough of the rudiments of VTR's account are by now in place to begin asking questions about it. Perhaps the most obvious question concerns why they think that cognition's dependence on sensorimotor activities, even granting that these activities will lead different kinds of organisms to different conceptions of the world, implies rejection of a "pregiven" world. The so-called chicken position is consistent with the claim that perception and action are co-dependent, and that the knowledge of the world they provide depends on the properties of the perceptual and bodily systems.

Perhaps motivating VTR's dismissal of a pregiven world is their lengthy analysis of color perception. As we shall see in more detail in the next chapter, VTR believe that color does not exist in the world, but is rather like what John Locke long ago described as a secondary quality: a power to produce an experience that does not resemble any real quality in the world. Experience of color, for VTR, is a response of a properly tuned perceptual system to certain non-colored properties in the world. But even granting this analysis of color, there is no reason to expect that a similar analysis holds for all other properties. How does the fact, if it is one, that color is a secondary quality justify the conclusion that *all* properties are secondary qualities? If colors are the product of an interaction between a particular kind of perceptual system and particular kinds of external properties, must *shape* also be a secondary quality? *Length?* What of atomic properties, properties of planets, and temporal properties? Using color as a model for all such properties, given the unique cluster of philosophical puzzles that color has for so long generated, seems a profoundly dubious choice.

But of greater moment than VTR's rejection of a pregiven world for understanding their conception of embodiment is their idea that an investigation of embodied action requires a new approach to cognition. According to this approach, which they call the *enactive* approach, "the point of departure ... is the study of how the perceiver can guide his actions in his local situation" (1991: 173). As with their denial of a pregiven world, this claim too seems to leap, rather than step, from their comments about embodiment. One may grant that a perceiver's ability to guide his actions in his local situation is indeed a worthy object of investigation without further supposing that an interest in sensorimotor capacities drives one to investigate *only* this. Furthermore, VTR do little to reveal why pursuit of this investigation could not unfold within the computational framework of standard cognitive science. They suggest that the dynamic nature of the perception-action loop is not suited to a computational explanation, but their reasons for this suspicion are not clearly developed.

In sum, VTR's claims about embodiment are less precise than provocative. Clearly important in their view is that embodiment involves a deep connection between perception and action. It also involves a rejection of the idea that cognition should be construed as the representation of given features of the world. Cognizers make their world, in some sense, as a result of activities that reflect the idiosyncrasies of their bodies and perceptual systems. Although, as we have seen, VTR's presentation of these ideas contains various gaps, the ideas themselves have resonated in a number of ways in the embodied cognition community, and in coming chapters we shall see how they might be more carefully developed.

3.3 Thelen: Representation *Lite*

Esther Thelen's pioneering application of dynamical systems theory to cognitive phenomena has earned her royal status in the embodied cognition community. The details of dynamical systems theory needn't concern us at this time. We shall examine these details more carefully in chapter 5. The immediate task before us is to understand Thelen's conception of embodiment. In an article co-authored with Schöner, Scheier, and Smith, Thelen says:

> To say that cognition is embodied means that it arises from bodily interactions with the world. From this point of view, cognition depends on the kinds of experiences that come from having a body with particular perceptual and motor capabilities that are inseparably linked and that together form the matrix within which reasoning, memory, emotion, language, and all other aspects of mental life are meshed.
>
> (2001: 1)

Moreover, Thelen, et al. see their embodied approach to cognition as marking a challenge to traditional cognitivist approaches. They say that embodied cognition "stands in contrast to the prevailing cognitivist stance which sees the mind as a device to manipulate symbols, and is thus concerned with the formal rules and processes by which the symbols appropriately represent the real world" (2001: 1).

These remarks raise a number of questions, but perhaps the most immediate is this: Why should the claim that cognition arises from interactions between the body and world demand that its investigation proceed without the cognitivist's apparatus of symbols, rules, and representations? Indeed, no cognitivist would deny that cognition arises from interactions between body and world. How else, a cognitivist might wonder, could it arise? An organism's body is its interface with the world – it is the world's point of contact with an organism. The cognitivist believes that the sensory surfaces on an organism's body translate (transduce) stimulation from the environment into a symbolic code that the brain then processes. But, this is not inconsistent with the idea that cognition has its origins in body/world interactions.

Clearly, Thelen, et al. must mean something more by *embodiment* than the banal fact that cognition arises from interactions between body and world. An indication of a more interesting suggestion comes in the remark that "cognition depends on the kinds of experiences that come from having a body with particular perceptual and motor capabilities that are inseparably linked." The meaning of this claim becomes clear only in the context of Thelen, et al.'s broader research interests.

Among these interests is what is called *perseverative* behavior in infants. Perseverative behavior is simply behavior that one perseveres in producing despite the behavior's current inappropriateness. For instance, when I moved from a house that had a trash can under the kitchen sink to one where the trash can was located underneath a counter top, I persevered in opening the cabinet beneath the sink when needing to dispose of trash. In fact, years have passed and I still, on occasion, open the cabinet beneath the sink in order to throw something away. The behavior perseveres despite its inappropriateness.

Studies of so-called A-not-B errors in infants reveal that certain kinds of perseverative behavior emerge at the age of six or seven months, remain until the infant is about twelve months old, and then disappear again (Thelen, Schöner, Scheier, and Smith 2001; Smith and Thelen 2003; Clearfield, Diedrich, Smith, and Thelen 2006). Of special interest to developmental psychologists is the question why perseverative behavior, once in place in the seven- to twelve-month-old infant, then goes away. In seeking an answer to this question, a task that the developmental psychologist Piaget (1954) described has become a focal point.

The basic form of the task is this. An infant sits on its parent's lap in front of a table. On the table are two identical cups (or boxes, or handkerchiefs), A and B. The experimenter captures the infant's attention and the infant then observes the experimenter hiding an attractive object such as a toy under A. The surface on which the cups sit is then moved to within the infant's reach, and the infant will typically reach toward A in order to retrieve the hidden object. This process is repeated several more times, with the infant finding the toy under A on each occasion. On the test trial, the experimenter shows the infant the attractive object and then, as the infant watches, places it under B. When reaching for the toy on this trial, the infant does something peculiar. Rather than reaching toward B, where it has seen the experimenter place the toy, the infant will reach toward A. The infant perseveres in reaching toward A, committing the A-not-B error.

Piaget's (1954) explanation of this behavior portrays the infant's behavior as evidence of a confused object concept. According to Piaget, very young infants lack the concept of an object as something that endures and exists independently of the infant. During this first stage of cognitive development, the infant conceives of objects as existing for only as long as they are observable. Once out of sight, they no longer exist. By the age of twelve months, the infant has finally formed the concept of object permanence, and understands that objects continue to exist even when hidden from view or otherwise removed from sight (Smith and Thelen 2003). At the age when infants commit the A-not-B error, they are in a stage of cognitive development when their representation of objecthood is undergoing transformation. They now conceive of objects as things that continue to exist when out of sight, and they are thus prepared to search for hidden objects. However, the infant does not yet understand that objects exist independently of their own actions. The infant conceives of an object as in part comprising the motor actions that lead to its observation. Because the object that is now at location B has been observed when reaching toward location A, the infant will continue to reach toward A in its efforts to retrieve the object that is hidden at B. The infant's concept of the object is something like "thing that requires reaching toward location A."

The crucial element of Piaget's explanation is the concept of object permanence. This concept is absent in newborns, wholly present in one-year-olds, and in various transitional forms during the intervening months. The A-not-B error, on this view, is revelatory of the content of the object concept in its final stages of development. Moreover, although Piaget's early explanation of the A-not-B error was not dressed in full computational clothing, it was an explanation that computationalists might easily absorb. The changing representations of objects might be conceived as rule-governed transformations of an early-stage representation into something more complex. At the very least, the infant's development is viewed as a kind of cognitive maturation – a progression through representational stages, much as computational vision describes the stages of vision as a series of increasingly detailed representations (Marr 1982).

Many cognitive scientists who have studied the A-not-B error have by now rejected the details of Piaget's account, but retain his idea of an object concept. One finding that motivates a rejection of Piaget's explanation is this. Although infants' *reaching* behavior is perseverative, their *looking* behavior is not. Length of gazing time is a common variable for measuring an infant's expectations. A longer looking time indicates a violation of the infant's expectations. Using this method, it was found that infants who have been trained to reach toward cup A to retrieve an object do indeed expect the object to be under cup B during the test trial, *even though they continue to reach toward cup A to retrieve it* (Ahmed and Ruffman 1998). This finding has led cognitive psychologists to hypothesize that looking and reaching are guided by different kinds of object concepts, or that reaching involves performance errors to which looking is not subject, or that looking can tap implicit knowledge that is unavailable to reaching (see Ahmed and Ruffman 1998 for a discussion of all of these proposals). Common to all these hypotheses is the idea that infants possess an object concept and that this concept is explanatorily significant in understanding the A-not-B behavior.

Other difficulties with the Piagetian explanation of the A-not-B error center on the *brittleness* of the phenomenon. Small changes in the experimental task make the error disappear. For instance, the error seems to depend on the amount of time between when the object is hidden beneath cup B and when the child reaches for the object. The error is more frequent as the delay between hiding and searching grows. Also making a difference to the infant's performance is the distinctiveness of the cups (e.g. whether they are brightly colored) under which the object is hidden, whether reaching toward B involves roughly the same motor processes that the reach toward A requires, the number of reaches toward A before the B trial, and still other factors. Why, it is fair to ask Piaget, should variables unrelated to object permanence make such a difference in an infant's ability to retrieve an object if, as Piaget claims, an impoverished conception of object permanence is the correct explanation of the A-not-B error?

On Thelen, et al.'s view, there is no object concept; there is no dissociation between what the infant knows about the location of the object and what the infant reaches for; there is no developmental program involving step-like changes through increasingly sophisticated representations. "Indeed," they say, "the cornerstone of our dynamic model is that 'knowing' is perceiving, moving, and remembering as they evolve over time, and that the error can be understood simply and completely in terms of these coupled processes" (2001: 4). Let's now try to understand how this is so.

Technical niceties aside, the idea is this. In place of an object representation that guides behavior, there is instead a collection of processes that, in the course of their interactions, produces the A-not-B error. The error is emergent, in the sense that the processes involved "are coordinated without an executive agent or programme that produces the organized pattern. Rather, the coherence is generated solely in the relationships between the organic components and the constraints and opportunities of the environment" (Smith and Thelen 2003: 343–4). The most significant relationship is between the infant's past history of reaching and its current reaching behavior. A history of reaching toward cup A will create a tendency in the infant to reach toward cup A, i.e. past behavior is self-reinforcing. Hence, the more training an infant has in reaching toward A before having to reach toward B, the more effort is required to overcome the tendency to reach toward A.

If you think of the task confronting the infant as one of having to break a habit, then other parameters in Thelen's model begin to make sense. One parameter is the salience of the hiding situation. The infant is less likely to make the error if the experimenter takes extra care to draw the infant's attention to the B location (she might wave the object around before hiding it, or cup B might be decorated in an especially attractive way). Similarly, the infant is less likely to err if allowed to reach toward B within just a few seconds of hiding the object there. In this case, the location of the object is "fresh" in the infant's mind, and the tendency to reach toward A is, during this brief time span, overwhelmed by the novelty of seeing the object placed in a new location. If attempting to reach just a few seconds later, the infant will have fallen into its old pattern of behavior, and will find itself reaching toward cup A. Still another parameter concerns the motor operations the infant uses in reaching toward B. If the infant is required to use novel patterns of movement or different amounts of force, such as would occur if the infant had initially practiced reaching from a sitting position and then was required to reach for B from a standing position, or if a weight is attached to the infant's arm in the A trials but removed in the B trials, then the reaching would not fall into the old rut that the A trials had created. And, indeed, this is the case. The infant succeeds in reaching toward B when doing so requires that it change its motor plan.

Let's now consider how the model Thelen and colleagues devised to explain perseverative behavior supports her comments about embodiment. Recall that Thelen sees cognition as depending "on the kinds of experiences that come from having a body with particular perceptual and motor capabilities that are inseparably linked" (2001: 1). We wondered at the time why this assertion marks a departure from standard cognitive science. No standard cognitive scientist would deny that cognition depends in some sense on the kind of body one has, nor would she resist the idea that perception and action are linked. True enough, Thelen might respond, but the cognitivist errs in thinking that in addition to perceptual and motor capacities there must also be structures like cognitive programs, representations, and concepts. In describing their model, Smith and Thelen allege that it explains the full range of behavior surrounding the A-not-B phenomenon "without invoking constructs of 'object representation,' or other knowledge structures. Rather, the infants' behavior of 'knowing' or 'not-knowing' to go to the 'correct' target is emergent from the complex and interacting processes of looking, reaching, and remembering integrated within a motor decision field" (2003: 27). In effect, the A-not-B error is hardly more mysterious, hardly more in need of an explanation in terms of rules and representations, than the fact that a road map is more likely to be folded along its old crease lines than new ones, or that a book is more likely to open on a favorite page than to a seldom-read one. Cognition is embodied insofar as it emerges not from an intricately unfolding cognitive program, but from a dynamic dance in which body, perception, and world guide each other's steps.

3.4 Clark: Thinking with the Body

The philosopher Andy Clark is not only one of embodied cognition's most eloquent and enthusiastic spokespersons, but his careful and cogent presentations of embodied cognition have helped to shape and orient a number of research programs within embodied cognition. My intent in this section is mainly to summarize Clark's most recent statement of those features he sees as characteristic of embodied cognition. We'll have ample time in chapter 6 to fill in details and examine more closely the coherence of Clark's conception of embodied cognition.

Clark describes six distinguishing attributes of work in embodied cognition.[1] To contend that these attributes are *essential* features of embodied cognition, or are individually necessary and jointly sufficient, would, I think, be an error. Clark's intent is rather to capture the distinctive *flavor* of research in embodied cognition. Thus, a given research project may not include all six of these elements, but its adoption of several should suffice to distinguish it from research within more standard cognitive science, as well as to ally it with other embodied approaches. I shall first label these elements and will then elaborate.

1 Nontrivial Causal Spread
2 Principle of Ecological Assembly
3 Open Channel Perception
4 Information Self-structuring
5 Perception as Sensorimotor Experience
6 Dynamic-Computational Complementarity

1. Nontrivial Causal Spread   A slinky's descent down a staircase is marvelous to watch. Despite lacking joints, gyros, and power sources, the slinky manages to take each step with what appears to be wary deliberation. It accomplishes the feat passively – leaving itself to the mercy of gravity, friction, and the tension in its own coils. Too much or too little gravity, friction, or tension, and the slinky's careful creeping will be foiled. In contrast, the ability of robots like Honda's Asimo to descend stairs depends on a number of mechanisms – servomotors, drive units, control units, gyroscopes, accelerator and foot sensors, batteries – that require extensive programming. Despite all this fancy gear, Asimo cannot beat the slinky for grace.

The slinky is an example of nontrivial causal spread. It exhibits a behavior "we might have expected to be achieved by a certain well-demarcated system [which] turns out to involve the exploitation of more far-flung factors and forces" (Clark 2008: 7, note omitted). Unlike Asimo, whose progress down a flight of stairs is largely a product of his own internal workings, the slinky depends largely on forces external to itself (gravity and friction) to carry it safely to the bottom of the stairs. Proponents of embodied cognition expect that many behaviors that might, given their versatility, tempt one to seek explanations in terms of sophisticated internal mechanisms, instead have explanations that are in fact nearer the passive end of the spectrum. Indeed, bipedal robots have been devised that take advantage of the kinds of passive dynamics that animate a slinky (Collins, Ruina, Tedrake, and Wisse, 2005). Collins, et al. remark of their robot, "[i]n contrast to mainstream robots, which actively control every joint angle at all times, passive-dynamic walkers do not control any joint angle at any time. Although these walkers have no actuation or control, they can walk downhill with startlingly human-like gaits" (2005: 1083). These robots display nontrivial causal spread: the canny utilization of external factors and forces to perform duties that otherwise would require costly internal organization.

2. Principle of Ecological Assembly   As task demands change, so too do the resources and strategies necessary to meet them. For instance, suppose you are shown a pattern of six tiles of different colors and are then asked to replicate the pattern using tiles on a work surface in front of you. The strategies you use to perform this task are likely to differ depending on whether you are free to examine the pattern as you attempt to replicate it, or whether you are allowed only a quick glance of the pattern before trying to copy it. In the latter case, you must rely on your memory to guide your performance; in the former case, you need only glance back and forth between the pattern and the workspace to insure success.

The assumption in embodied cognition is that a cognizer "*tends to recruit, on the spot, whatever mix of problem-solving resources will yield an acceptable result with a minimum effort*" (Clark 2008: 13). Problem solving, according to the Principle of Ecological Assembly, is a function of the resources an organism has available to it in its surrounding environ. This makes problem solving an ecological affair: What an organism brings to the solution of a problem, and what it depends on its environment to provide, will vary in concert with the offerings in its surroundings; and organisms can exploit this fact, abandoning strategies that no longer "fit" for more efficient ones. Using the environment, the organism will be able to reduce or simplify abstract and difficult cognitive tasks to more primitive tasks involving perception and action.

> *3. Open Channel Perception*   This idea builds on points that I introduced in chapter 2's discussion of Gibson. Gibson, recall, described invariants in the optic array that correlate reliably with features of the world. Perceiving, on Gibson's view, is a matter of picking up the information that these invariants convey. Thus, to return to an earlier example, in order to maintain a particular heading, one need only make sure that the object or landmark that marks the destination remains at the point of zero optical flow. There is no need for complicated procedures of reckoning. As you move forward, just be sure that your target never flows, i.e. never appears to smear as would the portions of the optic array that are not directly in front of you. Perceptual systems, from the perspective of embodied cognition, are precisely tuned to exploit the sorts of invariances that Gibson sought to identify, thus forgoing computationally lavish mechanisms in favor of cheaper and more efficient alternatives.

An important feature of this account of navigation concerns the nature of the connection that the perceptual system bears to the world. An alternative account of navigation might require that you build an internal representation of your environment, plot a course, and consult the world only sporadically to ensure that your progress matches your expectations. When using the Gibsonian solution, however, you are constantly monitoring the world. The channel between the perceptual system and the world is constantly open. This way, the point of zero flow can act like a magnet that will pull you along unless you shift your gaze. The invariant works for only as long as you are in contact with it.

> *4. Information Self-structuring*   Within the fields of robotics and artificial intelligence, researchers are beginning to develop quantitative models that reveal the importance of morphological design (Lungarella and Sporns 2005) and action (Fitzpatrick, Metta, Natale, Rao, and Sandini 2003) for various cognitive operations. This idea, like that of open channel perception mentioned above, also has roots in Gibson's theory of perception. As Gibson conceived of perception as an active process, requiring that an organism move about its environment in an effort to uncover invariants in stimulation, so roboticists are discovering that robots can learn about their environments more effectively if they engage in actions that create or structure information available to perceptual systems. For instance, Fitzpatrick, et al. (2003) showed that a robot can learn about an object – its shape, its pattern of motion – by tapping, pushing, and slapping it. This example, though simple, illustrates a productive interplay between perception and action. Actions of the right sort can take some of the guesswork out of perception. If one thinks of perception as a process that generates hypotheses about the contents of the surrounding environment, the point of self-structuring information is to enhance the evidence available to this process; to enrich, or refine the evidence so that the burden on the perceptual system correspondingly lightens.

Motion parallax presents an obvious case of information self-structuring in the visual realm. Stereopsis is of very limited use in detecting relative depth. Distant objects do not produce enough disparity on the retinas to indicate their relative depth. Motion parallax, on the other hand, provides a very strong monocular cue of relative depth. If you fixate on an object in middle distance and move your head, you'll notice that objects between you and the point of fixation appear to move in a direction opposite to that in which your head is moving; objects beyond the point of fixation move in the same direction. Head movements are thus a means by which information is structured for purposes of depth perception.

Moreover, we should expect that, depending on an organism's morphology, different kinds of actions might be necessary to reveal the same kinds of information. Pigeons, for example, bob their heads up and down to recover depth information.[2] The more general point, however, is that embodiment matters to cognition "because *the presence of an active, self-controlled, sensing body allows an agent to create or elicit appropriate inputs, generating good data*," for cognitive processing (Clark 2008: 21).

> *5. Perception as Sensorimotor Experience*   The philosopher Alva Noë and psychologist J. Kevin O'Regan have developed a theory of perceptual experience that identifies this experience with a kind of knowledge of sensorimotor dependencies. Experience with the world, Noë and O'Regan, argue, leads one to acquire certain expectations about how one's movements will change one's experiences. For instance, as one moves around a cube, or moves a cube in one's grasp, sides and corners that were once visible may no longer be so; previously invisible sides and edges come into view. In contrast, the stimulation a spherical object presents will remain invariant under transformation. Moreover, how one's perception of objects changes through motion depends not only on the nature of the object, but also on the qualities of the perceptual apparatus. For example, because the retinal surface is concave, a straight line will form a great arc on the retina's surface as one's gaze shifts from the line to a point above or below the line (O'Regan and Noë 2001).

The knowledge one attains of these sensorimotor contingencies, knowledge that is for the most part tacit, creates expectations about how objects should look were one to engage them in various ways. Noë (2004) argues that these expectations explain why things look as they do. Moreover, because the sensorimotor dependencies that are tied to one perceptual modality, e.g. vision, differ from those that characterize another, e.g. touch, one can appeal to distinct classes of sensorimotor dependencies to explain why the phenomenology of, say, visual experiences differs from the phenomenology of tactile experiences.

The special significance Noë and O'Regan's account of perceptual experience has for Clark is its suggestion that the locus of perceptual experience is not, as might ordinarily be thought, the brain, but is instead spread out across cycles of organism-world interactions (Clark 2008: 23). Although this claim seems in keeping with Noë and O'Regan's own view, we shall have to examine it more carefully before hoping to make sense of it. As I will explain in chapter 6, there is a question that claims like Clark's face having to do with a distinction between *constitution* and *causation*. The idea that bodily actions *constitute* perceptual experience or other mental states differs importantly from the idea that bodily actions *influence* or *cause* perceptual experience or other mental states. Becoming clear on how work like Noë and O'Regan's accommodates this distinction between constitution and causation will be vital to its assessment.

> 6. Dynamic-Computational Complementarity   This final plank of Clark's embodied cognition platform offers a conciliatory message. Despite his fervent defense of embodied cognition, Clark believes that there remains a role in cognitive science for more traditional explanatory concepts such as computation and representation. In seeing no need to exorcise these central elements from cognitive science, and, indeed, in thinking that these concepts are ineliminable for understanding some aspects of cognition, Clark is obviously creating a divide between his vision of embodied cognition and one of the sort Thelen endorses. Whereas Thelen would have cognitive science abandon altogether the framework of computation, Clark's position seems to be that cognitive science might retain this framework, but would do well to focus its energies on understanding the extent to which body and world are factors in cognitive processes.

In summary, the six ideas that Clark sees as characteristic of embodied cognition are intended to mark a shift away from thinking of the body as a mere container for the brain, or, slightly better, a contributor to the brain's activities, and toward recognizing the body as the brain's partner in the production of cognition. The body incorporates passive dynamics, structures information, and determines unique sensory signatures that help to create perceptual experience. The body and brain divide the labor of cognition between them, sharing in processes that neither could complete on its own.

Clark's vision of embodied cognition is doubtless enticing, but raises a number of tough questions that will occupy us in future chapters. For instance, much of the work from which Clark draws inspiration is on the perceptual end of the cognitive scale. One might wonder how much of cognition actually depends on the body in the ways Clark describes. Might the body have a more prominent role in perceptual functions than it does in functions involving more abstract, conceptual, cognitive tasks? There also remain questions of the sort Noë faces concerning the distinction between constitution and causation. What motivates Clark's belief that the body is a genuine constituent in cognitive processing rather than a contributing player to cognitive processes that occur exclusively in the brain? On occasion, as we shall see, Clark suggests that the interplay between brain, body, and world is so thoroughly integrated as to make artificial any distinction between these things when explaining cognition. This is a claim that deserves more careful consideration. Finally, Clark's description of embodied cognition does not clearly mark a break from standard cognitive science and, indeed, embraces some of the concepts central to that tradition. We must decide whether embodied cognition is, as some researchers have suggested, a "Copernican revolution,"[3] or whether, less dramatically, it marks a more modest shift in emphasis.

3.5 Summary

If philosophy begins with perplexity, then the descriptions of embodied cognition I have presented in this chapter would seem to offer philosophers a ripe fruit indeed. One conclusion that seems immediately tempting is that the label "embodied cognition" cannot attach to a single, unified, conception of the mind. In fact, as just remarked, Clark's view of embodied cognition, insofar as it finds a place for representational accounts of the mind, is actually inconsistent with Thelen's anti-representationalism; and yet both Clark and Thelen are widely perceived as having had a significant role in defining the contours of embodied cognition.

Of course, one might hope that from some sufficiently distant vantage point it might be possible to locate among the claims of Varela, Thompson, and Rosch, Thelen, and Clark some common core. Differences are easy to find under a microscope, but, stand far enough away, and more general resemblances might begin to show themselves. The question, of course, is just how much distance must one take in order to find shared ground beneath the variety of claims we have scouted in this chapter. Too much distance and one might have trouble distinguishing embodied cognition from the more traditional conception of cognitive science. Too little distance and we are stuck again trying to come to terms with why a project like Varela, et al.'s world building should draw the interest of Thelen, who is intent on establishing dynamical systems theory as the way forward for cognitive science, or Clark, who seems most concerned with understanding how the body and world can, through their interactions, simplify or do work that was once seen as the exclusive business of the brain.

The issue of unity is too difficult to settle at this point. Before hoping to resolve it, we must first develop a more detailed understanding of the goals, methods, and conceptual resources of those who consider themselves to be pursuing embodied cognition. Fortunately, the efforts of the present chapter put us in a good position to proceed with this project, for, although finding common ground among the views I have discussed might appear difficult or impossible, the work we've sampled does, I submit, represent three prominent research agendas into which much of embodied cognition can be sorted.

More specifically, Varela, Thompson, and Rosch's focus on world building is an example of research that fits into a broader effort that I shall call the hypothesis of *Conceptualization*. Work falling under the Conceptualization heading seeks to show that an organism's understanding of the world – the concepts it uses to partition the world into understandable chunks – is determined in some sense by the properties of its body and sensory organs. Whether the truth of Conceptualization requires that one abandon the idea of an objective world, as Varela, et al. seem to suggest, is an issue we will have to consider. But of greater interest is an evaluation of the research that purports to lend support to Conceptualization. Discussion of Conceptualization will be the business of the next chapter.

Thelen provides an example of research that might more broadly be seen as supporting the hypothesis of *Replacement*. Those engaged in Replacement projects are convinced that the computational and representational tools that have for so long dominated standard cognitive science are in fact irremediably defective, and so must be abandoned in favor of new tools and approaches. These approaches, it is claimed, capture the important elements of cognition, but do so without recourse to a vocabulary pregnant with computational concepts. Dynamical systems theory is one such approach, as is the roboticist Rodney Brooks's subsumption architecture. But whether these strategies can truly account for all of cognition, and whether they really are free of any representational residue, are topics that will require careful attention.

Finally, Clark's fairly encompassing view of embodied cognition is engaged in a *Constitution* project. The distinguishing feature of projects in support of the hypothesis of Constitution is a commitment to the idea that the constituents of the mind might comprise objects and properties apart from those found in the head. Those who endorse Constitution believe that in an important sense, but one which we must take pains to clarify, mental activity includes the brain, the body, and the world, or interactions among these things.

As I mentioned in the Introduction, my division of embodied cognition into three categories should not be taken to suggest that the categories are exclusive. Many proponents of embodied cognition are conducting research that might fall into more than a single category, and, indeed, a conclusive case for any single category may well require evidence that lends support to the other two. However, if I am right that Conceptualization, Replacement, and Constitution define categories into which most work in embodied cognition might be sorted, then a detailed discussion of each should take us a long way toward understanding what embodied cognition is and to what extent it stands as a genuine alternative to standard cognitive science. Time to begin.

3.6 Suggested Reading

Clark, A. (1997a). Being There: Putting Brain, Body and World Together Again (Cambridge: MIT Press).

Clark, A. (2008). Supersizing the Mind: Embodiment, Action, and Cognitive Extension (Oxford: Oxford University Press).

Shapiro, L. (2007). "The Embodied Cognition Research Programme," Philosophy Compass 2: 338–46.

Shapiro, L. (forthcoming). "Embodied Cognition," in E. Margolis, R. Samuels, and S. Stich (eds.) Oxford Handbook of Philosophy and Cognitive Science (Oxford: Oxford University Press).

Smith, L. and Thelen, E. (2003). "Development as a Dynamic System," Trends in Cognitive Sciences 7: 343–8.

Varela, F., Thompson, E., and Rosch, E. (1991). The Embodied Mind: Cognitive Science and Human Experience (Cambridge: MIT Press).

Wilson, M. (2002). "Six Views of Embodied Cognition," Psychological Bulletin and Review 9: 625–36.

4

EMBODIED COGNITION

THE CONCEPTUALIZATION HYPOTHESIS

4.1 Conceptualization

The question "How do you conceptualize the world?" will undoubtedly elicit a variety of answers. Consider a more specific question: "How do you conceptualize a morel mushroom?" Perhaps an equivalent but clearer form of this question is this: "What is your concept of a morel mushroom?" or "What do you include in your concept of a morel mushroom?" No doubt these questions, too, will prompt distinct answers, but a reasonable hypothesis is that whatever features are mentioned in the answers will be a function of how much one knows about morels, how much experience with morels one has had, and also subjective considerations involving preferences. Thus, Sally the mycologist might conceive of a morel as an epigeous ascocarp; Charles the Provençal chef might conceive of the morel as a delicacy to be sautéed in butter; and Lucy the child might conceive of morels as yucky stuff that she must eat before being allowed dessert. As a result of these different conceptions of morels, we should expect Sally, Charles, and Lucy to behave differently, or to differ in their attitudes, towards morels. For instance, if a morel were placed on a table alongside the cup-shaped *disciotis venosa* fungus, a truffle, and boiled spinach, and Sally, Charles, and Lucy were instructed to choose the item most like a morel, Sally might choose the *disciotis venosa* fungus because it is in the same family as the morel and also has an epigeous ascocarp, Charles might choose the truffle because it too is a delicacy, and Lucy might choose the spinach because, like the morel, it is (in her callow eyes) a yucky obstacle to dessert.

Taking the example a bit further, we might imagine Lucy growing up and changing her conception of morels. She might come to conceive of a morel as something like a parsnip – worth eating if it's in front of you, but certainly not a treasure of great value. Alternatively, Lucy might have become a mycologist or a chef, and might now conceive of morels just as Sally or Charles once did. But notice that whereas there is nothing in principle to prevent Lucy from developing the same morel concept as either Sally or Charles, Lucy may never be able to develop the same concept *loud* that Sally and Charles possess if Lucy is deaf. Furthermore, because guns make loud sounds, Lucy's concept of a gun may well differ from the concept that normally hearing individuals have of guns. Lucy may never have quite the same concept of *loud* that Sally and Charles do because she cannot hear; and she may never have quite the same concepts that Sally and Charles do of those things that Sally and Charles associate with loudness.

In this chapter we are going to consider research in embodied cognition that purports to show a relationship between the kind of body an organism possesses and the kinds of concepts an organism can acquire. In its most dramatic form, the hypothesis under review is this: to conceive of the world as a human being does requires having a body like a human being's. Admittedly, this hypothesis is not precise. It does not tell us what it means to "conceive of the world as a human being does;" nor does it say what it means to have a body "like" a human being's. However, the hypothesis is, I think, clear enough to be sensible. As we take time to inspect the arguments that linguists and psychologists have offered in support of this hypothesis, we will have opportunities to refine its content. Of help in this regard will be an examination of some parallel ideas in linguistics that seek to defend the thesis of linguistic determinism. Linguistic determinism is not itself a prominent view within embodied cognition, but because of the similarity it bears to Conceptualization, a study of its motivations and difficulties will make a final evaluation of Conceptualization that much easier.

4.2 Linguistic Determinism

The linguist Benjamin Whorf famously claimed that "[w]e dissect nature along lines laid down by our native language ... all observers are not led by the same physical evidence to the same picture of the universe, unless their linguistic backgrounds are similar ..." (1956: 212–14). Put another way, Whorf's claim is that people have the same picture of the universe only if they share a language. Of course, "picture of the universe" is metaphoric. No one really has a picture of the universe. Whorf probably had in mind something like the point I made above. How one views or conceives of objects in the world is relative. However, whereas I suggested that Sally, Charles, and Lucy's conceptions of the morel were determined by what they knew or cared about, Whorf believed that one's thoughts are determined by the language one speaks: "Language shapes the way we think, and determines what we can think about" (1956). Whorf's hypothesis has a checkered history, but the idea that how we think is relative to the language we speak has enjoyed a revival in recent years. Understanding what counts as evidence for linguistic determinism and the limitations the hypothesis faces will help us to understand the hypothesis of Conceptualization.

In place of the question whether language determines one's picture of the universe, the psychologist Lera Boroditsky has asked whether language might selectively bias cognition, causing one to reason about or represent particular domains in a way that would differ were one's language to differ. I shall present two of Boroditsky's studies that, she claims, reveal such a bias. The first investigates the effect that language has on reasoning about time; the second examines the consequences that grammatical gender has for object representation.

4.2.1 The Linguistic Determination of Time Conceptions

Time is an abstract concept in the sense that many of its properties are not observable. We cannot see time, and so cannot see it as moving in a particular direction. However, the English language is equipped with spatial terms that have been co-opted for the purpose of describing time. Time is described as marching forward; the future lies ahead; the past is back then; one might be behind on her rent. The choice of spatial words that describe time as moving horizontally – from back to forward – is, presumably, arbitrary. Indeed, Mandarin, as well as using horizontal spatial terms, also describes time with vertical spatial terms. A Mandarin speaker would describe future events as down and the past as up.[1] Thus, a Mandarin speaker might say in January that February is down but December is up.

The question Boroditsky asked is whether differences in how English and Mandarin speakers talk about time determine differences in how they represent and reason about time. To answer this question, Boroditsky used a standard experimental method within cognitive psychology called priming. In a priming experiment, a subject is exposed to the priming stimulus and then the target stimulus. Of interest is the effect that the priming stimulus has on the subject's ability to respond to the target stimulus. Typically, the psychologist gauges the effect of the prime through a measure of the time the subject needs to act on the target stimulus (the subject's reaction time). For instance, a subject might be asked to push a button as soon as she recognizes a word (the target stimulus). If primed with a picture of a circle, the subject will require less time to respond to the word "circle" than she would to the word "chair;" and she may take longer to respond to the word "square" than she would to either "circle" or "chair." This would reveal something about the organization of knowledge in the subject.

Boroditsky exposed native English-speaking subjects and native Mandarin speakers who were fluent in English to primes like those in Figure 4.1.

After exposure to the primes, subjects were then shown an English target sentence about time to which they had to respond with a true/false response. An example of a target sentence is "March comes earlier than April." The temporal descriptors in the target sentences were pure, meaning that they did not draw on spatial metaphors. This insured that nothing in the target sentence would by itself suggest a horizontal or vertical spatial alignment.

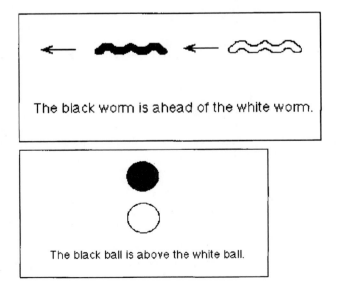

Figure 4.1 Examples of horizontal spatial prime (top) and a vertical spatial prime (bottom). Boroditsky (2001: 7–8).

Boroditsky found that most English speakers were quicker to respond to target sentences after horizontal primes than they were after vertical primes; most Mandarin speakers showed the opposite effect. This is evidence, Boroditsky claims, "that experience with a language can shape the way one thinks" (2001: 12). More specifically, because time, in English, is described as having horizontal dimensions, and in Mandarin is described in vertical dimensions, English and Mandarin speakers will think differently about time. Because of these different ways of representing time, primes that facilitate temporal thinking for an English speaker will fail to do so for a Mandarin speaker, and vice versa. This conclusion is, of course, much more modest than the Whorfian idea that language determines *everything* about thought, but this is to its advantage. Boroditsky's focus is narrow – representations of *time* – and the aspects of language of concern to her – spatial metaphors for time – are readily identifiable. What her work lacks in grandeur it gains in precision.

4.2.2 *Sex With Syntax*

Many languages assign gender to objects that clearly have no gender. These assignments are made in the grammar of the nouns used to refer to these objects. In Greek, for instance, the word for *dog* has a masculine ending, and the word for *cat* a feminine ending, but this is not because all Greek dogs are male and all Greek cats are female. There seems neither rhyme nor reason to the gender assignments that languages make. Just as there is no fact about time that makes horizontal descriptions of it better than vertical ones, there is no reason a key or a bridge should have one gender or another. But, given that some languages require that genderless objects be en-gendered, the question arises whether this creates in the speakers of these languages habits of thought that they would otherwise not have. Does a grammatical gender system determine a way of thinking about objects?

Because gender assignments to sexless objects appear to be arbitrary, learning the genders of nouns might require representing objects in a manner that makes this task easier. For instance, if the word for *cat* is feminine, a strategy for learning this might be to focus on those properties of a cat that are stereotypically feminine, such as its grace. Likewise, conceiving of dogs as aggressive or loud might aid in learning that "dog" is masculine. If this suggestion is on the right track, then a gendered language imposes on its speakers a tendency to think of objects in terms of stereotypically female and male characteristics.

In a study involving native speakers of either Spanish or German but conducted in English, Boroditsky, et al. displayed to each subject a list of twenty-four object names. The names selected were of opposite genders in Spanish and German. The subject's task was to write down the first three adjectives that popped into mind when describing each object. After collecting the adjectives, a third group of native English speakers was assigned the job of rating the adjectives as describing masculine or feminine properties. "As predicted," Boroditsky, et al. report, "Spanish and German speakers generated adjectives that were rated more masculine for items whose names were grammatically masculine in their native language than for items whose names were grammatically feminine" (2003: 70). For example, German speakers tended to describe a key, which has a masculine name in German, with "virile" adjectives such as "hard, heavy, jagged, metal, serrated, and useful." Spanish speakers, who use a feminine name for key, tended to describe keys with "feminine" adjectives such as "golden, intricate, little, lovely, shiny, and tiny." I leave it to the reader to guess the gender of "bridge" in German and Spanish. You need know only that Germans described bridges as "beautiful, elegant, fragile, peaceful, pretty, and slender;" Spaniards described them as "big, dangerous, long, strong, sturdy, and towering."

As with the earlier study on time, Boroditsky's investigation of object representation forsakes a *general* question about linguistic determinism for a narrower question about whether grammatical gender might determine biases in how one thinks about objects. I make this point again because it says something important about scientific reasoning that we must bear in mind when considering research in support of Conceptualization. An empirical test of the claim that language structures *all* thought is difficult to imagine. Rather, the scientist does better to chop this general hypothesis into smaller, more readily testable, pieces. Boroditsky's research attempts to do just this — narrowing its sights on particular linguistic structures and making explicit which observations would lend support for her hypotheses.

A final feature of Boroditsky's work worth mentioning before turning to the hypothesis of Conceptualization is the care she takes to distinguish between cognition that is in service of speaking a particular language and cognition more generally (Slobin 1996).[2] Naturally, a Spaniard's thought processes must differ from those of an English speaker's to some extent simply because the grammars of the language differ. For instance, because a Spanish speaker must take care to use nouns with the proper gender, her speech production requires that she *remember* the gender of nouns and that she *remember* how to inflect the noun correctly. These are tasks with which an

English speaker needn't bother. Similarly, a Greek speaker must think about how to transform nouns into the vocative case when addressing others, whereas, because there is no such case in English, Spanish, or German, speakers of these languages needn't spend cognitive resources on recalling and applying the rules for vocative constructions. These are examples of differences between speakers of different languages, but they are not surprising differences. There is no surprise that one must engage in whatever cognitive processes are necessary to speak Spanish, English, or Greek if one is to speak Spanish, English, or Greek, and naturally these processes will differ, given that the languages they support differ.

Making the thesis of linguistic determinism interesting is the possibility that language alters one's nonlinguistic thinking. If, for instance, speakers of different languages drew category boundaries differently, were quicker or slower to recognize certain relations, or attached different emotional valences to different objects or situations, *because* of differences in their languages, this would be a more startling discovery. Boroditsky believes that her subjects represent objects differently in virtue of the genders their various languages assign to objects. Some of her subjects conceive of keys as feminine and others conceive of them as masculine. Devising experiments that unambiguously indicate nonlinguistic differences requires tremendous ingenuity. We shall see when reviewing support for Conceptualization that a distinction analogous to that between linguistic and nonlinguistic thinking is important to draw. Not all researchers who investigate Conceptualization are attentive to this need.

4.3 Concepts and Conceptualizations

Despite the careful studies that Boroditsky has undertaken in support of linguistic determinism, one might harbor doubts that the evidence she has collected really does show that language informs or constrains a speaker's concepts. Here is one way to motivate these doubts. At the start of this chapter, I mentioned three individuals, Sally, Charles, and Lucy, who, I said, had different concepts of a morel mushroom. But perhaps this was too quick. Further interviews with Sally, Charles, and Lucy might reveal that each applies the predicate "is a morel mushroom" to exactly the same objects. When presented with a hundred mushrooms of various sorts, suppose, each selects from the collection all and only morels. On the basis of this finding, we might insist that Sally, Charles, and Lucy have the same morel concept.

How, then, do Sally, Charles, and Lucy differ? Simply, they think differently about morels; or, we might say, they have different conceptions of morels. Because Sally is a mycologist, she has certain thoughts about morels that Charles the chef and Lucy the child do not. Similarly, Charles's interest in cooking leads him to conceive differently, or form a different conception of, morels than do either Sally or Lucy.

The distinction between a concept and a conception is even clearer in those cases where the meaning of a concept is quite explicit. Consider the concept BACHELOR. This concept applies to all and only unmarried men. But, even though two people can share this concept, they may still differ in their conceptions of bachelors. Jane might think of bachelors as sexually aggressive Lotharios, whereas Ann thinks of them as lonely souls who need to find a good woman. Despite these very different conceptions of bachelors, Jane and Ann nevertheless possess the same bachelor concept – they never disagree about who is and who is not a bachelor.

One might go further and note that if concepts were indeed nothing more than what I have been calling conceptions, then the chance that any two individuals ever share a concept is terribly unlikely. Insofar as each of us is unique, with our own experiences, preferences, tastes, educations, cultural backgrounds, and so on, the probability is quite high that no two of us share *exactly* the same thoughts about anything. But, of course, we *can* agree about claims like "Bachelors are unmarried men;" "Squares are four-sided equilaterals;" "Widows are women whose husbands have died" and so on. Moreover, we judge those who disagree with these claims to have defective concepts, rather than simply different concepts. Whereas Jane and Ann may differ in their conceptions of bachelors, they should not disagree that bachelors must be male, and if one them does this would show her to lack the BACHELOR concept.

On this view, Boroditsky's experiments do not support the conclusion that speakers of different languages have different concepts. Rather, her studies show only that, e.g., Mandarin and English speakers differ in their conceptions of time; and that Spanish and German speakers differ in their conceptions of keys and bridges. True, distinct conceptions might flow from differences in language, and also true is that one might be able to predict, say, how a given individual is likely to conceive of something, given the language he or she speaks. Nevertheless, if concepts do differ from conceptions, one might press Boroditsky to justify her claim that language does indeed determine concepts rather than merely conceptions. Her data are consistent with the possibility that members of distinct linguistic communities differ in conceptions while nevertheless sharing concepts. While conceiving of keys and bridges differently, perhaps Spaniards and Germans retain the same concepts KEY and BRIDGE.

Many of the issues that arise when seeking answers to these questions remain matters of intense controversy among psychologists and philosophers. For instance, some psychologists and philosophers have questioned whether so-called classical concepts like BACHELOR, that can be defined in terms of necessary and sufficient conditions, actually exist (Smith and Medin 1981; Quine 1951). One does not have to become too creative to wonder at the adequacy of "unmarried man" as a strict definition of "bachelor." Are priests bachelors? Are gay men bachelors, and if so, would this change if laws forbidding homosexuals to marry were abolished (perhaps single gay men are bachelors in states where they can wed, but are not in states where the option is unavailable)? Moreover, even granting that some concepts can be defined with necessary and sufficient conditions, that all can, is implausible. Wittgenstein (1953/1958) made this point with the example of a game. No sooner does one develop a list of individually necessary and jointly sufficient conditions for something to be a game than a counterexample appears. Finally, psychologists have known for quite a while that people do not appear to use concepts as they would if they really did express necessary and sufficient conditions. Thus, people tend to think of things as being more or less representative of a concept (Smith and Medin 1981). For instance, subjects might rate a rabbit as being more mammal-like than a whale; or a robin as more bird-like than an ostrich. If MAMMAL and BIRD really were concepts in the classical sense they should not apply more or less well to particular individuals – they should admit of no degree.

The upshot of these reflections is that prior to a theory of what concepts are there can be no assessing the weight of support for linguistic determinism. Boroditksy's data make linguistic determinism plausible if concepts are nothing more than conceptions. On the other hand, if concepts are something else, Boroditsky faces the task of showing that her experiments have isolated the correct notion of concept rather than targeting mere conceptions. Because this is not the place to advance and defend a theory of what concepts are, we should treat the issues above as a ground for caution. Whether linguistic determinism is true depends on whether language determines concepts, and similarly, whether Conceptualization is true depends on whether bodies determine concepts. It is a significant shortcoming in the research surrounding linguistic determinism and Conceptualization that more time is not devoted to examining the concept of a concept.

4.4 Testing Hypotheses

One final detour is necessary before finally turning to the hypothesis of Conceptualization. In describing Conceptualization, as well as Replacement and Constitution, as *hypotheses*, I am adopting the attitude that these theses should be testable. In part, this attitude simply reflects the idea that the claims emerging from embodied cognition should derive from an empirical investigation of psychological capacities rather than armchair speculations about what might be true. But the meaning of testability extends beyond the mere requirement of empirical investigation. I shall have in mind something more precise when I speak of testability. In particular, in saying that hypothesis H1 is testable, I shall mean that H1 implies observations (or makes predictions) that would give it a higher *likelihood* than some rival hypothesis H2.

The notion of likelihood is a technical one. To say that hypothesis H1 has higher likelihood than H2 is to say that the former makes some observation O more probable than the latter does. Thus, suppose I open the cookie jar only to find that its contents have been stolen. I notice crumbs on the counter. I then consider two hypotheses: my daughter Sophia, who tends to be very messy, stole the cookies. Alternatively, Sophia's sister Thalia, who is always very neat, stole the cookies. The observation that there are crumbs on the counter gives higher likelihood to the hypothesis that Sophia stole the cookies than it does that Thalia stole the cookies. Crumbs on the counter are more probable given that Sophia is the thief than they are given that Thalia is. This is reflected in the claim that the former hypothesis has higher likelihood than the latter.

Importantly, likelihood and probability are measures of different quantities. The hypothesis that Sophia is the thief can have a very high likelihood even if it remains improbable that Sophia stole the cookies. Maybe Sophia is known far and wide for her honesty. Likelihood is simply a measure of how strongly one should expect certain observations *given* some hypothesis. If Sophia is messy and Thalia is not, one should expect to find crumbs on the counter *given* that Sophia stole the cookies, but one should be surprised to find crumbs *given* that Thalia was the culprit. Higher likelihood attaches to the hypothesis that leads one to expect some observation; lower likelihood belongs to the hypothesis that makes the same observation surprising. The *probability* of the hypotheses is another matter.

In framing matters in this way, testability turns out to be a contrastive notion: H is testable only with respect to some rival hypothesis R (Sober

1999). The reason to treat testability as contrastive becomes clearer when one remembers that evidence always underdetermines theory. This means simply that for any piece of evidence there are an indefinite number of hypotheses that the evidence "fits." For instance, if I find that the cookie jar is empty and that there are crumbs on the counter, I might take the crumbs to be evidence that Sophia has stolen the cookies. But the evidence doesn't clinch the case against her. Other hypotheses might predict the same evidence. Perhaps my wife, who is also untidy, was the perpetrator. Perhaps Thalia, who is devious, is framing her sister. The evidence does not decide between these hypotheses – they have the same likelihood because they lead us to expect the same observation.[3] Rather than *determining* one hypothesis to be better than another, the observation of crumbs *underdetermines* the choice between hypotheses.

The importance of treating testability as a contrastive relation should now be apparent. The claim that evidence might support a hypothesis *full stop* carries little information, for the same evidence can support countless others as well, making the very idea of *support* difficult to assess. For instance, suppose I claim that the cookie crumbs are evidence that Sophia stole the cookies. But if there are a hundred other hypotheses that also predict the presence of crumbs on the counter, then the claim that the evidence *supports* the hypothesis about Sophia is peculiar. If "support" means simply "is consistent with," then the evidence does support the hypothesis, but it supports innumerable others as well.

However, one can still make sense of the claim that a piece of evidence gives one hypothesis higher likelihood *than another*. We saw this when comparing the hypotheses about Sophia and Thalia. If hypothesis H1 predicts O but hypothesis H2 makes no such prediction, then the discovery of O yields more support for H1 than it does for H2. Thus, whereas the presence of crumbs is not good evidence for distinguishing between the hypotheses that (i) Sophia stole the cookies, and (ii) my wife did (because they are both untidy), it may be quite good evidence for distinguishing the hypothesis about sloppy Sophia from the hypothesis about tidy Thalia. The general point is simply that evidence is useful when it can distinguish between competing hypotheses. This is why testability is helpfully interpreted as a contrastive exercise.

We see this methodology at work in Boroditsky's studies. Consider again her investigation of conceptions of time. The hypothesis Boroditsky sought to test was this: English and Mandarin speakers conceive of time differently. The hypothesis against which this was to be tested was simply this: English and Mandarin speakers have similar conceptions of time. The evidence, in the form of reaction times to target questions after exposure to identical primes, favored the first hypothesis over the second, for the first hypothesis predicts that English and Mandarin subjects ought to react differently in response to the primes whereas such a finding, if the second hypothesis were true, would be surprising. What Boroditsky took care not to do was devise an experiment that would reveal differences in what she called linguistic thinking. Proponents of both linguistic determinism and its rival agree that speakers of different languages will differ in the cognitive activities that are required to speak their different languages. Evidence that this is true thus lends support to neither side. The valuable experiments are those that produce evidence that either the linguistic determinist or her rival should not expect.

In the remainder of this chapter as well as in chapters to follow, we must keep these points about testability in mind as we try to articulate the hypotheses that proponents of embodied cognition offer and as we try to understand the role that evidence plays in their evaluation. Boroditsky's experiments, while perhaps an especially useful guide to the work on Conceptualization, are also of more general interest for the lessons they teach about hypothesis testing.

4.5 The Embodiment of Color

Varela, Thompson, and Rosch offer the example of color vision as "[p]erhaps the best example" of embodiment in a living system (1991: 157). Moreover, they claim, the choice to explicate embodiment through the example of color vision is especially appropriate, because "color provides a microcosm of cognitive science," insofar as our understanding of color draws from the disciplines of psychology, linguistics, philosophy, neuroscience, and artificial intelligence (1991: 157). The first step in assessing the success of VTR's analysis of color vision is to understand what they intend the example to show.

VTR aim to show that the human capacity for color vision is the product of a "history of coupling" between a human being and particular properties of the world. The special sort of coupling involved in color vision is supposed to "stand in sharp contrast to systems whose coupling with the environment is specified through input/output relations" (1991: 157). The digital computer, VTR say, is an example of this latter type of system. The suggestion, then, is that color vision emerges from a kind of coupling that is beyond the capacity of a computer. A corollary of this suggestion is that standard cognitive science, insofar as it adopts a computational theory of mind, cannot explain color vision. Still another conclusion VTR wish to draw is that "color provides a paradigm of a cognitive domain that is neither pregiven nor represented but rather experiential and enacted" (1991: 171). This second conclusion brings us close to the hypothesis of Conceptualization, for it expresses the idea that colors are created in experience through a kind of activity, where this activity is the product of specialized equipment that in turn creates opportunities for a unique sort of coupling. Thus, the human experience of color would differ from the experiences that emerge from different kinds of coupling: "the vastly different histories of structural coupling for birds, fishes, insects, and primates have enacted or brought forth different perceived worlds of color" (1991: 183).

Let's examine these conclusions in reverse order. Stated more precisely, VTR seem to be offering the following hypothesis:

> *Color Conceptualization*: color experience is created through a unique sort of embodied coupling.

Frustratingly, VTR say little about the meaning of "coupling," but hints to its meaning surface in their presentation of the details of color vision. The important details are these: there is no single physical property with which experiences of a single color correlate. Color experience is the product of the interaction of three different sorts of cells in the retina known as cones. Distinguishing the three sorts of cones is their sensitivity to different portions of the visible light spectrum. There are cones sensitive to short, medium, and long wavelengths. Perceived color is a function of the ratio of the excitations of these three types of cone. However, an infinite number of different combinations of light can produce identical ratios of excitation. Thus, from the experience of, say, *green* it is impossible to infer any conclusions about the composition of light in the world that is causing the experience, except to say that the composition of light suffices to fix a ratio of cone firings that creates an experience of green.

Another important point is that the structure of color experience depends on how the three types of cones interact. Determining the experience of red and green is the difference in firing rates of the long- and medium-wave cones, whereas the experience of blue and yellow is determined by the difference of the sum of long- and medium-wave cone excitation minus short-wave cone excitation. Because of these interactions, red and green "oppose" each other, as do blue and yellow. The red/green channel can never indicate red and green at the same time, and likewise for the blue/yellow channel. Thus, the wiring of the cones explains why it is impossible to see something as reddish green or bluish yellow. The opponency system explains other features of color experience as well, for instance the fact that red, green, yellow, and blue are unique hues — can be experienced as containing no other hue — in contrast to a binary color like orange, which appears as a reddish yellow.

A final point to make about the color vision system concerns its response to contrast and changes in illumination. A surface that projects a single collection of wavelength frequencies may appear to be one color at one time and another color at another time. This is because the color vision system is sensitive to contrast. Thus, moving a color patch from one surface to another can change its experienced hue despite the fact that it continues to reflect the same frequencies of light. On the other hand, a patch can seem to retain a single color despite the fact that under different illuminations it reflects different frequencies of light. This phenomenon, called color constancy, is readily apparent when we note that the surfaces that surround us do not appear to change their colors as the sun slowly sets.

These facts about color vision, VTR summarize, show "that we will not be able to explain color if we seek to locate it in a world independent of our perceptual capacities. Instead, we must locate color in the perceived or experiential world that is brought forth from our history of structural coupling" (1991: 165). Perhaps VTR mean this. There are no colors in the world — "colors are not 'out there' independent of our perceptual and cognitive capacities" (1991: 172). Rather, color emerges from the interaction (coupling) between a visual system with a particular variety and arrangement of specialized cells and certain properties in the world. Thus, the hypothesis of color conceptualization, that color experience is created through a unique sort of embodied coupling, is correct. Moreover, because many non-human organisms have visual systems with different characteristics, e.g., pigeons have perhaps as many as six types of cone cells and goldfish have four, we should expect that the world of color they "bring forth" will differ from the world of color that human beings experience.

If my interpretation of VTR has been reasonably accurate, it would seem to face some very serious challenges. Let's begin with their claim that there are no colors "out there." Here's a reconstruction of the argument that seems to lead VTR to this conclusion:

Argument Against Colors in the World

1   The color experiences that the visual system determines do not corre-
     spond one-to-one with properties in the world.
2   If color experiences do not correspond one-to-one with properties in
     the world, then there are no colors in the world.
3   Therefore, there are no colors in the world.

If this indeed is the argument against colors being "pregiven," then
it should be rejected. The first premise is fine, but the second is not. The
problem is that there is no logical connection between a failure of correspondence and the existence of properties. Everything VTR say about the
operation of the color system may be true, and so it may be true that there
is not just one property in the world that corresponds to each experienced
color. Indeed, we can assume that for every experienced color there are an
infinite number of distinct properties to which the experienced color might
correspond. But to move from these assumptions to the rejection of colors
"out there," VTR require an additional assumption.

One candidate would be this: if there were colors in the world, color
perception would be accurate. To see why this assumption might be necessary, consider a color theorist who insists that colors (but not experiences of
color) do correspond to unique collections of surface spectral reflectances.[4]
Thus, green "out there" is identical to a certain way that an object reflects
light. VTR would here object that an experience of green correlates with a
potentially infinite number of different combinations of light frequencies,
and so there is no real, objective green "out there." But, from the color
theorist's perspective, this shows just that most experiences of green do not
track actual green. The possibility that most experiences of green – even *all*
experiences of green – are mistaken does not imply that there is no green
"out there." That is, the color theorist might reject the assumption above:
the fact that color perception is often inaccurate does not show that colors
do not exist in the world. To think otherwise would be akin to denying the
existence of gold because one is unable to distinguish real gold from many
things that only appear to be gold.

But rather than belaboring problems with VTR's rejection of a pregiven
world, the more significant challenge they face is to explain why the hypothesis I have called color conceptualization is at all interesting. According to
this hypothesis, color experience emerges from the special properties of a
visual system; thus organisms with different kinds of visual systems will
have different color experiences. But surely there is nothing surprising

about this hypothesis. Indeed, we should be more surprised if differences in visual systems *never* created differences in experience.

This criticism becomes even more damaging when we recall that VTR look to color as a "paradigm of a cognitive domain that is neither pregiven nor represented but rather experiential and enacted" (1991: 171). Being experiential and enacted is, for VTR, what it means to be embodied. Now, however, it would appear that all there is to being embodied is having experiences that are a function of a particular sort of nervous system. Yet, there is nothing in this claim that should encourage the first of VTR's conclusions that I mentioned above, viz. that the study of cognition must abandon the computational and representational framework of standard cognitive science. Far from it, vision researchers are busily constructing computational theories of color vision in the attempt to discover algorithms that, for instance, explain the experience of color constancy through changing conditions of illumination (e.g. Barnard, Finlayson, and Funt 1997).

I introduced this chapter with a discussion of linguistic determinism because I hoped that understanding that thesis and its relation to evidence might put us in a position to grasp more easily the hypothesis of Conceptualization. We might now apply some lessons from that discussion to the issues at hand. The hypothesis of linguistic determinism has a clear competitor – the view that language does not influence nonlinguistic cognition. One must design an experiment that will yield observations that either linguistic determinism or its rival predicts. The data then provide evidence on behalf of one or the other thesis. Boroditsky, recall, took care to distinguish data that would reveal differences in nonlinguistic thinking from those that would show differences only in linguistic thinking. The reason for this is simple: both the thesis of linguistic determinism and its rival are consistent with the possibility that speakers of different languages will show some differences in cognition. No one denies that speakers of different languages show differences in cognition. The issue is whether there are differences in cognition *beyond* those that one would predict, given differences in language.

We can now see how VTR fall short in their goal to supplant standard cognitive science with embodied cognitive science. Their thesis of color conceptualization, which, recall, is their *best case* for an embodied approach, predicts nothing that a dyed-in-the-wool traditional cognitivist wouldn't also predict. Both the cognitivist and VTR can agree that color experience emerges from interactions of the nervous system with the world. Both camps can agree that organisms with distinct nervous systems may very well have distinct color experiences. Of course, VTR also argue that on their view there are no "pregiven" colors, but, even if I am wrong that this conclusion is unwarranted, we can also now see that the point is a red herring. Those who agree on details of a cognitivist explanation of color vision are free to, and often do, disagree about what these details say about the nature of color. Disputes about the ontological status of color – whether, for instance, colors are "in the head" or "out there" – are orthogonal to the question whether standard cognitive science can explain color vision and its associated phenomena.

4.6 Embodiment and Metaphor

One of the most provocative defenses of Conceptualization builds on a compelling analysis of the role of metaphor in thought. The linguist George Lakoff and philosopher Mark Johnson are the primary figures in this area. Of particular interest to us is their claim that "the peculiar nature of our bodies shapes our very possibilities for conceptualization and categorization" (1999: 19). This hypothesis sounds close to the idea of linguistic determinism that we examined earlier, with the "peculiar nature of our bodies" rather than the properties of language being the focus of investigation. Unfortunately, the thesis also shares the vagueness in Whorf's assertion that "[l]anguage shapes the way we think, and determines what we can think about" (1956). Boroditsky manages to sidestep the imprecision in Whorf's statement by narrowing her sights to particular properties of language, e.g. the use of gender constructions, and to particular ways of thinking, e.g. tendencies to associate particular properties with objects. Thus, although her experiments cannot demonstrate linguistic determinism *tout court*, they can provide evidence that specific features of language influence specific cognitive capacities. We shall have to see whether Lakoff and Johnson can similarly adjust for the imprecision in the hypothesis they offer.

Defense of their hypothesis begins with observations about the importance of metaphor in the development of concepts. "The essence of metaphor," they say, "is understanding and experiencing one kind of thing or experience in terms of another" (1980: 5). Metaphor is a method for *expanding* understanding. Given that one already understands A, B, and C, one can use this knowledge to help in coming to understand some new concept or idea D. To do this, one must draw connections between A, B, and C, on the one hand, and D on the other.

For instance, to explain the concept of an intimate relationship to a child, one might resort to a metaphor that ties relationships to a journey – something with which the child is presumably already familiar. The *relationships are a journey* metaphor acts as a scaffold for framing the various aspects of relationships that would otherwise be difficult or impossible to articulate. Thus, lovers choose to *travel the path* of life together, they may face a *bumpy stretch* or two, or find themselves at *crossroads*, or pursuing a *course* that is ultimately a *dead-end street, going nowhere*, until they *go their separate ways*. Or, more optimistically, they can *get back on the right track*, find the *sailing smooth*, and *ride into the sunset* together.

But more than simply helping to elucidate concepts, Lakoff and Johnson argue that metaphors actually determine, at least in part, the meanings of concepts. The *relationships are a journey* metaphor imposes a structure on how we think about relationships. The metaphor sanctions some descriptions of relationships, or inferences about relationships, or *ways of thinking* about relationships, while prohibiting others. A disappointed lover might say to a partner "we'd *come so far* together, how could you possibly *stray*?" We can make sense of this remark because we do think of relationships as journeys. In contrast, the cuckolded lover could not say "we'd climbed to the top of the tree, how could you possibly break a branch?" because *relationships are trees* is a not metaphor that we use to inform our conception of relationships. Thus, metaphors contribute to the meanings of concepts insofar as they license certain ways of using concepts, describing concepts, and understanding concepts.

When attending closely to language, one might be surprised to find how extensively metaphors insinuate themselves. Lakoff and Johnson remark that "metaphor pervades our normal conceptual system. Because so many of the concepts that are important to us are either abstract or not clearly delineated in experience ... we need to get a grasp on them by means of other concepts that we understand in clearer terms ..." (1980: 115). Concepts like *time* (for which we have already seen metaphorical spatial associations), *God, peace, life, infinity*, and many others are impossible, or nearly so, to understand without recourse to metaphor. But, not every concept depends on a metaphorical explication. Concepts must "bottom out" at some point or else the metaphors we use to give meaning to new concepts would themselves involve concepts that would have to depend on metaphors for their meaning, and so on. The solution to this problem, Lakoff and Johnson argue, lies in embodiment.

Those concepts that we can learn without resort to metaphor – *basic concepts* – derive from "direct physical experience" (1980: 57). For instance, consider the concept *up*. Lakoff and Johnson contend that we come to understand this concept through our experience with motion through space: "[w]e have bodies and we stand erect. Almost every movement we make involves a motor program that either changes our up-down orientation, maintains it, presupposes it, or takes it into account in some way" (1980: 56). The concept *up* is something we come to understand simply in virtue of our embodiment. Of course, we must still learn that, in English, "up" is the word that designates this concept, but the concept itself needs, as it were, no further introduction. Similarly, the experiences that come from having a body of the sort we do also explain how we come to understand concepts like *front* and *back*. Moreover, the basic actions of which our bodies are capable ground our understanding of concepts that involve force: "pushing, pulling, propelling, supporting, and balance" (1999: 36). Basic concepts, then, do not rest on other concepts, but instead have roots in the particulars of our bodies and the actions that they perform.

If our understanding of abstract concepts depends on a metaphorical expansion of more familiar concepts, and our understanding of more familiar concepts depends on a metaphorical expansion of basic concepts, then we can begin to see the motivation for Lakoff and Johnson's hypothesis that "the peculiar nature of our bodies shapes our very possibilities for conceptualization and categorization" (1999: 19). Human bodies are oriented vertically, have a front and back, move in the direction of their front side, have joints with specific degrees of freedom, possess most of their sensory organs at their top end, and so on. These features of human bodies will endow human psychology with a distinctive suite of basic concepts, which in turn will influence the meanings of familiar concepts, which in turn will influence the meanings of more abstract concepts. This "trickle up" effect explains the sense in which human bodies determine human concepts.

Lakoff and Johnson add some vibrancy to their hypothesis with the following thought experiment. "Imagine," they say, "a spherical being living outside of any gravitational field, with no knowledge or imagination of any other kind of experience. What could UP possibly mean to such a being?" (1980: 57). Similarly, they say, the concepts *front* and *back* "make sense only for beings with fronts and backs. If all beings on this planet were uniform stationary spheres floating in some medium and perceiving equally in all directions, they would have no concepts of *front* and *back*" (1999: 34). These examples give further shape to Lakoff and Johnson's hypothesis that the body determines the concepts one can acquire. Lacking bodies of the "right" sort, organisms are unable to develop basic concepts such as up, front, or back.

Furthermore, because of the "trickle up" from basic concepts, through familiar concepts, and onward to more abstract concepts, we should predict that the spherical beings Lakoff and Johnson imagine differ from human beings with respect to most or all of the concepts they possess.

4.6.1 Putting Lakoff and Johnson's Conceptualization Thesis to the Test

Having before us Lakoff and Johnson's case for their version of Conceptualization, we can now begin to evaluate it. An obvious place to begin is with their claim about the conceptual abilities of their imaginary spherical beings. Why, we might wonder, should the acquisition of concepts like front, and back be impossible for a spherical being? Perhaps they cannot learn these concepts through experience with their own body, but can they not learn the concepts through their experience with other objects? Lakoff and Johnson think not. "We project fronts and backs onto objects," they concede (1999: 34). But, "[w]hat we understand as the front of a stationary artifact, like a TV or a computer or a stove, is the side we normally interact with using our fronts" (1999: 34). Apparently, they think, it takes a front to know a front. But I do not see why this must be so. Why not think of an object's front as the side of the object that usually approaches us, or the side it shows us as we approach it? Spherical beings may not have fronts, but objects can still approach them, and they can still approach objects. If the objects that approach them always do so with the same side "forward," or always turn the same side towards approaching spherical beings, then this may suffice to endow the spherical beings with a concept of front.

More generally, Lakoff and Johnson's confidence that similarity in concepts requires similarity in body seems too strong. Perhaps similar concepts can be acquired through different means. An organism for which front is not a basic concept may yet have other basic concepts from which front can be derived. If so, the "trickling up" of conceptual differences could be blocked early on – permitting sameness of more abstract concepts. Whether this is possible is surely an empirical question, and so it is appropriate to ask how one might go about testing Lakoff and Johnson's hypothesis.

We have seen how Boroditsky tests specific hypotheses of linguistic determinism. To do so, she designs experiments that involve two distinct linguistic populations. Linguistic determinism predicts that these populations will exhibit cognitive differences in virtue of differences in the languages they speak. What Boroditsky does not do is compare an English-speaking population to an imaginary population that speaks an imaginary language. While such thought experiments are not completely worthless – they might, for instance, help refine ideas or suggest experimental designs – they should not serve as the sole basis for empirical conclusions. However, this would seem to be precisely Lakoff and Johnson's *modus operandi*. The doubter who objects, as I did above, that similar basic concepts might arise in a variety of ways would find little reassurance in a discussion of what imaginary beings would find possible to learn.

There is also an interesting parallel to draw between Boroditsky's distinction between linguistic/nonlinguistic thought and a distinction between cognitive processes that are necessary to "run" a particular sort of body and cognitive processes that are not geared toward a particular sort of body. Although Lakoff and Johnson never consider this distinction, one might find it plausible in the present context. As an example, consider that an organism that possesses two eyes with overlapping visual fields can derive relative depth information from information about retinal disparity. But the algorithm for recovering depth information must be tailored to the specific features of the organism's ocular anatomy. An organism with eyes that are four inches apart would be ill-served by cognitive algorithms that have been "designed" for eyes two inches apart. Similarly, algorithms that recover depth from binocular vision would, presumably, fail to recover depth from tri-ocular vision. So, just as there are cognitive processes that are necessary for competence in a *particular* language, surely there are cognitive processes that are necessary to exploit the anatomical properties of particular sorts of bodies.

Likewise, just as Boroditsky was interested in discovering whether differences in language might create differences in nonlinguistic cognitive processes, we should wonder whether whatever conceptual differences there may be between organisms with different bodies go beyond just those that are necessary to operate the different bodies. The fact that organisms with different bodies differ in the cognitive processes necessary to "run" their bodies is banal. Far more interesting would be a demonstration that these organisms differ in other cognitive ways. Perhaps they differ in their capacities for memory, or attention. Perhaps the bodily differences influence their abilities to solve problems or learn languages. Perhaps, as Lakoff and Johnson suspect, they would partition the contents of the world in inconsistent ways. Unfortunately, populations of cognitive beings with distinct morphologies are not as easy to find as populations of beings who speak distinct languages. This presents a serious obstacle to efforts to confirm Lakoff and Johnson's hypothesis.[5]

4.6.2 Second-Generation Cognitive Science

Even if there are problems in the details of Lakoff and Johnson's program, one might wonder whether the emphasis they place on the body's role in cognition suffices to establish a break from standard cognitive science. They believe that it does. On their view, standard cognitive science, or what they call first-generation cognitive science, is doomed or already dead. In its place is second-generation cognitive science, or the cognitive science of the embodied mind (Lakoff and Johnson 1999: 77; Lakoff 2003). Lakoff (2003) provides a summary of, in his view, the essential features of first-generation cognitive science as well as a description of their replacements in second-generation cognitive science.[6]

According to Lakoff, first-generation cognitive science clings to four ideas that, surprisingly, are rooted in a priori philosophical considerations rather than having an empirical foundation (2003: 2–3; see also Lakoff and Johnson 1999: 78–9 for the same charge). This is surprising, for in earlier chapters we have seen work in standard cognitive science that is apparently committed to empirical investigation. And, although the studies we have examined (e.g. Sternberg's work on recall) do not try to test fundamental assumptions in standard cognitive science, we might nevertheless see the success of these research projects as evidence in favor of these basic assumptions. If these projects were not successful – if the predictions and explanations they offered were rarely accurate or enlightening – then one would expect that in time the basic computational assumptions would become the focus of critical attention. And, indeed, as we saw, connectionists have made ventures in this direction. But, again, this is even more reason to believe that first-generation cognitive science rests on empirical rather than a priori foundations.

The four assumptions that Lakoff identifies as fundamental in traditional, or first-generation, cognitive science are these:

1   Mind is symbolic and cognitive processes are algorithmic.
2   Thought is disembodied and abstract.
3   Mind is limited to conscious awareness.
4   Thought is literal and consistent, and thus suitable for modeling with logic.

The descendents of these first-generation ideas that now populate second-generation cognitive science are these:

1'. Mind is "biological and neural, not a matter of symbols" (2003: 3).

2'. Thought is embodied: "physical in nature, with concepts precisely and exquisitely sculpted by neural circuitry that evolved to run a body ... The peculiar structures of our concepts reflect the peculiarities of our bodies ..." (2003: 3).

3'. Approximately 95% of the mind is unconscious.

4'. Abstract thought "is largely metaphorical, making use of the same sensory-motor system that runs the body."

(2003: 3)

Let's examine pairs of the "old" and "new" in turn. Lakoff is correct that standard cognitive science conceives of the mind as computational. But, as I explained in §1.3, one can have a commitment to the computational mind while at the same time believing that minds are biological and neural. An object can be a vase and a collection of molecules at the same time. But perhaps this response is unfair. Lakoff doubtless means that a symbolic description of the mind is, for some reason, wrong. His reason for thinking this brings us to the second difference between first- and second-generation cognitive science.

The charge that standard cognitive science portrays the mind as disembodied has some merit. As we saw in chapter 1, the idea that the mind consists in algorithmic processes does indeed encourage a picture of minds as abstract entities that can be studied in isolation from the hardware on which they are implemented. The prominent cognitive scientist Jerry Fodor has gone so far as to say that neurophysiology is irrelevant to psychology (1975: 17). If standard cognitive scientists are correct that the mind/brain relationship is like the program/computer relationship, then minds would seem to be autonomous from the brain.[7] After all, one needn't know how computers operate in order to write a program.

But we should ask whether Lakoff's alternative – embodiment – is truly irreconcilable with the computational theory of mind. Where Lakoff sees tension between his claim that the "peculiar structures of our concepts reflect the peculiarities of our bodies" and the view that thought is computational, I see opportunities for rapprochement. Suppose, for the sake of argument, that Lakoff and Johnson's account of concept acquisition is correct, and that the concepts human beings develop owe something, in some sense, to the particularities of their bodies. This idea is close to Varela, et al.'s earlier point that concepts or experiences of color reflect the properties of retinal cone cells. Indeed, Lakoff looks to color perception as another example of embodiment (2003: 9). However, there is nothing inimical in the computational theory of mind to these observations. If properties of the body do indeed "shape" how we experience the world, then the standard cognitive scientist should insist that the relevant properties of the body be represented in the algorithms that constitute cognition. On this view, the "problem" with first-generation cognitive science is not that it adopts a computational framework, but that it fails to include in its description of the mind's programs information about the body.

As an example to illustrate this suggestion, consider that sound localization is possible in virtue of the fact that an organism's ears are separated from each other. Because of this separation sound waves will typically enter one ear before they enter the other, (this is called the *interaural time difference*, or ITD) and this difference, though small, suffices to indicate the location of the sound source. The ITD for a given organism will depend on the distance between its ears: the larger the distance, the larger the ITD. These facts seem to be just the sort that impress Varela, et al. as well as Lakoff and Johnson. Our perception of the location of objects is *embodied*. Now suppose further that a standard cognitive scientist wished to write an algorithm that modeled sound localization. Lakoff seems to think that such an algorithm cannot succeed, because it must ignore the peculiarities of the body. But, while it is true that the algorithm would fail if it neglected to represent the ITD, there is no reason to believe that it *cannot* represent the ITD. Presumably, a symbolic representation of ITD would be an integral part of the algorithm. I conclude that embodiment, as Lakoff describes it, is not inconsistent with computationalism.

The third pair of assumptions that Lakoff discusses is the most curious. Recall that he thinks that first-generation cognitive science is committed to the view that all cognitive processes are conscious, whereas second-generation cognitive science allows that as much as 95% of cognition is unconscious. "Descartes was in error," Lakoff intones (2003: 3). Making these remarks curious is the obvious and irrefutable *wrongness* of Lakoff's description of standard cognitive science. Virtually none of the cognitive processes we have so far examined – memory retrieval strategies, the computation of depth from disparity, linguistic effects on time and object representation – was thought by their investigators to be completely available to consciousness. Without a doubt, one can safely say that *almost all* research in standard cognitive science examines processes that are unconscious, and *all* cognitive scientists would admit to the existence of unconscious cognitive processes.

This leaves us with the fourth difference between first- and second-genera-tion cognitive science. Lakoff contends that standard cognitive science insists on the literalness and consistency of thought, but that thought is, in fact, "largely metaphorical, making use of the same sensory-motor system that runs the body" (2003: 3). I shall address the point about the sensory-motor system in more detail later in this chapter when discussing mirror neurons. For now, I wish to raise two issues. First, the sense in which standard cogni-tive scientists have insisted that thought be literal and consistent is not clear. Perhaps Lakoff's reasoning is this: if thought is computation, and computa-tion requires literalness and consistency, then thought, for the standard cogni-tive scientist, must be literal and consistent. However, if this is truly Lakoff's reasoning, then its error is easy to spot. An important aim of cognitive science is to understand how human minds work — how, a bit more tendentiously, they think. But commitment to a computational theory of mind does not commit one to the view that cognition must be literal and consistent. Indeed, cognitive psychologists have long been interested in instances of what appears to be irrationality, as when, for instance, subjects are able to apply material implication in one context but not in other contexts (the so-called Wason selection task (Oaksford and Chater 1994)), or when subjects make errors in probabilistic reasoning (e.g. the base rate fallacy (Gigerenzer and Hoffrage 1995)). I see no reason that computational models of non-literal and incon-sistent thinking are impossible. In fact, as Lakoff must be aware, there exist computational models of metaphor (see, e.g., Martin 1990).

Second, Lakoff's focus on thought is too narrow. Thought, as ordi-narily conceived, is at the upper end of cognitive abilities. Accordingly, condemning *all* of standard cognitive science for a problem it purportedly has with explaining processes at the upper end is inappropriate. Lakoff fails to appreciate the diversity of research interests that comprise cognitive science. Criticisms that stick to one research program may leave untouched other programs.

To summarize this section, Lakoff and Johnson have sought to distinguish standard cognitive science from embodied cognitive science on a number of points. Where, on their view, standard cognitive science is hobbled by its inability to attend to the important role the body plays in cognition, and must conceive of thought as literal and consistent, embodied cogni-tion embraces the body's significance, and appreciates the prominence of metaphorical thinking. I have argued that this contrast between "old" and "new" is, for the most part, unsustainable. What may be true, however, is that standard cognitive scientists do not realize the extent to which cognition is indebted to the body. We shall pursue this possibility further in the following sections.

4.7 The Symbol Grounding Problem

A number of psychologists have recently turned to embodiment in an effort to solve the so-called *symbol grounding problem*. This problem is, on their view, an artifact of the computational theory of mind. In this section I will present the problem and its association to standard cognitive science. In the next we will see how theories of embodied cognition bear on the problem. Additionally, although the connection between these issues and the hypothesis of Conceptualization is more tenuous than that between Conceptualization and research we have examined so far, this chapter is a natural home for the present discussion.

Psychologists concerned with the symbol grounding problem (e.g. Glenberg 1997; Barsalou 1999; Glenberg and Robertson 2000; Glenberg and Kaschak 2002; Glenberg, Havas, Becker, and Rinck 2005; Zwaan and Madden 2005) typically appeal to a famous thought experiment for its illustration: John Searle's Chinese Room (Searle 1980). The thought experiment (simplified for present purposes) centers on an English speaker, call him "JS," who knows nothing about the Chinese language. JS sits in a room with only a slot in a wall for access to the outside world. Through this slot come slips of paper with Chinese characters written on them. Perhaps JS recognizes the characters as Chinese, but, for all he knows, they may not be linguistic symbols at all. In the room are instruction manuals, written in English, that tell JS which Chinese symbols to write on a piece of paper in response to the symbols on the slip of paper he has just received through the room's slot. Having accomplished this, JS passes his handiwork back through the slot. In time, JS becomes so proficient at following the instructions that he is able to produce a string of symbols fairly quickly. To the Chinese speakers outside, the Chinese Room appears to understand Chinese. A speaker writes a question (in Chinese), e.g. "What do you make of Oedipus' decision to stab out his eyes?" and passes it through the slot. Moments later comes the response JS has created which, unbeknownst to JS, says something like, "Rather extreme, but then who am I to judge?"

The consensus among psychologists interested in embodiment is that the Chinese Room thought experiment shows definitively that symbols do not acquire meaning simply in virtue of bearing relationships to other symbols. Glenberg and Robertson, for instance, say of the Chinese Room that it "is meant to demonstrate that abstract, arbitrary symbols, such as words, need to be grounded in something other than relations to more abstract arbitrary symbols if any of those symbols are to be meaningful" (2000: 381). How does the Chinese Room demonstrate this conclusion? The idea is that if relations between abstract and arbitrary symbols sufficed for meaning, then JS would be able to understand Chinese, because he understands (thanks to his manuals) how Chinese symbols are related to each other. But, of course, JS does not understand Chinese, and so meaning cannot emerge simply from knowledge of permissible symbol associations.

The force of the Chinese Room as a criticism of standard cognitive science should be apparent. If standard cognitive scientists think that minds operate like computers, and computational processes range over abstract, arbitrary symbols, then it follows that standard cognitive science cannot account for the obvious fact that people *understand* language: that language is meaningful. If JS is "to learn the meaning of the Chinese symbols, those symbols must be grounded in something other than additional Chinese symbols" (Glenberg, Havas, Becker, and Rinck 2005).

The symbol grounding problem, then, is just the problem of how linguistic thought, or thoughts more generally, acquire meaning. Searle's Chinese Room is taken to show that computational processes are not enough to ground meaning. Meaningless symbols do not become meaningful simply in virtue of their associations with other meaningless symbols. Here is where embodiment enters. Symbols are grounded – acquire their meaning – through embodiment.

Although the description of the symbol grounding problem I have just provided echoes its mainstream interpretation (e.g. Harnad 1990), it contains an ambiguity that threatens to derail efforts to assess how it might be solved. The ambiguity is in the notion of meaning. As we have just seen, those who work on the symbol grounding problem present it as a problem about how symbols come to mean, or be about, or represent features of the world. However, conflated with this problem appears to be another, concerning how people come to *understand* the meanings of symbols. Although this distinction between how a symbol becomes meaningful and how meanings come to be understood is seldom noted, further reflection on the Chinese Room shows both questions at play.[9]

Consider first that, strictly speaking, the symbols that JS is manipulating in the Chinese Room *are* meaningful. They *do* have meanings. Precisely because they have meanings are Chinese speakers able to use them to describe all manner of people, places, and things. So, there is something peculiar in

Glenberg and Robertson's claim that the Chinese Room shows that symbols cannot acquire meaning merely through their relationships with other symbols. There is simply no reason to accept at this point that the Chinese symbols, which, I have just noted, *are* meaningful, have become meaningful merely through their relations to other symbols.

Furthermore, if the symbol grounding problem *were* just the problem of how symbols become meaningful, then there would seem to be quite a number of viable solutions. Philosophers have been especially interested in how thoughts, *qua* symbolic expressions in a language of thought, come to be meaningful. This interest aligns neatly with the computational theory of mind that standard cognitive scientists favor, for if, as this theory contends, mental states are akin to symbols like those found in a computer, some account of how these mental states become meaningful is necessary. In virtue of what, theories of mental content ask, does a thought come to mean *red corvette* or *wheelbarrow* or *enchilada*? In chapter 5 we will examine one prominent answer – Fred Dretske's – to this question. For now, however, the points to note are: (i) there are a variety of plausible explanations for how symbols become meaningful, and (ii) many of these theories deny that meaning does or could arise merely through associations between symbols, and so would deny that activities taking place within the Chinese Room are of the proper sort to endow symbols with meaning.

So if, as I have argued, the symbols in the Chinese Room *are* meaningful, and if many philosophers sympathetic to the computational theory of mind believe that the operations that take place in the Chinese Room are *not* of the sort that would endow symbols with meaning in the first place, then Searle's Chinese Room is a dreadful example to use to motivate the symbol grounding problem.[10] Why, then, do many psychologists rely on the thought experiment to explicate the symbol grounding problem? The answer, I suspect, is that they are interested not in the problem of how symbols come to be meaningful, but in the problem of how symbol *users* come to *understand* the meanings of the symbols that they use. Theories of content like Dretske's are designed to address problems of the first kind, but they have nothing to say about problems of the second kind. Put another way, one can imagine that philosophers have discovered the true theory of meaning while psychologists remain at a loss to explain how people come to understand the meanings of the expressions they use, or one can imagine that psychologists have discovered how people come to understand language, despite philosophers' failure to explain how symbols, including linguistic ones, acquire their meaning in the first place.

If these observations are correct, then we can make sense of psychologists' interest in the Chinese Room. JS is manipulating symbols, indeed (we saw) he is manipulating *meaningful* symbols, yet intuitively he doesn't know what he's "talking" about. The symbols mean nothing *to him* and no amount of practice relating strings of symbols with other strings of symbols will change this fact. Moreover, granting that JS is performing the same kind of computational operations that, according to standard cognitive science, take place inside the head of a human being, standard cognitive science cannot explain how human beings understand meanings. If JS is "to learn the meaning of the Chinese symbols, those symbols must be grounded in something other than additional Chinese symbols" (Glenberg, Havas, Becker, and Rinck 2005). Against this background we can now examine one attempt to explain how symbols become meaningful *to someone*.

4.8 The Indexical Hypothesis

The psychologist Art Glenberg and colleagues have offered perhaps the most sustained defense of embodiment as a means for explaining how human beings come to understand linguistic symbols. The details of Glenberg's view take shape in what he calls the *indexical hypothesis*. I'll first present the indexical hypothesis and will then discuss some experimental results that Glenberg offers in its support. Finally I'll explain what all this has to do with Conceptualization.

The indexical hypothesis offers an account of how linguistic symbols become meaningful for someone. Granting that the Chinese Room argument establishes the inadequacy of symbol manipulation as a basis, all on its own, for understanding meaning, Glenberg proposes that understanding is the result of a three-stage process. In the first stage, words are "indexed," or mapped, to *perceptual symbols*. In the second stage, *affordances* are derived from the perceptual symbols. In the final stage, affordances are *meshed*, yielding an understanding of the linguistic symbols. Obviously, all this requires some explaining. Let's begin with the concept of *perceptual symbol*.

4.8.1 Perceptual Symbols

The psychologist Larry Barsalou (1999) developed the idea of perceptual symbols in part to recognize a distinction between amodal and modal symbols. When we perceive objects in the world, we perceive them through various channels or modes. Thus, I may *see* a cardinal-bird outside my window but not hear it, or I may *hear* the cardinal but not see it. In the first case, I am perceiving the cardinal through (or *in*) the visual mode; in the second, through (or *in*) the auditory mode. We may also say that in the first case a visual representation leads to a belief that a cardinal is present but that in the second case it is an auditory representation that leads to that belief. The word "cardinal" is also a representation, but it is amodal insofar as it does not present its content (a cardinal) *as* appearing visually or aurally. The word "cardinal" takes one directly to cardinals without need of visual or auditory intermediaries. In addition to being amodal, words (typically) bear only arbitrary connections to their referents.[11] There's nothing about the word "whale" that makes it especially suited to represent whales. Some other word would have done just as well. Indeed, in languages other than English, other words *do* do just as well.

As Barsalou, Glenberg, and others understand standard cognitive science, the symbols over which cognitive processes range are conceived as amodal and arbitrary. The stimulation that hits the various sensory surfaces is transduced (translated) into a neurally realized code that is then processed further into amodal and arbitrary symbols in a language of thought. Thus, while the *sound* of a cardinal and the *sight* of a cardinal must initially take the form of distinct codes – one the product of the auditory system and the other via the visual system – later cognitive stages unify these modal representations into a single representation that no longer bears any trace of its sensory origins. From various sights and sounds comes the deliverance of the amodal and arbitrary CARDINAL symbol that is now available for whatever further consideration one cares to give it (Barsalou 1999: 578–9). The Chinese symbols with which JS wrestles are amodal and arbitrary. Presumably, this at least partly explains why JS cannot understand Chinese despite the apparent fluency that Chinese speakers attribute to him.

Barsalou proposes that the transition from modal representations – representations in the visual, or auditory, or etc., mode – to amodal representations is unnecessary. Cognitive processes do not need to detach modal information from the representations on which they operate. Rather, cognition can avail itself of the modal representations that constitute the initial deliverances of the perceptual systems. "Cognition is inherently perceptual," he argues, "sharing systems with perception at both the cognitive and neural levels" (1999: 577). Perceptual symbols are simply reconstructions, for the purpose of later cognitive processing, of representations as they appeared in their original perceptual coding. For instance, assume that you are both seeing and hearing a cardinal. Barsalou argues that your later thoughts about the cardinal will draw on representations of visual and auditory encodings of the cardinal. The same perceptual processes that captured the visual and auditory aspects of the cardinal come into play again when remembering the cardinal, forming beliefs about the cardinal, answering questions about the cardinal, and so on. Perceptual symbols, as Glenberg and Kaschak summarize, are "based on the brain states underlying the perception of the referent" (2002: 559).

4.8.2 Affordances

The second piece of Glenberg's Indexical Hypothesis is the idea of an *affordance*, which comes from Gibson (1979). Because the theory of affordances came late in the development of Gibson's thought (Gibson 1979), and has proved something of a vexed topic, I chose not to muddy the waters with a discussion of it in chapter 2. For present purposes, the following remarks about affordances should suffice. Gibson stressed the importance of the organism/environment relationship for understanding perception (this is in part why Gibson is seen as the father of *ecological* psychology). Organisms evolved in particular kinds of environments, and, accordingly, their perceptual equipment is tuned to recover information particular to their environments. However, there is more to it than that. Organisms, depending on their evolutionary history, should respond only to certain features of their environments, or should respond to similar features in different ways, depending on their evolutionarily installed goals. Reflecting this idea is the concept of an organism's *niche*. Members of different species may share an environment but still live in distinct niches because the properties of the environment that are relevant to their survival — the features to which they have developed adaptations — may be quite diverse. Thus, a blossoming tree may provide food for a bee but not a bird; and may provide shelter for a bird, but not a bee. The same tree, that is, may figure differently into any number of niches.

Gibson (1979) called properties that, in a sense, *matter* to an organism *affordances*, and he would speak of objects affording different things to different kinds of organisms. The blossoming tree affords food to a bee and shelter to a bird; the sandy beach affords a breeding ground for a turtle and home for a fiddler crab. Gibson's most controversial claim was that affordances could be directly perceived — a bird, for instance, could perceive directly, with no cognitive intervention of any sort, that a branch affords perching. Evaluation of this claim would take us too far afield. Important for understanding Glenberg's Indexical Hypothesis is Gibson's idea that organisms can recognize the affordances of objects and that what an object affords depends on the needs and properties of an organism. The branch that affords a resting place for a bird would not do so for a pig; and "a chair affords sitting for adult humans, but not for mice or elephants, who have the wrong sorts of body to sit in an ordinary chair" (Glenberg and Kaschak 2002: 558–9).

4.8.3 Meshing

We come now to the final piece of the indexical hypothesis, and its explanation will require tying together the previous discussions of perceptual symbols and affordances. To this end, an example will be useful. Suppose that you see an upright vacuum cleaner. If Barsalou is correct, future reasoning about vacuum cleaners now has available a modal representation of a vacuum cleaner. Thus, when considering whether a vacuum cleaner might be used as a coat rack, the original visual representation of the vacuum cleaner is reconstituted. But determining whether a vacuum cleaner might serve as a place to hang a coat requires that one attribute a nonstandard use to the vacuum cleaner. One must be able to recognize whether a vacuum cleaner "affords" coat hanging. Similarly, one must be able to recognize that the properties of a coat "afford" being hung on a vacuum cleaner. From the perceptual symbols of a vacuum cleaner and a coat, one is able to derive the affordances of these objects. Glenberg uses the term "meshing" to describe the complementarity of affordances. Because upright vacuum cleaners afford "being hung on" and coats afford "being hang-able," the two affordances "mesh." In contrast, coffee cups do not afford "being hung on" and so the affordance of a cup does not mesh with the hang-able affordance of the coat.

   Suppose further that one is asked to evaluate the sensibility of the sentence "Hang the coat on the vacuum cleaner."[12] Reflection on the demands of this task returns us, finally, to discussion of the symbol grounding problem. On the interpretation that psychologists assign to this problem, it is about understanding meaning (rather than about how symbols acquire their meaning in the first place). Glenberg and others take Searle's Chinese Room to show that linguistic symbols cannot become meaningful to someone simply in virtue of following instructions for associating them with other symbols. Understanding must somehow be grounded. Bereft of the proper grounding, one could not understand the words "coat" and "vacuum cleaner," and so one would be unable to judge whether the sentence "Hang the coat on the vacuum cleaner" is sensible. The indexical hypothesis explains, Glenberg claims, how understanding becomes grounded and so how sentences can be understood. Understanding is possible because the symbols involved in linguistic thought "are modal and nonarbitrary. They are based on the brain states underlying the perception of the referent" (Glenberg and Kaschak 2002: 559). The modality of perceptual symbols, Glenberg thinks, allows the derivation of affordances: "[u]nlike the case with arbitrary symbols, new affordances can be derived from perceptual symbols because perceptual symbols are not arbitrarily related to their referents" (Glenberg and Kaschak 2002: 559).

In brief, the indexical hypothesis states that "meaning is embodied – that is, that it derives from the biomechanical nature of bodies and perceptual systems" (Glenberg and Kaschak 2002: 558). This way of putting the hypothesis makes its relation to Conceptualization clearer. The understanding of a *situation*, on this view, "consists of the set of actions available to the animal in the situation" (Glenberg and Kaschak 2002: 558). The understanding of a *sentence* consists in the set of actions that derive from the affordances belonging to the referents of the sentence. Understanding is embodied because properties of the body in part determine affordances. Just as the sentence "Hang the coat on the cup" is judged as nonsensical because cups do not afford hanging on, so too, Glenberg would presumably claim, the sentence "climb the pencil" is judged to be nonsensical, because pencils do not afford climbing for organisms with bodies like ours, although they might for insects. Thus, sentence comprehension depends on embodiment and, because different kinds of bodies create different kinds of affordances, we should expect that differently embodied organisms will diverge in their understandings of identical situations (or sentences). They will "see" the world differently in virtue of the differences in affordances they recognize. In this way, the indexical hypothesis aligns itself with Conceptualization.

4.8.4 Experimental Evidence for the Indexical Hypothesis: The Action-Sentence Compatibility Effect

Consider a collection of sentences, some of which imply movement toward the body and others of which imply movement away from the body. An example of a "toward" sentence would be "Open the drawer" or "Put your finger under your nose;" an "away" sentence might be "Close the drawer" or "Put your finger under the faucet."[13] Also in this collection are nonsense sentences that express no direction, such as "Boil the air." Glenberg and Kaschak (2002) asked subjects to judge whether each sentence they viewed was sensible or not. To score their judgment, a subject was equipped with a box to be held in a way that put the five buttons on its top surface in a vertical alignment with the subject, so that the first button was nearest the subject and the fifth furthest away. Subjects would press the center button to cause presentation of a sentence on a computer screen. Subjects would then have to release the button to press the "yes" button if the sentence was sensible and the "no" button if not.

For subjects in the "yes-is-near" group, the "yes" button was closest to their body and the "no" button furthest from their body, forcing them to move their hand toward their body to indicate a yes and away to indicate a no. The position of the buttons was reversed for the "yes-is-far" group.[14] The question the experiment addressed was whether responses that required one to move one's hand *away from* or *toward* one's body would interfere in judgments of the sensibility of sentences that indicated movements *toward* or *away* from one's body. Would, that is, a subject be slower to recognize the sensibility of the sentence "Open the drawer" if she had to move her hand away from herself to indicate "yes," or if she had to bring her hand toward herself when judging the sensibility of the sentence "Close the drawer?" The crucial measure was the amount of time the subject spent with a finger on the middle button before lifting the finger to make the sensibility response.

Glenberg and Kaschak (2002) found that subjects were indeed slower to make a sensibility response when the direction of motion of the response was opposite to the direction of motion implied by the target sentence. This *action-sentence compatibility effect,* they say, "supports the notion that language understanding is grounded in bodily action" (2002: 562). Were language understanding *not* so grounded, the movements required by the subjects would not have interfered with their sensibility judgments. Moreover, those sentences that subjects judged not to be sensible are precisely those in which affordances could not be made to mesh. A sentence like "Hang the coat on the cup" is judged nonsensical because the actions that coats and cups afford cannot be meshed in a manner that permits the hanging of the former on the latter. So, understanding is grounded in affordances, drawn from perceptual symbols, and sensitive to the idiosyncrasies of embodiment.

4.9 Assessing the Indexical Hypothesis

A critical examination of the indexical hypothesis might take a variety of approaches. I intend to focus on three issues that Glenberg's defense of the hypothesis raises. The first concerns whether standard cognitive science can accommodate those aspects of the indexical hypothesis that Glenberg believes require a departure from computationalism. The second issue regards Glenberg and Kaschak's equation of sensibility judgments with a subject's understanding of a sentence's meaning. Finally, we must consider whether, as Glenberg and Kaschak believe, standard cognitive science cannot account for the action-sentence compatibility effect.

4.9.1 Meaningfulness in Amodal Representation

An impetus for Glenberg's Indexical Hypothesis, as well as Barsalou's theory of perceptual symbols, is the firm conviction that symbols of the sort that are present in computers, and likewise minds if one accepts that cognition is computational, cannot be "made" meaningful to their possessor. But, certainly fair to ask is how the indexical hypothesis explains the advent of meaningfulness. The crucial move seems to be Glenberg's adoption of modal symbols in place of the amodal symbols that appear in computational processes. Glenberg's idea seems to be that modal symbols are already meaningful to their possessors, so that one needs no further account of how they come to be understood. Whereas some account is necessary to explain how one derives an understanding of the amodal symbol CARDINAL, no such account is required to explain how one comes to understand a modal, e.g., a visual, representation of a cardinal. This is so, presumably, because when one actually sees a cardinal, one understands what one sees. And this is so, presumably, because, rather than being associated simply with other symbols, the perceptual representation of the cardinal is associated with an actual object in the world – a cardinal.

According to the indexical hypothesis, when one is thinking about cardinals on occasions when not actually seeing or hearing cardinals, tokens of the same type of representational states that were created when perceiving cardinals are created again for thoughts about cardinals. These states, like the original perceptual states, carry their meaning with them. They are offspring of the original perceptions of a cardinal and inherit their meaningfulness from their ancestors. The original perceptual states were meaningful (were understood to be about cardinals) because of their association with cardinals, and future thoughts about cardinals are understood to be about cardinals because they are replicas of the original perceptual states.

But, even if this account of how understanding comes about is correct,[15] one should wonder why standard cognitive science cannot help itself to a similar account. In developing his theory of modal symbols, Barsalou claims that modal symbols are necessary because there is no account of "how amodal symbols become mapped back to perceptual states and entities in the world" (1999: 580). But why shouldn't standard cognitive scientists help themselves to the very account that Barsalou offers on behalf of modal symbols? Barsalou claims that the meaning of perceptual symbols can be understood because they are grounded in the neural states that arose initially in the perceptual system. But now consider an amodal symbol like CARDINAL. This symbol may also be grounded in the neural states that arise in a perceptual system as a result of stimulation. All that is necessary is an additional causal step – from the modal representation of a cardinal to an amodal representation. Barsalou and the standard cognitive scientist can agree that symbols must be grounded in relationships between perceptual states and the world. The standard cognitive scientist need only insist that these amodal symbols bear the right sort of relationship to modal symbols which, in turn, must bear the correct relationship to stimulation. These considerations suggest that the complaints against standard cognitive science that drive Barsalou, Glenberg, and others to look to embodiment as a means for symbol grounding are perhaps misguided.

Moreover, making sense of Barsalou's account of perceptual symbols is difficult without supposing that, at some point, modal representations *do* give rise to amodal ones. Consider that, for Barsalou, a cardinal might be represented in the visual mode and in the auditory mode. But what makes both of these representations mean *cardinal*? What binds the visual representation of the cardinal to the auditory representation, so that the two are understood to be about the same object rather than different objects? Another way to ask this question is this: why should visual representations of cardinals be associated with auditory representations of cardinals rather than with auditory representations of, say, elephants? One way to solve this problem is to assume that some more abstract, amodal, representation of a cardinal emerges from the various modal representations. Indeed, Barsalou, Simmons, Barbey, and Wilson (2003) suggest a solution like this when speculating about the need for conjunctive neurons in an association area that combine information from the various sensory representations. In sum, if modal symbols can be understood because they are connected in the right way to the world, perhaps amodal symbols can be understood when connected in the right way to modal symbols, and, furthermore, amodal symbols do seem necessary as a means for integrating modally disparate representations of the same object.

4.9.2 *Sensibility Judgments*

Fred Adams (forthcoming) asks an interesting question about Glenberg, et al.'s experimental work. Recall that Glenberg has subjects judge whether a given sentence is *sensible*. Sensible sentences, Glenberg reasons, are those from which subjects are able to derive affordances that complement, or mesh with, each other. Thus, the sentence "Hang the coat on the vacuum cleaner" is judged as sensible because the subject derives the affordances of "hang-able on" from "vacuum cleaner" and "hang*able*" from "coat" and understands that these affordances complement each other. On the other hand, "[i]f the affordances do not mesh in a way that can guide action (e.g. how could one hang a coat on a cup?), understanding is incomplete, or the sentence is judged nonsensical, even though all of the words and syntactic relations may be commonplace" (Glenberg and Kaschak 2002: 559). So, a sentence like "Climb the pencil" would be judged nonsensical because the subject cannot mesh the action of climbing with the affordances of a pencil (unless, I suppose, the subject were a literate insect).

But, Adams points out, although subjects might judge "Climb the pencil" to be nonsensical, they still know what it *means*. They still *understand* the sentence. Indeed, subjects are likely judge it to be nonsense *because* they understand it. The contrast between (i) not understanding and (ii) thinking something to be nonsense, is clear in the contrast between responding with a "huh?" and with a comment like "that's silly, I can't do that." In the former case, you simply don't get it; in the latter, you get it, but don't see how you can possibly accomplish what's asked of you.

The problem for Glenberg is that his request for sensibility judgments seems to entail that subjects have already understood the sentences that they have read, and so comes too late to reveal the processes involved in understanding. The question that the action-sentence compatibility effect seems more directly to address is this: how do subjects determine whether certain actions (e.g. hanging a coat on a cup or climbing a pencil) are possible for them to perform? Perhaps subjects do indeed derive affordances from perceptual representations of the referents of linguistic symbols in order to determine the possibility of various actions. But even so, this tells us nothing about how subjects come to understand language in the first place.

If this criticism is correct, then the action-sentence compatibility effect does not support Conceptualization, for Conceptualization is a thesis about the connection between bodies and conceptual abilities. But Glenberg, et al. have not shown that different embodiments lead to different capacities for understanding. At most they have shown that different embodiments might lead to different judgments about whether a particular action is possible (for someone with a body like X). But the fact that, say, a person in a wheelchair would judge stairs to be unclimbable whereas a bipedal person would not is hardly interesting. More interesting, but far from established, is that the person in the wheelchair would not be able even to *understand* the sentence "Climb the stairs."

4.9.3 Standard Cognitive Science and the Action-Sentence Compatibility Effect

Doubts about the explanation that Glenberg and Kaschak offer for their experimental results do nothing to obviate the need for *some* explanation. Why should movements in a direction opposite to that which a sentence implies interfere with judgments about the sensibility of the sentence? One answer that we will consider in more detail in chapter 6 emphasizes the role of the sensorimotor system in cognition. If responses to language draw on the sensorimotor system, then possibly those processes involved in judgments of linguistic sensibility can find themselves at odds with processes that cause movement, and Glenberg and Kaschak's experimental paradigm induces just such a tension.

For now, it is appropriate to wonder whether the standard cognitive scientist is without resources to explain the action-sentence compatibility effect. In terms I introduced earlier, is it true that the indexical hypothesis predicts the action-sentence compatibility effect but that the hypothesis that cognition consists in computational processes does not? One point to note immediately is that present uncertainties about the content of the indexical hypothesis must reduce confidence that it does truly imply the action-sentence compatibility effect. If the indexical hypothesis is, as Glenberg intends, an account of language understanding, but the action-sentence compatibility effect, as Adams argues, does not concern understanding, then we should doubt that the effects Glenberg and Kaschak discovered do indeed follow from the indexical hypothesis.

Of greater moment, however, is whether the action-sentence compati-bility effect really is inconsistent with standard cognitive science. One reason to think not is the extensive array of priming and interference phenomena that cognitive scientists have studied. We have come across priming before in our discussion of Boroditsky's studies of temporal language. Exposure to vertically aligned pictures primes Mandarin speakers to make certain judg-ments about sentences with temporal indicators but does not prime English speakers when making judgments about the same sentences. This is a case where perception of a picture influences linguistic processing. Boroditsky never assumes, and no one to my knowledge has ever suggested, that such priming could not occur without the involvement of modal symbols like those Barsalou (1999) describes. Similarly, explaining the action-sentence compatibility effect might be the simple fact that the sentences subjects read prime a motor response that is in conflict with the motor response the subject is required to perform.

Yet the question remains why a sentence should initiate a motor response in the first place. Perhaps understanding a sentence causes one to imagine performing the action the sentence describes, which in turn generates activity in the motor cortex. When this activity conflicts with the actions required for a response, there will be interference. This account is signif-icant in two respects. First, it assumes that understanding comes prior to motor cortex activity – thus it denies Glenberg's assumption that action is somehow part of understanding. Second, it is consistent with traditional conceptions of symbols as amodal and arbitrary. There is no reason to suppose that the representation of the action that a sentence causes one to imagine, nor the motor commands that generate the subject's movement, cannot have as their vehicles amodal and arbitrary symbols.

Some interpret recent neurophysiological findings as evidence that the connection between action and perception is inconsistent with the sugges-tion I made above. The sequence of events I sketched has too many steps. Understanding certain sentences involves a motor component directly. We shall close this chapter by examining this suggestion in more detail.

4.10 The Body in the Brain

An analogy will help to introduce the significance that neurophysiological research may have for the hypothesis of Conceptualization. Suppose some circuitry in your brain becomes tangled up so that every object you see as yellow also causes you to experience a lemony taste. You see a banana, a school bus, sunflowers, and in each case you would swear that you've just licked a lemon slice. Over time, you no longer conceive yellow objects as distinct from lemony tasting objects. Your conception of yellow objects is now a yellow-lemony conception. This new way of conceiving yellow objects directly reflects a fact about your neural circuitry: that yellow and lemony-tasting are "coded" together.[16]

The recent discovery of canonical and mirror neurons in the premotor cortex of some primates, including human beings, has been embraced by many embodied cognition researchers as evidence that there is a common code for perception and action, and thus objects are conceived partly in terms of how an organism with a body like so would interact with them. The premotor cortex is the area of the brain that is active during motor planning. Its processing influences the motor cortex, which is responsible for executing the motor activities that comprise an action. The canonical neurons and mirror neurons in the premotor cortex are bimodal, meaning that their activity correlates with two distinct sorts of properties (Rizzolatti and Craighero 2004; Gabarini and Adenzato 2004; Gallese and Lakoff 2005). The same canonical neuron that fires when a monkey sees an object the size of a tennis ball is the one that would fire were the monkey actually to grasp an object of that size. If the monkey is shown an object smaller than a tennis ball, one that would require a precision grip rather than a whole-hand grip, different canonical neurons would fire. Thus, canonical neurons can be quite selective. Their activation reflects both the particular visual properties of objects the monkey observes (size and shape) and the particular motor actions required to interact with these objects.

The properties of mirror neurons are even more surprising. Mirror neurons fire in response to the observation of transitive actions. For instance, a monkey observing another monkey (or human being) placing food into its mouth or reaching for a banana will cause mirror neurons within its premotor cortex to fire. If, on the other hand, there is no object toward which the hand is reaching, the mirror neurons remain quiet. Some mirror neurons fire only in response to the observation of actions involving tools, for instance the use of a rake to draw an object toward oneself (Ferrari, Rozzi, and Fogassi 2005). The observations that activate a mirror neuron needn't be only visual. The sounds of actions suffice to trigger some mirror neurons. Indeed, there is a class of mirror neurons that fire in response to either the sight or sound of an action (Rizzolatti and Craighero 2004). Like canonical neurons, mirror neurons are bimodal. Their activity reflects both the sight (or sound) of an action and whatever activities the monkey would need to execute to perform the same action. Significantly, it's the *action* that counts – not merely the motor activity. Observing a monkey reaching for an object will cause a mirror neuron to fire, but observing identical motions when no object is present will not. Likewise, observing *different* motions that comprise the *same* reaching action will cause activation in the same mirror neurons.[17]

The properties of canonical and mirror neurons have inspired some researchers to claim that the perception and categorization of objects and actions is embodied (Richardson, Spivey, and Cheung 2001; Gabarini and Adenzato 2004; Gallese and Lakoff 2005). Just as in the situation we imagined at the beginning of this section, in which scrambled neural circuitry causes one to conceive of objects as yellow-lemony tasting, canonical and mirror neurons cause one to conceive of objects and organisms in a manner modulated by one's body. The tennis ball, for instance, is perceived not just as a sphere, but as a *sphere-graspable-with-my-whole-hand*. The ping pong ball is perceived as a *sphere-graspable-with-finger-and-thumb*. The agent whose arm extends toward the banana is perceived as *reaching for* the banana, and the one who moves an object toward itself with a rake is seen as *trying to retrieve* the object.

This interpretation of the neurophysiological data has an obvious tie to Conceptualization. How one interacts with objects in the world and which actions one can expect to accomplish, depend on the properties of one's body. Thus, the same ball that is represented as *graspable-with-finger-and-thumb* by one kind of primate might be represented as *graspable-with-whole-hand* by a smaller kind of primate. Similarly, whether an organism represents a given sequence of movements as an action may well depend on whether its body is capable of producing the same or similar sorts of action. Perhaps the large primate sees another as *reaching* for the fruit with a rake, but the smaller primate sees only the larger primate *moving* the rake. The more general idea is that cognition is embodied insofar as representations of the world are constituted in part by a motor component, and thus are stamped with the body's imprint.

If this account of canonical and mirror neurons is on track, it might prove valuable in addressing difficulties that we have so far encountered with the hypothesis of Conceptualization. Consider first the issue of testability that haunts Lakoff and Johnson. If it is true that the type of body one has determines (in part) how one experiences the world, then differently embodied organisms should experience the world differently. But, we asked, how might one test this hypothesis? The extraterrestrial creature

Lakoff and Johnson summon to illustrate their claim has yet to volunteer as a psychological subject. However, suppose we find that the canonical and mirror neurons of different kinds of primates are tuned differently, so that, as I suggested above, an object that triggers the *graspable-with-whole-hand* neuron in a smaller primate triggers the *graspable-with-finger-and-thumb* neuron in larger primates. This may be taken as offering experimental confirmation of Lakoff and Johnson's speculation: a difference in the size of the primates' bodies leads them to conceive similarly-sized objects in different ways.

The existence of mirror neurons might also speak in favor of Glenberg, et al.'s interpretation of the action-sentence compatibility effect (Richardson, Spivey, and Cheung 2001).The idea is that a subject has difficulty responding with an *away* motion to a sentence that describes a *toward* motion because the sentence has activated mirror neurons that are involved with *toward* motions. There is now a contest between the neurons involved in planning the action that the instructions require, and mirror neurons that are busy simulating the action suggested by the sentence. This explanation differs from the priming explanation I proposed in the previous section. The priming explanation goes like this: the subject first understands the sentence, then imagines the situation it describes, then acts. The action is delayed because it conflicts with the action which the subject's imagination has primed. In contrast, the mirror neuron explanation of the action-sentence compatibility effect has fewer steps: understanding the sentence excites mirror neurons immediately – indeed, the activity of the mirror neurons is a component in the process of understanding the sentence. The delay in the subject's response is a result of interference between the *action-informed* understanding of the sentence and the action required by the experimental task.

Provocative as these various suggestions are, any discussion of the relation between canonical and mirror neurons and Conceptualization must proceed with extreme caution. Too much about these neurons is not presently known. For instance, although correlations have been found between the firing of mirror neurons and the observation of actions, evidence that this has any influence on how an organism *conceives* actions is still scant.[18] Perhaps the activity of mirror neurons plays no role at all in a primate's conceptual abilities. Perhaps their response to observed action has no cognitive function at all. No doubt the properties of canonical and mirror neurons are intriguing, but any verdict on their support for Conceptualization must await further investigation.

4.11 Summary

The focus of this chapter has been on a particular hypothesis that some researchers of embodied cognition have sought to defend. The hypothesis, Conceptualization, sees a connection between the kind of body an organism possesses and the concepts it is capable of acquiring. The connection is a constraining one: properties of the body determine which concepts are obtainable. Conceptualization predicts that at least some differences between types of body will create differences in conceptual capacities. Different kinds of organism will "bring forth" different worlds. For Varela, Thompson, and Rosch, color experience exemplifies these ideas. Facts about neurophysiology determine the nature of an organism's color experience. Were the neurophysiological facts to differ, so would the experiences of color. For Lakoff and Johnson, facts about the body determine basic concepts, which then participate in metaphors, which in turn permeate just about every learned concept. For Glenberg, et al., an understanding of language, which reflects an understanding of the world, builds from the capacity to derive affordances, the meanings of which are a function of the properties of bodies. Common to all these thinkers is the conviction that standard cognitive science has not, and cannot, illuminate certain fundamental cognitive phenomena – color perception, concept acquisition, language comprehension – because it neglects the significance of embodiment.

In examining some of the research and arguments that have been used to bolster Conceptualization, we have come across various problems. One challenge is to make a case for Conceptualization that does not reduce to triviality. VTR face this problem: of course color experience is a product of neurophysiological processes; of course color experiences would differ were these processes to differ. VTR's "best case" of embodiment appears to express little more than a rejection of dualism. Glenberg, et al.'s defense of Conceptualization is also in danger of sliding into triviality. The experimental evidence they collect in support of the indexical hypothesis might more easily be explained as the result of an ordinary sort of priming effect than as the product of a multistage process involving perceptual symbols, affordances, and meshing. Additionally, the experimental task Glenberg, et al.'s subjects perform may not really be testing their ability to understand language but instead testing whether they can imagine acting in a manner that the sentence describes.

The dissatisfaction with standard cognitive science that the defenders of Conceptualization in this chapter profess is puzzling in many respects. In some cases, the phenomena that "simply can't be explained" from a computational perspective – color experience, metaphorical reasoning, concept acquisition – have extant computational explanations. Perhaps these explanations are incorrect, but there is no reason to believe that their faults lie in the computational framework on which they are built rather than in the details of the algorithms they postulate. More unsettling is an apparent failure to understand basic elements of the very science these authors seek to topple. Lakoff is especially notable in this respect, charging cognitive science with resting on a priori assumptions and having an interest only in the conscious mind. Neither of these accusations is tenable. If standard cognitive science has shortcomings – and chapter 2's examination of Gibson, Hatfield, and connectionism suggests that it may indeed – the work we have studied in this chapter at best only hints at what they may be.

Although the prospects for Conceptualization do not, on the basis of what we have seen, appear hopeful, continuing study of canonical and mirror neurons may someday reveal that properties of organisms' bodies are somehow integrated with their conceptions of objects and actions. Worth bearing in mind is that Conceptualization is only one theme that embodied cognition researchers pursue. Now it is time to look at the second theme of embodied cognition that I identified in chapter 3: Replacement.

4.12 Suggested Reading

Gallese, V. and Lakoff, G. (2005). "The Brain's Concepts: The Role of the Sensory-Motor System in Reason and Language," *Cognitive Neuropsychology* 22: 455–79.

Glenberg, A. and Robertson, D. (2000). "Symbol Grounding and Meaning: A Comparison of High-Dimensional and Embodied Theories of Meaning," *Journal of Memory and Language* 43: 379–401.

Lakoff, G. and Johnson, M. (1980). *Metaphors We Live By* (Chicago: University of Chicago Press).

Lakoff, G. and Johnson, M. (1999). *Philosophy in the Flesh: The Embodied Mind and its Challenge to Western Thought* (New York: Basic Books).

Varela, F., Thompson, E., and Rosch, E. (1991). *The Embodied Mind: Cognitive Science and Human Experience* (Cambridge: MIT Press).

5

EMBODIED COGNITION

THE REPLACEMENT HYPOTHESIS

5.1 Replacement

Of the three themes around which I am organizing discussion of embodied cognition, Replacement is most self-consciously opposed to the computational framework that lies at the core of standard cognitive science. We saw in our discussion of Conceptualization that a number of cognitive scientists suspect that this core is rotten. Insofar as they have an alternative to offer, they are engaged in the Replacement project as well as Conceptualization. In this chapter the focus is strictly on Replacement. The work we will examine was developed with the goal of providing a *better* way to do cognitive science.

We had a small taste of Replacement in chapter 3, where we saw Thelen, et al.'s explanation of the A-not-B error. The error, they argue, is not the result of a flawed or undeveloped object concept, as a computationally-inclined cognitive scientist might conclude, but rather emerges from the interaction of a number of factors, including the infant's history of reaching behavior, the salience of the hidden object, the duration of the gap between hiding and searching, and the motions necessary to retrieve the object. When the factors are *just so*, the infant will commit the error. More generally, Thelen and her colleagues are tempted by the thought that many developmental transitions might be best explained as outcomes of dynamical interactions: "[d]evelopment can be envisioned, then, as a series of evolving and dissolving patterns of varying dynamic stability, rather than an inevitable march towards maturity" (Smith and Thelen 2003: 344). If this picture of development is correct, then dynamical systems theory, rather than computational theory, would seem to provide the right tools for its investigation.

Of course, we saw already in chapter 2 that the computational theory of mind is not "the only game in town." Gibson offers a theory of perception that is stubbornly anti-inferential and anti-representational. Furthermore, connectionist models of cognitive capacities show that symbol processing of the sort computationalists envision is not necessary for at least some types of cognitive processing. However, as we saw Hatfield arguing, rejecting the idea of symbol processing requires one neither to abandon a description of cognition as computation, nor to withhold from theories of cognition a role for representation. Connectionist networks do, after all, compute: they transform inputs into outputs. They also represent: they enter states that can be interpreted as being about features of the world; and the weightings that connections between nodes acquire can be interpreted as a form of knowledge about how to make particular discriminations on the basis of inputs.

Replacement goes further than connectionism in its resistance to standard cognitive science. Proponents of Replacement deny that cognition lends itself to any useful sort of computational description; they similarly question the utility of a concept that is central both to connectionist and computational theories of mind: representation. The two main sources of support for Replacement come from (i) work that treats cognition as emerging from a dynamical system; and (ii) studies of autonomous robots. Although dynamical systems approaches to cognition were developing alongside connectionism (see Beer forthcoming for discussion), and the two sometimes intersected (see, for example, Elman 1995), part of the motivation for dynamical systems approaches grew from dissatisfaction with some aspects of connectionism (van Gelder 1995, 1998; Elman 1998; Smith and Samuelson 2003). Gibson too, with his emphasis on the continuous interactions between organisms and environments, was an inspiration for dynamical systems approaches, particularly of the sort that Randy Beer has explored. Gibsonian perspectives, we shall see, also figure heavily in the design of autonomous robots that demonstrate surprising versatility, despite their computational simplicity.

In this chapter we will first examine the challenge to standard cognitive science that dynamical systems approaches to cognition pose and will then turn to the challenge coming from robotics. On the surface these challenges differ. The *dynamicists*, as I shall call them, think that computational theories of mind cannot account for certain features of cognition, and this helps to justify a move toward dynamical descriptions. On the other hand, the roboticists' strategy is to create a robot that exhibits intelligent behavior without recourse to the sort of architecture that computationalists insist is necessary for cognition. The next step is to argue that much or most of cognition can be built on the same principles that underlie the robot's intelligence. Although the dynamicists and the roboticists offer different reasons for rejecting standard cognitive science, they share a very deep commitment to *embodiment* and *situatedness*, finding in these concepts the resources by which to *replace* old cognitive science with a new and improved version.

5.2 Dynamical Systems

A dynamical system is any system that changes over time. Dynamical systems *theory* (DST) is the mathematical apparatus that describes how systems change over time. The first step in describing the behavior of a dynamical system is to identify those parts of it that change. The second step is to map out all the possible ways in which these parts might change. A change is described in DST as a change in *state*, and so the map of all possible changes is known as the *state space*. So, for instance, a familiar target of dynamical systems theory is a pendulum. As the pendulum swings back and forth, both its angular velocity (v) and its angle from a vertical position (θ) change. The state space for a pendulum comprises all possible velocities and positions that the pendulum could assume. The third step in devising a dynamical description is to identify a rule of evolution. This rule describes how the system evolves, or changes, from one instant to the next. Thus, given the rule of evolution for the pendulum, $v = d\theta/dt$, the angular velocity and position of the pendulum at time t_1 can be determined from the angular velocity and position of the pendulum at time t_0.

Often the rule of evolution of a dynamical system is in the form of differential equations. This is necessary for systems that change continuously through time. Some systems evolve in discrete or iterated steps (those familiar with Turing machines or cellular automata might think of these) and thus do not require differential equations for their description. Another concept from dynamical systems theory is that of an *orbit* or *trajectory*. If you pick as an initial state a particular velocity and position of the pendulum, the orbit or trajectory of this state is the set of all the states that emerge from this state over time. A dynamical system might also exhibit *attractor* points. Attractors are points toward which trajectories head. A pendulum has an obvious attractor point – starting from any state, the pendulum will eventually settle at zero velocity and a vertical position.

As another example of a dynamical system, consider Kelso's description of oil as it is heated in a frying pan (Kelso 1995). Initially, before being heated, the molecules of the oil are moving about randomly. At a critical temperature, however, the surface of the oil begins to roll and the molecules behave in a regular fashion. In this example, the temperature is a *control parameter*, because temperature affects, or controls, the state of the oil molecules. The amplitude of the convection rolls that eventually appear on the surface of the oil is called an *order parameter* or a *collective variable*, to express the idea that the amplitude of the rolls is the product of individual elements in the system (the molecules) that are now displaying collective behavior, or order.

The convection example illustrates two other features of (some) dynamical systems that impress embodied cognition researchers. First, the pattern that forms on the surface of the oil is *emergent*, or *self-organizing*. There are no rules or instructions that guide the oil molecules toward the rolling pattern. As Kelso says, "the control parameter does not prescribe or contain the code for the emerging pattern. It simply leads the system through the variety of possible patterns or states" (Kelso 1995: 7). Other examples of self-organization are the patterns of striping and spotting that appear on the skin of zebras, giraffes, tigers, and cheetahs. Interestingly, it was Alan Turing, one of the fathers of computer science, who was the first to discover the rules of evolution that predict these patterns.

The second feature of interest in the convection example is the cyclical pattern of causal events the system exhibits: "the order parameter is created by the cooperation of the individual parts of the system, here the fluid molecules. Conversely, it governs or constrains the behavior of the individual parts" (Kelso 1995: 9). The convection rolls appear as a result of the behavior of individual molecules, but then the behavior of the individual molecules becomes a function of the convection rolls. The convection rolls are a "higher-order" pattern that influences the behavior of its lower-order constituents, which in turn, through their motions, maintain the higher-order pattern.

An idea related to the cycle of causal activity that discussions of dynamical systems frequently mention is *coupling*. Systems, or parts of systems, are coupled when the mathematical description of the behavior of one must include a term that describes the behavior of the other. For instance, the seventeenth-century Dutch scientist Christiaan Huygens discovered that if he hung two pendulum clocks from a wooden beam, the motions of the pendulums would eventually become synchronized. To explain the behavior of the pendulums, the differential equation describing the dynamics of each pendulum would have to include a term describing the behavior of the other. The behaviors of the pendulums are thus *coupled*.

Given the generality of the description of dynamical systems – systems that change through time – almost any system is a dynamical system. Accordingly, dynamical systems theory can be used to explain just about everything. A natural question, then, is why some researchers think that the tools of dynamical systems theory should be applied to cognition and why the more traditional computational tools of standard cognitive science should not. In the next sections we will examine the philosopher Tim van Gelder's case for favoring a dynamical approach to cognition over the computational approach.

5.3 Van Gelder's Dynamical Hypothesis

Van Gelder's Dynamical Hypothesis (DH) has two parts. The first is about the *nature* of cognitive agents: "it specifies what they *are* (i.e. dynamical systems)" (1998: 619). The second is about how we are to understand cognition: "we can and should *understand* cognition dynamically" (1998: 619). Clearly, the two parts are related. If the claim about understanding is true, presumably the nature claim is too, for how could we understand cognition via dynamical systems theory unless cognition were in fact a dynamical system? At least, truth of the understanding claim would be evidence for the truth of the nature claim. But, as I observed above, just about everything is a dynamical system, so we must wonder why the nature claim is not just trivially true.[1]

In response to this worry, one should recall our earlier discussions of levels of description (§1.3). Many distinct but compatible descriptions are available for anything. A brain can be at once a collection of molecules, an organization of neurons, an information processor, and a dynamical system. I know a neuroscientist who frequently refers to the brain as a chemical battery. Decisions about how to describe an object depend on which of the object's capacities one hopes to understand. Thus, one might see the dispute between standard cognitive scientists and connectionists as concerning whether the brain's cognitive capacities are better understood from a computational or a connectionist perspective. On one view of this dispute, the connectionist sees a computational description of the brain as gratuitous, or strained, because it requires abstractions (e.g. rules, algorithms, discrete symbolic expressions) that turn out not to be necessary for understanding cognition. The computational description of the brain, according to the connectionist, is not the best one for explaining cognition. Van Gelder's DH might usefully be viewed as taking a similar stake on cognition, disowning even connectionism on the grounds that it contains the wrong tools for understanding cognition.[2]

Because, as I noted, the part of the dynamical hypothesis that makes a claim about *understanding* is evidence for the part about *nature*, the first step in assessing DH is to examine why dynamical systems theory might provide a better explanation of cognition than standard cognitive science does. Toward this goal, I will first present van Gelder's defense of dynamical explanations in a very different context: the Watt centrifugal governor.

5.4 Explaining Watt's Centrifugal Governor

Watt's centrifugal governor, named for the eighteenth-century Scottish engineer James Watt, is a mechanism for controlling, or *governing*, the power from a steam engine.[3] The engines for which the governor was adapted relied on a device known as a flywheel that would translate the up-and-down motion of pistons into a rotary motion that could be used for various industrial applications, which proved especially important for cotton mills. Prior to Watt's innovations, such engines could not be counted on to maintain a constant output, with the result that the speed of the flywheel would fluctuate inopportunely. The Watt governor changed all this, regulating the flow of steam from the boiler with a throttle valve so that when the flywheel slowed, the throttle valve would open, providing more power; and when too much power drove the flywheel's speed beyond the desired rate, the governor would close the valve, thereby slowing the flywheel.

Before examining how the centrifugal governor worked its magic, let's imagine that we are computer scientists who have been asked to write a program that, when implemented, would regulate engine speed. There's a thinly concealed motive for thinking about the problem from this perspective. Standard cognitive scientists routinely put on their programming caps when seeking to explain a cognitive process. Sometimes, as with Newell and Simon's *General Problem Solver*, and also in the efforts of computational vision theorists (see chapter 1 for details), the idea that a cognitive process consists in a program is quite explicit. In other cases, cognitive scientists will describe cognitive processes with diagrams, where connections between various boxes depict the flow of information, suggesting sequences of operations that might later be codified in an algorithm. So, in thinking about how a computer scientist might solve the governing problem, we are approaching it in the same way that a standard cognitive scientist might approach questions about cognitive processes.

Van Gelder offers the following algorithmic solution to the governing problem.

1   Measure the speed of the flywheel.
2   Compare the actual speed against the desired speed.
3   If there is no discrepancy, return to step 1. Otherwise,
    a   measure the current steam pressure;
    b   calculate the desired alteration in steam pressure;
    c   calculate the necessary throttle valve adjustment.
4   Make the throttle valve adjustment.
Return to step 1.

(1995: 348)

Several features of this algorithm are worth emphasizing. First, the steps involved are ordered, but there is a sense in which timing plays no role in the algorithm. For instance, the algorithm leaves unspecified how much time might elapse between steps, how much time each step might take, whether some steps must occur more quickly than others, and so on. Another point to notice is the centrality of representations in the algorithm. The algorithm can do its job only if it can store a representation of the desired speed, create representations of current speed, and then compare the latter to the former. The algorithm must also incorporate representations in its calculations of the adjustments needed to be made to steam pressure and the size of the throttle valve opening. For van Gelder, the presence of representations makes this solution to the governing problem computational: "it literally computes the desired change in throttle valve by manipulating symbols according to a schedule of rules. Those symbols, in the context of the device and its situation, have meaning, and the success of the governor in its task is owed to its symbol manipulations being in systematic accord with those meanings" (1995: 350).

So much for the computer scientist's solution to the governing problem. Let's now examine Watt's solution. To this end, a picture is worth at least a thousand words (Figure 5.1).

Here's how it works. The engine turns the flywheel at the bottom of the vertical shaft, which rotates the shaft. As the shaft spins, centrifugal force causes the flyballs to rise. When the flywheel turns beyond the desired speed, the rising flyballs decrease the throttle opening, reducing power to the engine, thereby slowing the flywheel. On the other hand, if the engine should not be generating enough power, the flywheel slows, the flyballs drop, the throttle valve opening enlarges, and the flow of steam to the engine increases.

Although the above description of the governing system is accurate, it is also misleading in an important way. The description suggests a *sequence* of events: first the flywheel turns, *then* the shaft rotates, *then* the flyballs rise, *then*

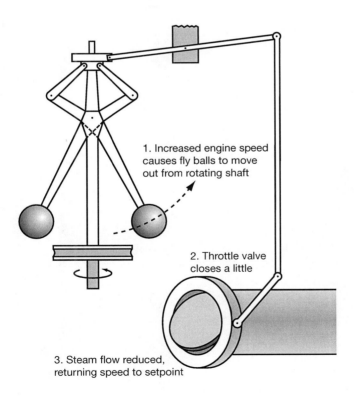

Figure 5.1 Watt's centrifugal governor.

the throttle valve closes, then the flywheel slows, then ... But, of course, the governing process has no first step or last step. I could have as easily begun a description of the governing process this way: first the throttle valve closes, then the flywheel slows, then the flyballs drop, then the throttle opens, then the flywheel speeds up, then ... In fact, the system of which the governor is a part provides a superb illustration of the cyclical pattern of causation and coupling that we discussed earlier. The speed of the flywheel, height of the flyballs, and opening of the throttle valve are continuously dependent on each other. Likewise, they are coupled: the equations that describe the changes in state of any one of them will contain terms that represent the states of the other two.[4] These facts explain why conceiving of the governing process as a sequence of discrete events is misguided.

Quite unsurprisingly, a system that exhibits the sort of cyclical causation and coupling present in the governing system is precisely the sort that dynamical systems theory is well-suited to describe. Just so, dynamical systems theorists have developed sets of differential equations that describe how parts of the steam engine change given changes in other parts. These equations reveal, for instance, how the speed of the flywheel changes as a function of its current speed given the current state of the throttle valve and the height of the flyballs. In short, these equations explain how the governor comes to be in its current state, and allow one to predict its next state. This, if anything, justifies the decision to use dynamical systems theory to understand the governing system for a steam engine.

But, of course, a reason to describe a system with the tools of dynamical systems theory is not a reason to refrain from using other explanatory strategies to understand the same system. We must ask, then, whether a computational description of the governing system might also be valuable. If van Gelder is correct, it is not. Computational clothes simply cannot be tailored to fit the governing system. There are two main reasons for this.[5] The first alludes to the point about temporality that I mentioned above. Computational descriptions have a beginning, a middle, and an end. An algorithm is essentially a recipe that makes explicit the steps involved in transforming an input into an output. However, apart from the ordering of the sequence of steps, timing is irrelevant. This is why a modern computer and a slowly plodding Turing machine may be said to be running the same algorithm despite the fact that the former might produce a solution millions of times faster than the latter.

In contrast, timing is an essential feature of the governing system. The differential equations that describe it owe their explanatory success to their ability to accommodate the idea of change – an essentially temporal concept. The size of the opening of the throttle valve is changing *as* the height of the flyballs is changing *as* the speed of the flywheel is changing. There is no first, middle, and last – no sequence of events. The coupling of the components in the governing system demands an explanatory apparatus that is equipped to handle simultaneous unfoldings, and so it is no wonder that a framework of sequential descriptions involving discrete and temporally isolated steps is unsuited to the task.

The second reason to reject a computational explanation of the governing system concerns the prominence of representations in these explanations. In our discussion of the computer scientist's approach to the governing problem we saw that representations of the current speed of the flywheel, of the desired speed of the flywheel, of the size of the throttle opening, and so on, were all necessary to compute the solution. However, van Gelder argues that attributions of representations to the centrifugal governing system are misguided. "[A] reliable way of telling whether a system contains them or not," he says, "is to ask whether there is any explanatory utility in describing the system in representational terms" (1995: 352). And, van Gelder continues, there is not. If one doubts this, one merely has to re-read the description of the governor's operation that I provided above. The description does indeed seem to explain how the system works, and yet nowhere does it refer to representations. Yet, matters may not be so clear, as we shall see later in this chapter (§5.9.1).

But, even if van Gelder is ultimately correct that the best explanation of the centrifugal governor is devoid of representations, this does not entail that explanations of *any* dynamical system can proceed without mentioning representations. Clark and Toribio, for instance, say "[i]n the case of the Governor, it is no surprise at all that the best story is told in non-representational terms" (1994: 422). Nevertheless they do believe that for understanding some dynamical systems, attributions of representations will be necessary. Even van Gelder, although often portrayed as a staunch anti-representationalist, foresees the possibility of adapting a conception of representation that might prove useful in understanding some dynamical systems (van Gelder 1995; 1998).[6] But before exploring these possibilities in more detail, we must first return to van Gelder's Dynamical Hypothesis. The discussion of the centrifugal governor is provocative, but can we really benefit from conceiving of cognitive processes as dynamical systems? Is it really true, as van Gelder muses, that "the Watt governor is preferable to the Turing machine as a landmark of models for cognition" (1995: 381)?

5.5 The Dynamics of Cognition

Why might dynamical systems theory be the right tool for investigating cognition? Why, to echo van Gelder, might the centrifugal governor be a better model for cognitive science than a computer? Those who advance the dynamical hypothesis emphasize several points. First, they point out that cognition happens in time. The components of a cognitive system are continuously changing and, just as an ability to model continuously changing events is crucial for understanding the centrifugal governor, we should expect no less to be true of a cognitive system.

This emphasis on change draws inspiration from Gibson's portrayal of perception as a kind of activity.[7] Whereas standard cognitive science often depicts perception as a sequential computational process in which a stimulus is sampled, symbolically represented, processed, and translated into a new form of representation that other cognitive processes might use, Gibson thought of perceivers as actively exploring their environments, and through their activities picking up information that would otherwise be unavailable. Action leads to perception, which creates opportunities for new actions, which result in new perceptions, and so on. Similarly, dynamicists conceive of cognitive processes as involved in a circle of causality, where, as we saw with the centrifugal governor, there are no principled partitions between beginning, middle, and end.

The circle of causality present in the governor involved components such as the throttle valve, the flyballs, and the flywheel. The circle of causality from which cognition emerges comprises the brain, the body, and the environment. From the perspective of the dynamical approach to cognition, *embodiment* refers to the fact that the brain is dynamically interacting with the body. The term "situated" is often used to draw attention to the fact that the body is embedded in and dynamically interacting with an environment. Thus, there is a coupling relationship between three components, each of which is itself a dynamical system. Beer (2003: 211) illustrates this idea (Figure 5.2).

That brain, body, and world are coupled is, then, the second reason dynamicists prefer their approach to the standard cognitive scientist's. Just as the coupling relation between the components of the governing system made understanding the behavior of one component necessary for understanding the behavior of another (remember that the equations that define the behavior of each component must include terms that describe the behaviors of the other components), so too, the dynamicist contends,

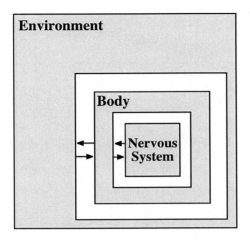

Figure 5.2 The environment, body, and nervous system are each dynamical systems and are in continuous interaction. The nervous system is *embodied*, and the body is *situated*.

there's no understanding the brain's activities without understanding activities taking place in the body and world. Van Gelder draws the contrast to standard cognitive science elegantly:

> [n]ote that because the cognitive system traffics only in symbolic representations, the human body and the physical environment can be dropped from consideration; it is possible to study the cognitive system as an autonomous, bodiless, and worldless system whose function is to transform input representations into output representations.
>
> (1995: 373)

Embodiment and situatedness are taken to broaden, literally, the boundaries of the cognitive system. Just as no single component of the governing system controls the speed of the steam engine, cognition belongs not just to the brain. Cognition emerges from dynamical interactions among the brain, body, and world.

As a side note, Beer criticizes connectionism for sharing with standard cognitive science the same commitment to "bodiless-ness" and "worldless-ness" about which van Gelder complains. As in typical computers, connectionist processing begins with settings to input nodes and ends with adjustments to output nodes. Understanding the activity in a connectionist net requires understanding features internal to the net: the number of hidden nodes, the weightings of connections between nodes, the learning algorithm, and so on. These are the properties that explain how connectionist nets compute their solutions – how they *cognize*. "In this sense," Beer says, "many connectionist models are still disembodied, unsituated, and computational (albeit distributed) in nature" (forthcoming: 20).

But proponents of dynamical system approaches offer two more reasons in support of the dynamical hypothesis. Smith and Thelen are impressed with the self-organizing ability of dynamical systems. We saw an example of self-organization in Kelso's discussion of convection rolls that emerge in oil as it is heated. Smith and Thelen's interest in *developmental* psychology perhaps explains their special fascination with self-organization. As we saw in our discussion of the A-not-B error (chapter 3), Thelen, et al. see the error as emerging from a number of interacting factors. In similar manner, Thelen and Smith explain the pattern of motor behavior that infants exhibit prior to walking – at a very young age they will make stepping motions when held aloft, then this behavior will cease, only to return again months later when they are finally ready to walk – in terms of the dynamical interactions between the legs' masses, the spring-like tension in the leg muscles, and the properties of the surface on which the feet make contact (or the medium through which the legs move) (Thelen and Smith 1994). The development of walking, rather than the product of some centralized cognitive plan, emerges from the dynamic interactions between masses, muscles, and surfaces. Insofar as the behavior is self-organizing, a computational description of its origin would be inaccurate – attributing the behavior to a progressively developing motor plan rather than to the properties and forces that really matter.

Finally, Beer finds in dynamical accounts the promise of a kind of unification. Approaching brain, body, and world as coupled dynamical systems allows one to apply the descriptive resources of dynamical systems theory to each. "Because all of the individual components are described in the same mathematical language," Beer notes, "it is much easier to approach questions involving their interaction" (2003: 212). In contrast, standard cognitive science makes no assumption that the computational resources it uses to understand how the brain produces cognition might also explain processes that take place in the body and in the environment. That standard cognitive science continues to insist on distinct forms of explanation to understand what takes place *in* the head and what takes place *outside* the head only reinforces, dynamicists charge, a lingering Cartesianism that would place an unscalable wall between the mental and the physical (van Gelder 1995: 381).

5.6 Categorical Perception from a Dynamical Perspective

I hope by now to have provided a sense of why an investigator might look to dynamical systems theory as a means for understanding the behavior of some systems and why cognitive systems might themselves be a viable target for a dynamical explanation. We have also seen an example (§3.3) in which a dynamical perspective toward a particular behavior – the A-not-B error – both explains the phenomena and makes novel predictions. But to appreciate more fully the riches that dynamical theories of cognition might provide, a careful study of Randy Beer's remarkable work on categorical perception is apposite.

Beer intends his study of categorical perception both to support his conception of an embodied and situated cognitive science and to demonstrate weaknesses in more traditional computational approaches to cognition. Because a brain is embodied, it "can utilize the natural biomechanics of its body, the geometry of its sensory surfaces, and its ability to actively control these surfaces to considerably simplify many problems" (2003: 211). Moreover, because bodies are situated, an agent "can utilize and manipulate the physical and functional organization of the space around it … to offload problems in its environment" (2003: 211). Embodiment and situatedness, we saw, lend themselves to a dynamical description, according to which cognitive behavior is seen as emerging from continuous interactions between brain, body, and world.

More technically, a dynamical systems explanation of cognition begins with the assumption that the brain, body, and environment constitute a dynamical system.[8] Within this system are states that change according to various rules of evolution. Identifying the correct state variables is one requirement for a dynamical explanation; another requirement is a characterization of the state space – the space of all possible states – so that trajectories from one state to the next can be traced. Control parameters that induce state changes and create collective behaviors must be isolated; the shapes of trajectories, the presence of attractors, and the effects of various perturbations must all be studied.

As complicated as this all sounds, in practice it is even more complicated. Indeed, a common criticism of dynamical approaches to cognition is that they are practically intractable except in the simplest cases. The equations that explain the behavior of the centrifugal governor are child's play compared to those that might be necessary to explain sophisticated cognitive processes. Appreciation of this complexity partly explains Beer's decision to examine the cognitive abilities of a simulated agent. The simulation enables Beer to have complete control over the architecture of the agent's nervous system, the properties of the agent's body, and the nature of the agent's environment. The mathematics involved in the dynamical description of the agent's behavior are still quite frightening, but certainly within the grasp of (a few) human beings.

The task Beer's agent performs is categorical perception. Categorical perception is a fundamental cognitive ability. Whenever you distinguish one phoneme from another, one color from another, one shape from another, you are making category judgments – you are carving nature into usable chunks. Beer's agent has just two categories to recognize. As it moves back and forth, it must decide whether the object falling from above is a circle or a diamond. If it is a circle, it must try to center itself beneath it in order to catch it; if a diamond, it must do its best to avoid it. The agent has seven "eyes," each of which has a single line of sight. The setup looks as shown in Figure 5.3.

The agent's nervous system consists of a continuous-time recurrent neural network (CTRNN). This is a special sort of connectionist network that is notable for its capacity to store the settings of the hidden nodes (or interneurons, as Beer calls them) so that earlier states of the nodes can be fed back into later states. CTRNNs are often analyzed with dynamical systems theory. The agent's nervous system has seven input nodes, each corresponding to one

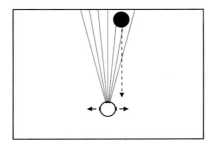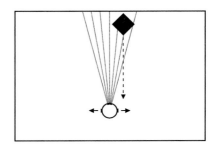

Figure 5.3 As the agent (open circle) moves back and forth, it must try to center itself beneath the falling circle, but avoid the falling diamond. From Beer (2003: 213).

of its seven eyes, five hidden nodes, and two output nodes which act as motor neurons, causing the agent to move toward circles or away from diamonds.

Beer trained a number of agents, allowing their nervous systems to evolve from various initial settings, and then chose a very successful one as a subject of his dynamical analysis. The point of the analysis was to understand how the agent manages to distinguish circles from diamonds. The answer, it turns out, requires attention to the changes that are happening simultaneously in the nervous system, body, and environment.

The successful agent has learned to engage in a pattern of actively scanning the falling object. As is clear from Figure 5.3, the diamond is wider than the circle, and so by moving back and forth beneath the falling object, the agent creates an opportunity for the object to break the lines of sight in a manner characteristic of its shape. The agent thus uses its body to simplify the categorical perception task. But the agent's ability to categorize is not perfect – it sometimes makes mistakes, classifying a circle as a diamond or a diamond as a circle. Figure 5.4 displays catching and avoidance performance

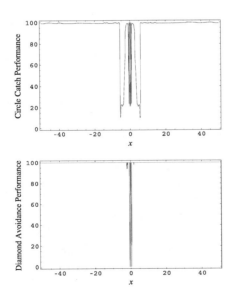

Figure 5.4 Catch performance (top) and avoidance performance (bottom) as a function of the initial position of the falling object. The agent is poor at catching circles and avoiding diamonds when it is roughly centered beneath the object as it begins to fall. From Beer (2003: 215).

as a function of the initial object location. As the figure illustrates, the agent is generally quite good at catching circles, but is likely to fail when the circle begins its descent from directly overhead or nearby. Interestingly, there is a region of high performance sandwiched between regions of low performance on each side of the agent's midline. In contrast, the agent fails to identify a diamond just in those cases where the diamond's descent is directly overhead.

Because the agent's environment is under Beer's control, variations in the environment that might shed light on the agent's categorization abilities are possible. In effect, Beer is in a position to perform psychophysical experiments on his agent. Thus, by slowly morphing the circle into a diamond, Beer can determine which features of the falling shape matter most to the agent's ability to distinguish circle from diamond. Likewise, Beer can drop the object from various heights in order to study how much time the agent needs to make a category judgment and whether it might change its mind several times before committing to a decision (it does). These, as well as the performance errors I mentioned above, are evidence that provide a portrait of the agent's cognitive capacities. It turns out that an appreciation of the dynamic interactions between the agent's nervous system, body, and the environment can make sense of all of them.

The dynamical analysis begins with the assignment of state variables. Beer selected an environmental state variable for the height of the falling object, a body state variable for the horizontal position of the agent relative to the falling object, and a neuronal state variable that takes values from the output of a single interneuron.[9] The analysis then proceeds to examine how the states of object, body, and neuron change as interactions between them occur.

Crucial for understanding the dynamical interactions is the extraction of a steady-state horizontal velocity field (SSHVF) for both circles and diamonds. Suppose that as a circle falls it becomes stuck, remaining frozen at a particular (x, y) coordinate. The agent's sensory neurons will now receive constant inputs from the object, and, in time, the agent's nervous system will settle into an equilibrium that causes the agent's body to move at a particular velocity — its steady-state velocity. The SSHVF for the circle is a map of all steady-state velocities the agent adopts for every possible position of the falling circle. The SSHVF for the diamond is produced in the same way. Representation of the agent's direction of horizontal motion is also possible in the SSHVFs for the circle and the diamond. Plate 5.1A shows SSHVFs for the circle and diamond.

The colors in the SSHVFs indicate in which direction and at what speed the agent would move, given its detection of an object frozen at some (x, y) pair of coordinates, for every possible pair of coordinates. When an object is within the blue regions, the agent will move toward the midline, centering the object above itself. The opposite is true when an object is within the red regions. An obvious difference in the SSHVFs for the circle and diamond is the height of the red regions in the centers. The red region extends higher in the SSHVF for the diamond because the agent needs to respond as soon as it can with avoidance movements – movements away from the midline – as the diamond approaches. Green regions are areas of multistability where the agent might move in either direction; and when the object is in a black region the agent does not move at all. The intensity of the colors indicates the velocity of the agent, with greater intensity standing for higher velocities. The white lines that divide the field mark areas that correspond to the number of lines of sight that the object touches. For reasons that will soon become apparent, it is important to understand that in the agent's actual world an object is always falling, and so the agent's nervous system never has time to enter the equilibrium points that generate the steady-state velocities that the SSHVFs map.

In Plate 5.1B the behavior of the agent in twenty-four successful catching trials (left) and twenty-four successful avoidance trials (right) is superimposed on the SSHVFs for the circle and diamond. At the top of the SSHVFs are the twenty-four different starting positions for the object. The descending trajectories describe the agent's motion in object-centered coordinates. Thus, although the object is falling in a straight line, if you were to imagine yourself sitting on top of the object and looking down at the agent as you fall, the agent would appear to be moving in a zig-zagging scanning pattern, centering itself beneath you if you were on top of a circle, and moving off to the left or right if you were riding a diamond. The colors code the agent's trajectory for direction and speed in the same way that they do in the SSHVFs; however, rather than showing the agent's steady-state velocity, the colors show the agent's instantaneous velocity. Thus, when the trajectory is red, the agent is moving at a particular speed and away from the midline. A blue trajectory shows the agent moving at a particular speed and toward the midline.

Plate 5.1B provides an opportunity for our first look at a dynamical explanation of some of the agent's perceptual abilities. Recall that the agent must actively scan the falling object in order to categorize it. We can see now how the agent's scanning motions emerge from the continuous interaction with the object as it falls, the nervous system as it senses the object and moves toward but never quite reaches the state that would generate a steady-state velocity, and the instantaneous horizontal velocity of the agent. Consider first the agent's behavior as a circle falls. As the circle begins to fall, the agent's sensors cause the nervous system to approach the equilibrium point that would generate a steady-state velocity in the direction of the midline. That is, the nervous system is always trying to generate the velocity that it would achieve if the object were frozen at a particular pair of (x, y) coordinates (it is always trying to match the color of its present trajectory to the background color in the SSHVF). However, the agent and the object are always moving, and so the nervous system is always in a game of "catch-up." This neuronal inertia causes the agent to move past the midline. Its trajectory turns red because it is now moving away from the midline, but because it continues to be in a blue region of the SSHVF – because it is "trying" to move toward the center – its horizontal direction will eventually reverse, represented with a blue trajectory, causing another midline crossing. Eventually, the agent finds itself directly beneath the circle.

The explanation for the agent's avoidance of diamonds is roughly the same. Because the red region extends higher into the SSHVF, the agent's nervous system will be pulled toward an equilibrium that would generate movement away from the midline. The red regions are wide enough, and the blue regions narrow enough, so that the nervous system's momentum is able to cross the agent through the blue regions without being sucked back toward the midline.

Finally, Plate 5.1C accounts for the misclassifications that Figure 5.4 illustrated. On occasion, the state of the agent's nervous system lags too far behind the state that would generate the SSHVF. That is, the difference between the current state of the nervous system and the state into which the nervous system would enter, had it all the time in the world to adjust to the current position of the falling object, becomes too great. The effect of this gap is most apparent in the misclassification of the diamond (Plate 5.1C). The first scanning reversal does not happen until much later than it normally would in cases of successful avoidance. It's too late for the poor agent, who becomes trapped in a blue region, causing it to move toward the midline where it is drawn into the black region of zero horizontal velocity.

In these accounts of why the agent adopts zig-zagging motions, and why on some occasions it misclassifies shapes, one must never lose sight of the coupled relationships between the agent's body, its nervous system, and the falling object. Just as descriptions of the centrifugal governor tempt one to read a sequence of events into a process that is in fact not sequential, so one must resist the idea that the agent's motions are simply responses to the falling object. Beer clarifies the difference:

> As the agent's state evolves from its current point, the agent's resulting actions and the environment's own dynamical evolution change the sensory input that the agent receives and modify the subsequent trajectories that are available to it. In this way, both the agent's dynamics and that of its environment continually shape the unfolding behavioral trajectory, as well as the future sensitivity of that trajectory to subsequent sensory input.
>
> (2003: 236).

Beer's description of his agent's behavior, and the capacity for perceptual categorization that this behavior illustrates, lends weight to van Gelder's speculation that the centrifugal governor, rather than the computer, might be a better model for cognitive science. But before passing judgment on this issue, we must take up the issue of explanation, for one might harbor misgivings about whether the dynamical analyses Beer has offered of categorical perception really are explanatory.

5.7 Do Dynamical Explanations Explain?

I have been at pains to describe Beer's research in detail because it brings to the fore many of the issues that we must consider in assessing whether and how dynamical approaches to cognition provide support for Replacement. One such issue concerns the nature of dynamical explanations. Another focuses on whether representations have a role to play in dynamical explanations. I shall consider the topic of explanation in this section and will turn to representation after presenting an embodied approach to robotics.

Explanations enlighten. They tell how something comes to be, or why things happen as they do. There are many philosophical theories of explanation. These theories might try to place conditions on the form an explanation can take. For instance, they might insist that explanations cite laws of nature, or that the phenomenon to be explained be deducible from a collection of laws and statements of initial conditions. Some theories of explanation might offer analyses of particular sorts of explanation, for instance mechanistic or causal or teleological explanation. Nevertheless, the basic idea that explanations should, above all else, enlighten seems secure.

The usual contrast to explanation is description. Whereas explanations tell you that Y happened *because* X happened, descriptions tell you that X happened *and then* Y happened. One way to make this difference between explanation and description more concrete is to consider *counterfactual* statements. What would happen if, contrary to fact, X had not happened? Would Y happen? If X's presence explains Y's presence, then we should think that in X's absence, Y should not happen. Moreover, we should expect explanations to address other sorts of counterfactuals. If X explains Y, we should have some idea how particular changes in X would bring about changes in Y, even if we had never observed these changes before. On the other hand, if all we have is a description − X happened and then Y happened − we have no reason to suspect that X's absence should make any difference to Y's happening. We should have no expectations about how Y might change as a result of changes in X. Descriptions do not tie events, or changes in events, together, whereas explanations do.

Another feature of explanations that distinguishes them from mere descriptions is their predictive power. If X explains Y, then X's presence *now* predicts Y's future presence; and the manner in which X is changing *now* predicts how Y will change in the future. David Hume, famously, exploited the fact that mere descriptions do not license predictions. If all we have are descriptions of events, if there is nothing to tie events together, we are not justified in believing that because Y followed X in the past it should follow X again in the future.

Because there is intense philosophical controversy over what, exactly, explanations are, why some explanations are better than others, whether scientific explanations differ from other sorts of explanations, and so on, I hope that the above comments are general enough to elude disagreement, and yet specific enough to raise some questions about dynamical approaches to cognition. However, before thinking about cognition, let's return to the centrifugal governor.

What explains how the governor regulates the engine speed? Two very different sorts of answers present themselves. One answer appeals to the features of the device itself. It's the fact that the flywheel is attached to the vertical shaft, on which are suspended the flyballs, and that this assemblage is then linked to the throttle valve, and that centrifugal force will cause the flyballs to rise as the flywheel spins faster. Indeed, in my initial description of how the governor works (§5.4), these mechanical devices and their connections were doing the explanatory work.

On the other hand, dynamical systems theory provides us with a number of differential equations that describe how changes in the state of one part of the system, e.g. the speed of the flywheel, change the way that states in other parts of the system, e.g. the height of the flyballs and the setting of the throttle valve, change. But one might wonder whether these equations are actually explanatory. They describe how the system changes, but do they explain *why* the system changes? Perhaps, to motivate a skeptical response to this question, the equations that describe the behavior of the governor's parts were discovered through observing and measuring the effects of their various interactions. Similarly, if the equations of motion were discovered by observing objects as they roll down an inclined plane, can they really be said to explain the objects' motions? They seem instead to fall into the category of mere description.

If this skeptical response is on track, then Beer's claim to be explaining the categorization abilities of his agent is in jeopardy. The sixteen differential equations that *describe* the system comprising agent, nervous system, and world would seem to do no more than that. Beer is aware of this concern. Indeed, his reason to examine the SSHVFs was in part to show that the dynamical relationships between the agent's body, nervous system, and world were explanatory. Consider his explanation of the scanning strategy that the agent adopts. Why does the agent zig and zag? How does this pattern of motion come about? The answer depends on identifying the interaction between the agent's instantaneous horizontal velocity and the agent's steady-state horizontal velocity. In its efforts to bring its instantaneous velocity in line with its steady-state horizontal velocity, the agent, when trying to catch a circle, will overshoot the midline and then be buffeted back. Likewise, Beer explains the agent's misclassifications by appeal to the fact that the gap between the agent's instantaneous velocity and steady-state velocity grows too large, which delays the time of the first reversal, which in turn has consequences for the agent's later behavior.

Both these explanations are counterfactual supporting. We can appeal to the SSHVFs to explain how the agent would behave given *any* starting position for the falling object. Beer tested twenty-four starting positions, but, using the explanatory strategy just sketched, he can easily answer the question "What if the object fell from this new position?" But this suffices to show as well that the explanation supports predictions. One prediction that Beer proceeded to confirm is that the agent will always take avoidance movements when the object starts at the far peripheries of the world, regardless of whether the object is a circle or a diamond. Examination of Plate 5.1C explains why. Objects that fall from the peripheries must cross through a large red region. The agent's instantaneous velocity toward the midline is not sufficient to overcome the pull of the agent's steady-state velocity away from the midline. Its trajectory sends it toward the world's edges.

Skepticism about whether dynamical systems theory is explanatory, rather than merely descriptive, thus seems misplaced. On reflection, this is perhaps not surprising. The equations of motion that describe the acceleration of a ball down an inclined plane are also explanatory in some sense. They explain why the ball is moving at this velocity in this instant. They predict its velocity in the next instant. If the minimal duty of an explanation is to enlighten, appeals to these equations seem to qualify. They tell us why, for instance, the system is in its current state, given its past state. They tell us what to expect from the system in the future.

Still, one might complain that something important is missing from Beer's explanation of his agent's behavior. Recall that I offered two possible explanations of the governor's behavior. The first focused on the actual mechanisms and the second on the equations that describe the mechanisms. Both, I am now prepared to say, are good explanations. Both provide an answer to the question "How does the governor work?" But so far Beer has provided an answer only of the second sort.

Yet, many prominent lines of research in cognitive science are concerned with offering explanations closer in spirit to the first explanation of the centrifugal governor I offered. The interest is in the mechanism itself – what its parts are, how they interact, the flow of information through them, and so on. This interest is perhaps nowhere clearer than in robotics laboratories, where the idea of understanding via mechanistic explanation receives vivid expression. Insofar as this is true, dynamical systems approaches to cognition need to show that they can accommodate mechanistic explanations if they are to offer a full-blown alternative to standard cognitive science.

Beer appears sensitive to this need, and thus embarks on an account of "how the agent dynamics … is actually instantiated in the evolved neural circuit" (2003: 231). The focus now shifts from an abstract mathematical characterization of agent dynamics to a careful study of the excitatory and inhibitory interactions between the agent's neurons. Study of the agent's nervous system explains, no less mechanistically than a study of the components of the centrifugal governor explains, why, for instance, the SSHVFs have the shape that they do, how the central black area in the SSHVF that is necessary for capturing circles appears, and why the agent overshoots the midline (Beer 2003: 231). The fact that examination of the nervous system explains these features of the agent's behavior does not compete with the claim that the agent's behavior is the product of dynamic interactions between its nervous system, body, and environment. Rather, it reveals the neural mechanisms that, when put in a certain sort of body, in a certain sort of environment, will produce the behavior that the equations of dynamics describe. Thus, Beer succeeds in producing a mechanistic as well as a mathematically abstract explanation of his agent's behavior, satisfying two sorts of explanatory goals that cognitive scientists have pursued.

Although those who adopt the framework of dynamical systems to understand cognition accept, along with standard cognitive science, the importance of mechanistic explanations, this should not be seen as conciliatory. These explanations, like that of the centrifugal governor, are not seen as drawing on the conceptual apparatus of standard cognitive science. From the perspective of dynamical systems, skepticism over the existence of representations is still well founded. On the strength of this, supporters of Replacement argue, we should be prepared to abandon those areas of cognitive science that are committed to representations. This, they are correct in surmising, would mean giving up pretty much everything. We will return to this issue below. However, dynamical perspectives are not the only source of representational skepticism. In the next section we will examine Rodney Brooks's work in robotics and the challenge to standard cognitive science that it poses.

5.8 Replacement and Robotics

Above I appealed to robotics as an example of a domain in which cognitive scientists are interested in the mechanisms that create intelligence, and I suggested that this interest might provide an explanation of cognition that dynamical systems theory on its own could not. The contrast is between the dynamicist's explanation of the centrifugal governor, which uses equations to describe the trajectory of the system through a state space, and the engineer's, which cites the mechanical properties of the governor, such as the connection between the throttle valve and the flyball assembly. Both sorts of explanation, I claimed, enlighten our understanding of what the system does and how it operates. In this context, Rodney Brooks's robots are particularly fascinating. Brooks's project is truly one of "understanding by building," but this difference in methodology does not prevent him from sharing the dynamicists' confidence that standard cognitive science is wrong and should be replaced with a more embodied cognitive science.

That Brooks finds himself allied with the dynamicists is perhaps no accident. The robots he builds are, as we shall see, near-implementations of the sort of agent that Beer's simulations describe. This suggests that a dynamical analysis of Brooks's robots is likely to meet with the same success, and so support the same conclusions about how to do cognitive science, that it does for Beer's agent. Interestingly, it also means that other forms of explanation – those that refer to the details of implementation rather than the abstractions of dynamics in order to understand cognitive behavior – might lead to the same skepticism about representation.

Part of the motivation for Brooks's departure from more traditional artificial intelligence (AI) was the apparent inability of its robotic products to perform even the simplest tasks – tasks any insect could perform – with much success. One such robot was Shakey, developed at the Stanford Research Institute in the late 1960s.

Shakey used a TV camera as a sensor, which would transmit images to an offboard computer for analysis. This computer would produce symbolic descriptions of the images so that they could be integrated with a symbolically encoded description of the world already in storage. A program called STRIPS planned Shakey's actions, using the symbolic descriptions of the world that the computer generated.

Shakey's tasks, which it received as typed input, included navigation through rooms while avoiding objects. But Shakey's environment was structured to make these tasks as easy as possible. The walls were uniformly lit, and a dark baseboard made their intersection with the floor quite conspicuous. The surfaces of the blocks and wedges that Shakey had to avoid or push were differently colored so that edges were easy to detect, making the shapes easier to analyze. Still, Shakey would require hours or days to complete the goals assigned to it.

Shakey illustrates what Brooks characterizes as a *sense-model-plan-act* framework (1991a: 1228). Shakey's TV camera senses the environment, a computer constructs a symbolic model from the TV inputs, the STRIPS program uses symbolic descriptions of the world to plan Shakey's action, and then Shakey acts on the instructions that STRIPS produces. Each iteration of this cycle, Brooks points out might take fifteen minutes or more.

More significantly for our purposes, Shakey illustrates how a standard cognitive scientist, instructed to build a robot, would likely proceed. The important steps – the steps that generate Shakey's behavior – take place in the offboard computer. Shakey's "brain" is quite literally disembodied. Once Shakey's sensor delivers an image, it is up to the computer to encode it, process it, apply various routines to it, and then derive a representation of an appropriate action that is then sent back to Shakey's body. Once the action occurs, the sequence of operations begins again. How else to build a robot?

Drawing inspiration from approaches to robotics that emphasized embodiment and situatedness, Brooks turned the sense-model-plan-act framework on its head. Brooks's understanding of the terms *embodiment* and *situatedness* is similar to Beer's. Brooks's robots are embodied because they "have bodies and experience the world directly – their actions are part of a dynamic with the world, and the actions have immediate feedback on the robot's own sensations" (1991a: 1227). His robots are situated in the world, meaning that "they do not deal with abstract descriptions, but with the 'here' and 'now' of the environment that directly influences the behavior of the system" (1991a: 1227). The embodiment and situatedness of Brooks's robots help to explain my earlier remark that these robots might be seen as implementations of the kind of agent Beer simulates. Just as the cognitive behavior of Beer's agent emerges from the continuous and instantaneous interchange between brain, body, and world, so Brooks has designed his robots to instantiate and exploit a coupling between the world, the robot's perception of the world, and the robot's actions on the world.

To realize his vision, Brooks replaces the standard sense-model-plan-act architecture with what he calls a *subsumption* architecture. The basic idea of subsumption is that, rather than decomposing the control system of the robot into components that transmit representations along a path that begins with sensation, moves through modeling, planning, and so on, resulting finally in behavior, the decomposition should be into components that connect sensing directly with behavior. Figure 5.5 depicts this contrast.

The result of a subsumption architecture is a *behavior-based* robot. Each layer within the control system produces a particular behavior in response to sensor activity, and because the layers have the power to inhibit or ignore each other, the overall behavior that emerges from the combined layers is surprisingly coherent and versatile.

Brooks's behavior-based robots might for good reason be called "Gibsonauts," for their design embodies a Gibsonian approach to perception. Sensing feeds directly into action without a representational middleman. No inferential steps from an impoverished input to a perceptual output are necessary. Gibson would have approved of Brooks's design for his "creatures:" "[e]ach activity producing layer connects perception to action directly. It is only the observer of the Creature who imputes a central representation

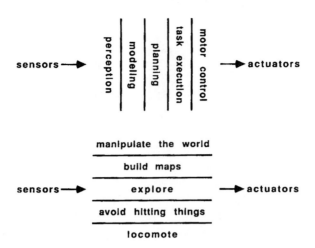

Figure 5.5 The top diagram illustrates a control system in which perception provides a representation of the world that is then transformed and used in various ways to produce behavior. The bottom diagram illustrates a control system in which perception leads directly to behavior. From Brooks (1991a: 1229).

or central control. The Creature itself has none ..." (Brooks 1991b: 144). Let's now see in more detail how the subsumption architecture works.

Brooks's earliest robot was Allen (named for Allen Newell, one of the designers of *General Problem Solver*). Allen's goals in life were similar to Shakey's, but he performed far better than Shakey did. Allen could move about a room, avoiding objects while actively exploring its environment.

Around Allen's circular base were twelve evenly spaced ultrasonic sonars that acted as Allen's sensors. The sensors provided Allen with information about his surroundings once every second. The sensors were connected directly to three behavior-generating layers: Avoid, Wander, and Explore. The Avoid layer caused Allen first to halt if the sonars detected an object in Allen's path, then turn, and then move forward. The Wander layer directed Allen toward a random heading every ten seconds, and the Explore layer chose distant targets and moved Allen toward them. If necessary, the Avoid layer could interrupt the activity that the Wander layer produced, to prevent Allen from wandering into an object. Similarly, the Explore layer could inhibit the Wander layer, keeping Allen on course, and could then re-orient Allen in the desired direction if the Avoid layer caused Allen to veer off course while avoiding an object. The robot, as Brooks observes, is thus "a collection of competing behaviors" (1991b: 144). And, like the other examples of self-organization we have seen, in which interacting parts coalesce into an organized pattern of behavior, from the various layers in Allen's control system "there emerges, in the eye of an observer, a coherent pattern of behavior" (Brooks 1991b: 144).

Brooks's later creations included Herbert (named for Herbert Simon, another designer of *General Problem Solver*). Relying on the same subsumption architecture, but one with additional layers of activity, Herbert could navigate through a cluttered office environment, collecting empty soda cans from desktops and depositing them in a recycling bin. Perhaps Brooks's grandest project is Cog, who, from the waist up, is humanoid in appearance. Cog has been designed to engage in social behaviors. For instance, he will nod to interlocuters if they nod, will point to visual targets, and will make and maintain visual eye contact (Brooks, et al. 1999). All of Brooks's creatures stay true to the ideals of embodiment and situatedness that, Brooks thinks, mark a radical departure from traditional AI.

I introduced this section with a discussion of Shakey, offered as an illustration of a robot that exemplifies fundamental assumptions of standard cognitive science. Brooks's embodied and situated robots are a stark alternative. Gone is the "reliance on monolithic internal models, on monolithic control, and on general purpose processing" (Brooks, et al. 1999: 54). In their place is a tight and uninterrupted connection to the world, and a sensory system that leads directly to behavior. Computations are not necessary to "figure out" how to respond to the deliverances of the sensory systems. Even representations, Brooks insists, are not necessary, for each of his creatures is able "to use the world as its own model" (1991b: 139). This last claim returns us to the topic of representation. Both the dynamicists and Brooks take a dim view of representation. The time has come to take up this issue.

5.9 The Case for Representational Skepticism

Perhaps the most radical claim of the dynamicists is that attributions of representational states to cognitive systems may be inappropriate. I make this point cautiously, because many dynamicists follow their bold anti-representational rhetoric with concessions of uncertainty about what the future may hold. Nevertheless, that many dynamicists are skeptical of the need for representations is clear. This is evident in van Gelder's musing that "the Watt governor is preferable to the Turing machine as a landmark of models for cognition" (1995: 381), given his belief that there are no representations in the centrifugal governor. Likewise, Thelen and Smith, summarizing their view of development, say "[w]e posit that development happens because of the time-locked pattern of activity across heterogeneous components. We are not building representations of the world by connecting temporally contingent ideas. We are not building representations at all!" (1994: 338). Finally, Beer remarks that "a dynamical approach to situated action raises important questions about the very necessity of notions of representation and computation in cognitive theorizing" (2003: 210).

Brooks is even more forceful than the dynamicists in disputing the need for representations. In an article called "Intelligence Without Representation," he claims that "[r]epresentation is the wrong unit of abstraction in building the bulkiest parts of intelligent systems" (1991b: 139), and "there need be no explicit representation of either the world or the intentions of the system to generate intelligent behaviors for a Creature" (1991b: 144). These anti-representational sentiments that Brooks and the dynamicists are eager to express raise perhaps the most serious challenge to standard cognitive science, for the computational theory of mind at the heart of standard cognitive science seems to depend on representation; or, at any rate, computation would seem to be of little value without representations over which to compute. In this section we will consider the arguments against representation and the responses that defenders of representation have offered. First, however, we need to say a bit more about what representations are.

Most basically, a representation is a "stand-in" for something else. A map is a representation insofar as it can be used to stand for the terrain that it maps. Likewise, one can use a photograph or painting of Niagara Falls as a stand-in for the real thing if one wants to answer questions about, perhaps, its appearance. But not only are representations stand-ins, many would insist that they must be *used as* stand-ins by someone or something to count as representations.[10] Thus, there is a sense in which the color of my skin stands for the amount of time I have spent in the sun. Being fair-skinned, the longer I spend in the sun, the redder I become, and so my skin color correlates with, or carries information about, my time in the sun. However, this correlation between the color of my skin and sun exposure does not by itself make my skin color a representation of sun exposure. There is nothing that uses my skin color as a representation of sun exposure. Of course, *were* one to use my skin color to determine whether and for how long I'd been soaking up the sun, then, arguably, my skin color might in fact become a representation.

To see this point more clearly, recall the computer scientist's solution to the governing problem. For the algorithm to work, it needs symbolic representations – stand-ins – for the current speed of the flywheel and the desired speed. The algorithm uses these stand-ins to compute the difference between how fast the flywheel is actually spinning and how fast it should be spinning. Having calculated the difference, the algorithm then calls for adjustments to the throttle valve in order to reduce the difference. So, the algorithm relies on stand-ins in order to do its job. The algorithm *uses* correlations, thereby elevating correlated states to the status of representational states.

Philosophers have for a long time been interested in explaining how a representation comes to stand for the things that it does. Although there seems to be nothing mysterious about how a map comes to represent terrain, or how a photograph might represent Niagara Falls, far less obvious is how states of the brain attain their representational powers. Thus, surely convention has a major role to play in representations like maps and photographs. By convention (e.g. let the color blue stand for water; red for roads, green for forest, brown for desert, and so on) a map comes to depict some terrain. But, presumably, appeals to convention cannot do similar work in explaining naturally occurring representations, like those that exist in the brain. The visual state you are in when seeing a red corvette represents the red corvette not by a conventional stipulation, but by some other process.

There are many different theories about how natural symbols acquire their content.[11] To consider just one – Fred Dretske's (1988; 1994) – a state of the brain B comes to represent a property F when tokens of B are reliably correlated with tokens of F. Dretske calls states that reliably correlate with particular properties in the world "indicators." Thus, part of the explanation for how a state of a frog's brain comes to represent FLY is that the state is an indicator of flies.

But, in addition to this correlation between the frog's brain state and flies, there needs to be a feature of the account that allows for the possibility of misrepresentation. Organisms capable of representation must also be capable of misrepresentation. Although the frog might be quite successful in spotting flies, we should expect on occasion that it might mistake a non-fly (e.g. a ball bearing) for a fly. But if this can happen, we should wonder why the correct description of the representational content of the frog's brain state is FLY rather than FLY OR BALL BEARING. After all, if a state in the frog's brain reliably indicates FLY, it indicates even more reliably FLY OR BALL BEARING. And, if the content is indeed FLY OR BALL BEARING, then when the frog's indicator fires in response to a ball bearing, it is no longer misrepresenting: it is correctly signaling the presence of something that is *either* a fly or a ball bearing.

Dretske's solution to this problem begins with the assumption that fly indicators of the sort the frog possesses have acquired the biological function of indicating flies – they evolved in the frog population because of their capacity to indicate flies. Now, when a frog snaps at a ball bearing, Dretske can say that the frog's indicator is not doing what it is *supposed* to be doing, where "supposed to" is analyzed in terms of the evolutionary function of the device. Because the indicator is failing to indicate that which it has the function to indicate, it misrepresents the ball bearing as a fly. Misrepresentation occurs when B, which has evolved the function to indicate F, indicates something else, thus failing to perform its function.

This sketch of Dretske's theory of representation is intended only to give something of the flavor of how a theory of representation might go. Of course, I have left out details. For instance, I mentioned above a visual state that represents a red corvette. Yet, the suggestion that human beings have visual states that have the biological function to represent corvettes is extremely unlikely. Dretske needs to explain how biological states can represent properties that have had no importance in a species' evolutionary history. He attempts such an explanation by appeal to processes of learning, whereby brain states, within the lifespan of an individual, become recruited for their abilities to indicate various properties. Of course, as I mentioned, Dretske's theory of representation is just one of many, but, for present purposes, I offer it only as a compelling account of how a state of a system might come to represent.

We can now ask whether there are any states in the dynamical systems we have examined, or in Brooks's creatures, that fit the characterization of representation I have just presented. Van Gelder, Beer, and Brooks think not. Let's first look at the possibility that there might be representations in the centrifugal governor.

5.9.1 Are There Representations in the Centrifugal Governor?

We have seen that van Gelder denies that an explanation of the centrifugal governor must refer to representational states. He denies, that is, that the governor contains any representational states. Of course, as an isolated example, excitement about this issue might seem curious. But because van Gelder wishes to apply lessons from the centrifugal governor to cognitive science, the issue gains importance. Van Gelder opposes ascribing representations to the governing system in part because he doubts that there is anything in the system that *uses* representations. Although it is true that the height of the flyballs is correlated with the speed of the flywheel, as well as with the size of the throttle valve's opening, there is nothing in the system that takes advantage of this correlation. The angle of the flyball arms therefore no more represents flywheel speed than the color of my skin represents the amount of time I have spent in the sun. This is why accounts of how the system works, as we have seen, needn't mention representations.

The philosopher William Bechtel, however, insists that the height of the flyballs, or, equivalently, what he calls the angle of the spindle arms, does in fact represent the speed of the flywheel. His reasoning is worth quoting at length:

> The fact that the angle of the spindle arms represents the speed of the flywheel becomes more clear when we consider why it was inserted into the mechanism to begin with. The flywheel itself has a speed, but there is no way to use this directly to open and close the valve. The spindle and arms were inserted so as to encode information about the speed in a format that could be used by the valve opening mechanism. The reason no one has to comment explicitly on the fact that the arm angles stand in for and thus represent the speed of the flywheel is that this system is very simple, and most people *see* the connection directly. But if someone does not understand how the governor works, the first thing one would draw attention to is how the spindle arm angle registers the speed of the flywheel.
>
> (1998: 303)

According to Bechtel, the angle of the flyballs not only correlates with (carries information about) the speed of the flywheel, but the governing system *uses* this correlation as a stand-in for the speed of the flywheel, hence the angle *represents* the speed of the flywheel.

The philosopher Jesse Prinz and psychologist Larry Barsalou make a similar point, although they frame it from the perspective of the theory of Dretske's that we examined above. For Dretske, recall, a state comes to represent X because (i) it correlates with X, and (ii) it has the function of correlating with X. For our purposes, Dretske's introduction of functions in clause (ii) might usefully be seen as a counterpart to the idea I expressed above about the significance of *use* in distinguishing mere correlations from representations. For a state to have the *function* of correlating with X, it must be present in the system *because* it correlates with X — its correlation with X is what it's there for. Like Bechtel, Prinz and Barsalou claim that the angle of the flyball arms represents flywheel speed because the system uses this angle and does so *because* it correlates with flywheel speed: "[i]f governor arms did not carry information about flywheel speed … they would not be able to carry out the functions for which they were designed" (2000: 57).

The crucial point for both Bechtel and Prinz and Barsalou concerns the necessity of the correlation between the angle of the flyball arms and the speed of the flywheel. Were this correlation not present, the system wouldn't work. There is reason for uncertainty, however, that this point suffices to show that the angle of the flyball arms does truly represent the speed of the flywheel. Van Gelder mentions one reason:

> notice that, because the arms are directly linked to the throttle valve, the angle of the arms is at all times determining the amount of steam entering the piston, and hence at all times the speed of the engine depends in some interesting way on the angle of the arms. Thus, arm angle and engine speed are at all times both determined by, and determining, each other's behavior.
>
> (1995: 353)

Van Gelder believes that the complexity present in this sort of coupling puts it beyond what "the standard conception of representation can handle" (1995: 353). Unfortunately, these remarks are rather cryptic and bring us only a little closer to understanding why one might think that the dynamical framework is hostile to representations. Why does the fact that arm angle is coupled with flywheel speed prevent the former from representing the latter? Is this fact intrinsic to the governor case, or are all systems that exhibit coupling nonrepresentational?

Perhaps van Gelder's point is this. Representations in computational systems are discrete states with determinate content that, in virtue of standing-in for some other feature, can serve in an algorithmic solution to a given problem. But this characterization of a representation seems not to apply to the height of the flyballs. The angle of the flyball arms varies continuously with the speed of the flywheel and the setting of the throttle valve. There is no step in the governing process in which the angle of the arms is frozen, measured, and then used to calculate adjustments to the speed of the flywheel. There is only a smoothly continuous interaction between arm angle, flywheel speed, and throttle opening.

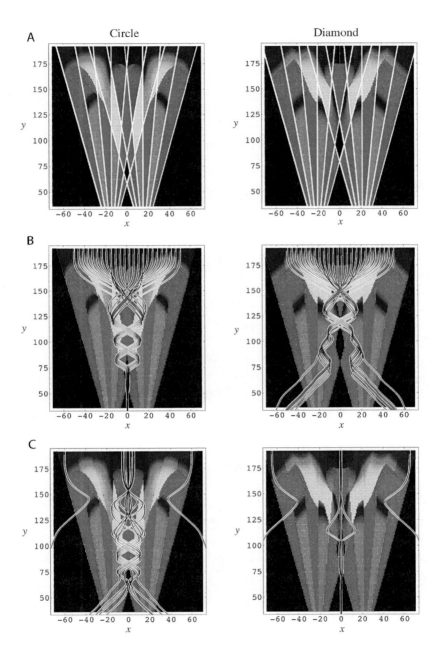

Plate 5.1A–C   Steady-state horizontal velocity fields (A); with superimposed successful trajectories (B); and instances of misclassification (C). From Beer (2003: 222). See text for further explanation.

Related to this point is the earlier observation that the cycle of causa-tion present in the governing system makes arbitrary any identification of a beginning, middle, and end of the process. Granting this, one must wonder why Bechtel and Prinz and Barsalou are so confident that it is arm angle that represents flywheel speed. Why not, instead, claim that flywheel speed represents arm angle; or that the throttle valve setting represents the flywheel speed or, for that matter, the arm angle? Bechtel, Prinz, and Barsalou might reply that arm angle represents flywheel speed but not vice versa because the height of the flyballs is used by the system to cause the flywheel to maintain a particular speed, but that the speed of the flywheel is not used to produce a particular flyball arm angle.

The difficulty with this response, of course, is its assertion that flywheel speed is not used to create a particular flyball height. This claim neglects the significance of coupling. Bechtel, Prinz, and Barsalou are laboring under the assumption that it is possible to yank one part from a coupled system and talk about how it behaves in isolation from its partners. In fact, the effect of arm angle on flywheel speed is a function of the effect of flywheel speed on arm angle. That the first carries information about the second is no more or less important than that the second carries information about the first. There is no reason to assign priority to the information that the arm angle carries, and so no reason to see the angle as representing the speed of the flywheel, rather than to see the speed of the flywheel as representing the angle of the flyball arms. This conclusion, although not establishing that coupled systems never contain representations, at least warns us that talk of representations in coupled systems may be too cheap, or too arbitrary, and thus adds little or nothing to an explanation of how these systems work.

Before leaving discussion of the governor, however, let's consider another reason to be suspicious of Bechtel's and Prinz and Barsalou's claim that the governing system contains representations. Bechtel, Prinz, and Barsalou claim that the flyball arms are *designed* to encode information about flywheel speed. If this were true, then on Dretske's analysis the angle of the arms would represent the speed of the flywheel, for to say that the flyball arms are *designed* to carry information is to say that carrying that information is the function of the flyball arms. But is it true, as Bechtel asserts, that "the spindle and arms were inserted so as to encode information about the speed" (1998: 303), or, as Prinz and Barsalou claim, that Watt "designed the arm angles to covary with engine speed" (2000: 55)?

I think that these claims hinge on a vagueness that permeates discus-sions of function and design. Consider another example. A light switch has two positions, with up typically correlated with the light being on and down correlated with it being off. Suppose, as is no doubt true, that light switches were designed to turn lights on and off. It so happens that the up position correlates with, and so carries information that, the light is on. Now, is it true that the switch was designed so that its two states (up and down) carry or encode the information that the light is on or off? I submit that a natural answer to this question is "no." It was designed to turn the light on and off. If it happens to carry information about the state of the light – indeed, if it cannot work *except* by carrying information about the state of the light – this still does not imply that the function of the switch is to carry information about the state of the light.

This point is clearer still when placed in the context of an imaginary conversation between an electrical engineer (EE) and the owner of a lighting company (LC):

LC: No one's buying my lights. Customers say they want some way to turn them on and off.

EE: I can build something that will do that for you, but you should know that the device I design will carry information about whether the light is on or off.

LC: I don't care whether it carries information about the number of sheep in New Zealand, just build it!

This conversation plays on the possibility that something can have a function to do X but not Y even when doing X requires doing Y. Perhaps in these circumstances the correct thing to say is that the system does Y *in order* to do X. The light switch carries information about the state of the light *in order* to turn the light on and off. Likewise, Watt's design of the centrifugal governor requires that the angle of the flyball arms carries information about the flywheel speed *in order* to regulate the speed. Still, the function of the flyball arms is not to carry information, but rather to play a role in regulating the speed of the flywheel.

Some devices surely do include components that have the function to carry information. The thermostat that Prinz and Barsalou, following Dretske (1988), discuss is such a device. Thermostats contain a bimetal strip because the behavior of this strip carries information about temperature, and the thermostat uses this information to regulate the temperature of the room. If I am right about the centrifugal governor, it is not a device like the thermostat. The governor does contain a component that carries information about the speed of the flywheel, but the governor does not use this information to regulate the speed of the flywheel. The flyball arms are not in the system in order to provide information, even if they happen to do this. This is, then, a second reason to side with van Gelder's conclusion that the centrifugal governor contains no representations, although, given its tight association with the structure of the governor, its usefulness as a *general* reason to dismiss representational talk from dynamical analyses is not so clear.

5.9.2 The Argument for Representational Skepticism

The centrifugal governor, is, for all its extraordinary proficiency, a simple device. Moreover, no one has suggested that it performs a *cognitive* task. Thus, even if van Gelder is right that it contains no representations, a defender of representation seems to have a powerful response: So what? To make a case against representations in *cognitive* systems, dynamicists need to show that dynamical analyses of *cognitive* systems needn't advert to representations.

Although tempting, this rejoinder may not be as compelling as supporters of representation would like to believe. The trouble is that van Gelder imagines that cognitive systems may be like the centrifugal governor *in those respects* that make the centrifugal governor an inappropriate subject for an explanation involving representation. Thus, if the reason that representational states have no place in a dynamical analysis of the governor is that there is, in a sense, *no room* for these states within a system of coupled components, and if cognitive systems also depend on coupled components, then this is a reason to doubt that they contain representations. The argument, in short, is that there is something about dynamical systems like the governor that makes attributions of representations to them inappropriate, and cognitive systems are dynamical systems like the governor.

Beer shares with van Gelder this idea that dynamical systems of a certain sort are simply inimical to representationalist treatment. In drawing a contrast between the embodied, dynamical conception of cognition and the computational conception, Beer claims that

> the focus shifts from accurately representing an environment to continuously engaging that environment with a body so as to stabilize coordinated patterns of behavior ... Rather than assigning representational content to neuronal states, the mathematical tools of dynamical systems theory are used to characterize the structure of the space of possible behavioral

trajectories and the internal and external forces that shape the particular trajectory that unfolds.

(2003: 210)

We must now ask what it is about dynamical systems like Beer's agent that makes representations an unneeded excrescence in explanations of their abilities.

The central argument that appears to lie behind both van Gelder and Beer's antagonism toward representation is this:

Argument for Representational Skepticism
1   Representations are stand-ins for actual objects.[12]
2   An agent is in continuous contact with the objects with which it needs to interact.
3   If an agent is in continuous contact with the objects with which it needs to interact, then it doesn't require stand-ins for these objects.
Therefore, an agent has no need for representational states that stand-in for actual objects.

Before assessing this argument, we should note its connection with Brooks's anti-representationalism. Brooks mentions several times that, rather than relying on representations, his creatures "use the world as its own best model" (1991b: 139, 144). In this sense, his creatures are quite similar to Beer's agent. Because Allen, for instance, is in constant contact with the world, receiving sonar readings from his environment every second, he has, according to Brooks, no need for representational stand-ins. The world makes itself known immediately. The argument above, then, seems also to lie behind Brooks's skepticism about the theoretical value, and thus existence, of representation.

To evaluate the argument, let's for now grant the first two premises. The third premise requires some additional comment. An example helps to reveal the motivation behind it. Compare these two cases. In the first, there is an apple in your grasp and you are asked to describe its shape. In the second, you drop the apple behind you and are then asked to describe its shape. In the second case, the task seems to require a representation of the apple. The apple is no longer present and so any questions about its shape require that you consult an internal representation of the apple. In the first case, this kind of consultation is not necessary. The apple is present in your hand, so rather than resorting to a representation of the apple to answer questions about its shape, you use the apple itself. The presence of the apple eliminates the need for a representational stand-in.

Yet, one might dispute that having continuous contact with the world obviates the need to represent the world. Consider again case one, in which the apple is present in your hand. You are in continuous contact with the apple, but does this imply, as Beer and Brooks intimate, that you needn't represent the apple to answer questions about its shape? Let's consider a third case. While you're holding the apple, a neuroscientist using a transcranial magnetic stimulation device temporarily knocks out the parts of your brain that process tactile information. As in case one, the apple is in your hand, but as in case two, any questions you are able to answer about the apple's shape require that you use representations, in the form of memories, of the apple. This shows that continuous contact with the apple, which you never lost, is not sufficient to answer questions about the apple.

What else is necessary? In addition to contact, you need access to the information that contact provides. When the parts of your brain that process tactile information cease to function, you've lost access to this information. But the states of the tactile processors that carry this information, quite plausibly, have the function to carry this information. They are present in the brain because their job is to carry information that the body's tactile contact with the world produces. But, as we've seen, on Dretske's understanding of what representations are, this suffices to make these states of the brain representations.

The lesson to learn from this discussion is that although Beer's agent and Brooks's creatures are in constant contact with the environment, this by itself does them no good unless they have the means to access the information that their contact with the environment yields. Contact without representation is useless. This shows that the third premise in the Argument for Representational Skepticism is false and so the argument is not sound.

Beer is prepared with a response to the misgivings I just presented. He agrees that his agent has internal states, but demurs when confronted with the possibility that these states might be representations:

> internal state is a property of physical systems in general, and these states can covary with states outside the system in quite complicated ways. Unless we wish to grant representational status to all physical states (does a thunderstorm represent the topography of the terrain over which it passes?), there must be additional conditions that license the modifier "representational."
>
> (forthcoming)

Beer is correct. Additional conditions are necessary to prevent representational promiscuity. However, as discussion of my unfortunate tendency to burn in the sun was intended to show, a reasonable additional condition on representational states is that they not just covary with their objects, but that their *function* within the system in which they are states is to so covary. Beer seems unaware of the consensus that this account of representation generally enjoys, saying that "there is very little agreement about what those additional conditions might be" (forthcoming). Perhaps, in the end, he would be willing to concede the presence of representations in his agent if they were no more substantial than the sort under discussion here.

The example of the apple introduces the possibility that representation comes in degrees. The representations you use to answer questions about the apple when the apple is no longer in your hand seem to differ from the representations you use when you remain in contact with the apple. Clark (1997b) helpfully distinguishes *weak internal representation* from *strong internal representation*. Weak internal representations are those, like in case one, that merely have the function of carrying information about some object that is in contact with sensory organs. Unlike a map or a picture, these representations persist for only as long as the link between them and the world remains unbroken. Once the apple leaves your hand, you are no longer weakly representing it. These weak representations are ideal for "inner systems that operate only so as to control immediate environmental interactions" (Clark 1997b: 464). Given that Beer's agent and Brooks's creatures are concerned only with what's happening *now*, they may need nothing more than weak internal representations for the tasks they perform.

Suppose, however, that an organism has concerns that go beyond the immediate. The second case I described, where you must answer questions about an apple that is now behind you, is such a case. Along these lines, Clark and Toribio (1994) identify classes of problems that are "representation-hungry." A problem is representation-hungry if either:

1   The problem involves reasoning about absent, non-existent, or counterfactual states of affairs.

2   The problem requires the agent to be selectively sensitive to parameters whose ambient physical manifestations are complex and unruly (for example, open-endedly disjunctive).

(Clark and Toribio 1994: 419)

The first condition is obvious. If weak internal representations provide information only about the here and now, they will be of no use in tasks that require reasoning about the absent, non-existent, or contrary-to-fact. The second condition requires a bit of explanation. Many of the properties to which organisms respond do not come nicely packaged with a single identifying physical mark. To be sure, some do. For instance, frogs eat flies, and in the frog's environment any spot of a particular size and moving at a particular speed is a fly. Thus, a frog equipped with a nervous system that responds to these properties of size and speed will (in its natural environment) have no trouble finding food. But now consider a property like *dangerous*. Certainly an organism benefits from being able to recognize dangers in its environment, but, unlike frog food, dangerous things may have no single identifying mark, or even a single collection of identifying marks, for which a nervous system can be specially designed. What, for instance, do spiders, snakes, guns, switchblades, and Rush Limbaugh have in common other than the fact that they can cause sickness or death? What they have in common is, apparently, nothing that a sensory system capable of producing only weak representations could capture.[13] Recognizing these things as dangerous would seem to require an ability to *represent* the various items *as* having those abstract features that are indicative of danger.

Clark and Toribio diagnose problems of both the first and second sort as requiring *strong* internal representations. Such representations can operate "off-line," enabling processes like abstraction in order to cover problems of the second sort, and processes like planning, imagination, and numerous other sorts of reasoning to cover problems of the first sort.

In light of Clark and Toribio's identification of representation-hungry problems, another response to the Argument for Representational Skepticism is available. Suppose, despite my earlier criticism of the argument's third premise, that the dynamicists and Brooks are correct that representations are not necessary for coordinated responses to an environment with which one is dynamically engaged. But this would support only the conclusion that agents do not require representations for certain kinds of activities. However, a stronger conclusion, for instance that cognition *never* requires representational states, does not follow. Given that organisms do engage in representation-hungry tasks of the sort Clark and Toribio describe, the Argument for Representational Skepticism suggests that there must be cognitive processes that are *not* good targets for dynamical explanations – a conclusion exactly contrary to that which the dynamicists intend.

5.9.3 The "They're Not Representations!" Argument against Representations

Beer and Brooks have another argument against attributing representations to agents and creatures. This argument focuses on the failure to identify within these systems a representational vehicle to which semantic content may be assigned. Representational vehicles are the token physical states that bear representational content. Written words are a paradigm case of representational vehicles. The word "martini" on a drinks menu is a collection of ink molecules, but it is a collection of ink molecules that has the content *martini*. Other kinds of representational vehicles – scribblings on a chalk board, vocalizations, skywriting – can have the same content despite their physical differences. Without a representational vehicle, there is nothing to bear content, in which case no sense is to be made of the presence of a representational state.

The standard cognitive scientist's commitment to a computational theory of mind entails a commitment to the type of representational vehicles that must be present in cognitive systems. These vehicles will be tokens of a language of thought. Like written words, they will have a form, will perhaps be composed of smaller representational vehicles, and can be written, read, erased and in other ways transformed by operations that are sensitive to their physical properties (properties they inherit, presumably, from their realization in brain matter).

Beer and Brooks both protest that there is nothing in their systems that can qualify as a representational vehicle, and so nothing that can count as a representation. Brooks, describing one of his creatures, says, "even at a local level we do not have traditional AI representations. We never use tokens which have any semantics that can be attached to them" (1991b: 144). Similarly, Beer, commenting on his agent, says, "[w]e have found no evidence for circle detectors or corner detectors within this agent's evolved nervous system, and even though we have shown that the agent's *behavior* is sensitive to object width, there is no evidence that any combination of interneuronal activity plays the role of re-presenting that width" (2003: 238). Because creatures and agents contain nothing that plays the role of representational vehicle – no traditional symbolic tokens to which content may be attached – they cannot possibly contain representational states.[14]

Clark, correctly in my view, recognizes that the "issues concerning representation thus reduce to questions about the isolability of inner content-bearing vehicles and the nature (weak or strong) of the standing-in relation itself" (1997b: 479). However, it is also important to note that settling issues concerning representation in dynamical systems and Brooks-like creatures may not settle issues concerning representation in cognition more broadly. As noted above, the existence of representation-hungry problems suggests that dynamical analyses of such problems must be equipped to handle strong representations; or, alternatively, dynamical analyses turn out not to be suited to an explanation of the full range of cognitive capacities.

In any case, the uncertainties about representational vehicles that Brooks and Beer express may not be as troubling as they fear. The idea that representational vehicles must be discrete entities, extractable from a system like a Godiva chocolate from a box, is indeed in keeping with standard cognitive science, but connectionists long ago showed us how to conceive of representational vehicles in other ways. Representations in connectionist nets may have as their vehicles patterns of activities that span networks of nodes. The reason to identify these patterns with representational vehicles do not differ from the reasons to count a word as a representational vehicle: within the system of which they are a part, the patterns of activity play the role of standing-in for various features.

But there is one last gambit for the representational skeptics. Beer argues that only by radically re-defining "representation" can one hope to make sense of the claim that dynamical systems contain representations. But this game of re-definition will only promote confusion in discussions of representation. Thus, better not to play: "if the mechanisms underlying situated, embodied cognitive behavior look nothing like re-presentations, and they act nothing like re-presentations, then they are not representations, and continuing to call them representations is just going to confuse everyone" (2003: 239).

This final argument, however, is unlikely to move defenders of representation. Naturally, if there is nothing in a cognitive system that looks or acts like a representation then there is no need to attribute a representation to that system. The real issue, of course, is whether a system can do all that we know cognitive systems are able to do without possessing anything that looks or acts like a representation. Can a representation-free system acquire language, reason its way through problems, entertain a variety of options when making a decision, form mental images, learn from past mistakes? Even granting that Beer is correct that his agent's behavior does not depend on representations, the question whether all cognition can do without representation is far from being settled in Beer's favor.

5.10 Summary

Within embodied cognition is a movement to overturn the computational commitments that define standard cognitive science, and in doing so to re-make cognitive science in a new image. Replacing the old vision of cognition as disembodied symbol processing, beginning with inputs from the sensory system and ending with commands to the motor system, is a new vision of cognition as emerging from continuous interactions between a body, a brain, and a world. Insofar as the behavior of such systems self-organizes from the coupling of its parts, dynamical systems theory, rather than computational theory, is, the assumption goes, a better tool for understanding this behavior. Likewise, a control system comprising multiple layers of sense-act cycles might be the best way to build such a system. Finally, insofar as dynamical analyses or subsumption control systems operate without need of representational states, embodied cognitive science can do without them.

Advocates of Replacement see embodiment and situatedness, rather than symbol manipulation, as the core explanatory concepts in their new cognitive science. The emphasis on embodiment is intended to draw attention to the role an organism's body plays in performing actions that influence how the brain responds to the world while at the same time influencing how the world presents itself to the brain. Similarly, the focus on situatedness is meant to reveal how the world's structure imposes constraints and opportunities relative to the type of body an organism has, and thus determines as well the nature of stimulation the brain receives. Within embodied and situated agents, the brain remains a crucial organ of cognition, but it must accept a downgrading in status from star to co-star, an equal partner in the creation of cognition alongside body and world.

I have argued that the case for Replacement coming from dynamical approaches to cognition and behavior-based approaches to robotics falls short. To date, the sorts of behavior that dynamicists have targeted, and the capacities of robots built on the principles that inspired Brooks's subsumption architecture, represent too thin a slice of the full cognitive spectrum to inspire much faith that embodiment and situatedness can account for all cognitive phenomena. Nevertheless, even if Replacement ultimately fails in its goal to topple standard cognitive science, there is no reason to dismiss as unimportant the contributions it has so far produced. Research programs like Thelen's, Beer's, and Brooks's have added to our understanding of cognition. Some tasks that were once thought to imply the existence of rules, models, plans, representations, and associated computational apparatus, turn out to depend on other tricks. For this reason, rather than Replacement, embodied cognition might do better to set its sights on rapprochement.

5.11 Suggested Reading

Beer, R. (forthcoming). "Dynamical Systems and Embedded Cognition," in K. Frankish and W. Ramsey (eds.) *The Cambridge Handbook of Artificial Intelligence* (Cambridge: Cambridge University Press).

Brooks, R. (1991b). "Intelligence Without Representation," *Artificial Intelligence* 47: 139–59.

Clark, A. and Toribio, J. (1994). "Doing Without Representing?" *Synthese* 101: 401–31.

Van Gelder, T. (1995). "What Might Cognition Be, If Not Computation," *Journal of Philosophy* 92: 345–81.

Van Gelder, T. (1998). "The Dynamical Hypothesis in Cognitive Science," *Behavioral and Brain Sciences* 21: 615–65.

6

EMBODIED COGNITION

THE CONSTITUTION HYPOTHESIS

6.1 Constitution

If embodied cognition is genuinely something new, something that advances, replaces, or otherwise supersedes standard cognitive science, then one should expect it to leave behind at least some of the methodological and conceptual commitments on which standard cognitive science rests. In our investigations of Conceptualization and, more explicitly, Replacement, we have seen arguments that embodied cognition does just this. Understanding the mind requires understanding the constraints that a body imposes on it, or requires an appreciation of the coupled interactions between brain, body, and world from which cognitive activity spontaneously emerges, and, for one reason or another, standard cognitive science is not equipped to accommodate these facts.

Proponents of the Constitution hypothesis also see themselves as upsetting the traditional cognitivist's apple cart. However, as we shall see, many of the resources on which standard cognitive science has relied remain in good standing even if Constitution is correct. The main point of disagreement concerns the constituents of the mind. Whereas standard cognitive science puts the computational processes constituting the mind completely within the brain, if Constitution is right, constituents of cognitive processes extend beyond the brain. Some advocates of Constitution thus assert that the body is, literally, part of the mind. More radically, some who defend Constitution claim that the mind extends even beyond the body, into the world. This latter view goes by the label *extended cognition*, and has been the source of some of the liveliest debate between embodied cognition theorists and more traditional cognitivists.

The main challenge that Constitution faces is to explain the sense in which the body or parts of the world are constituents of the mind. Making this especially difficult is the need to distinguish *constituents* of the mind from mere *causal influences* on the mind. Everyone, including standard cognitive scientists, agrees that events in the body affect the mind. Thus, turning one's head changes the stimulation that enters the eyes, and thus affects visual perception. However, this is not a reason to regard head motions as a *constituent* of perception: head motions may be just a causal contributor to those processes in which the *real* constituents of perception reside. Analogously, moving a video camera will affect the data the camera processes, but this is not a reason to include the motions of the camera as a constituent of, rather than a causal contributor to, the computational processes within the camera that actually create the image.

Before delving deeper into these issues, worth pausing to consider is a quick response to these examples. Why not, one might ask, simply define a mental process in a way that includes causal contributors to that process, thereby making Constitution true? Thus, if head motions are, suppose, necessary for certain visual perceptions (e.g. monocular depth perception), why not take them to be constituents of visual perception? Pressing the point, one might wonder whether the decision to limit the constituents of perception to processes within the brain isn't arbitrary. And if so, perhaps the entire dispute between those who would extend cognition beyond the brain and those who would keep it within the boundaries of the brain is entirely verbal – to be decided by stipulation rather than by anything more substantive.

We shall see that in some cases the debate over Constitution does tip dangerously close to a merely verbal dispute. However, insofar as there is a real difference between constituents and causes, there is reason to think that disagreement over Constitution is genuine, and, therefore, open to resolution. For now, we need to become clearer on the difference between constituent and cause.

There's an intuition that anchors the distinction between constituent and cause even though a precise account of the distinction can be frustratingly elusive. Consider an event like World War I. The war had many parts, or constituents, including naval battles, land battles, invasions, and so on. The war also had many causes, one of which was the assassination of Austria's Archduke. The intuition is that the assassination was not part of the war, but took place prior to the war. Similarly, one might distinguish the causes of an illness from the constituents of an illness. Among the constituents of diabetes are a reduction in the production of insulin and an increase in blood glucose levels. The *causes* of diabetes, on the other hand, are not well understood, and probably include both genetic and environmental factors. The genes and sugar consumption that cause diabetes are not part of the disease, just as the Archduke's assassination was not part of World War I.

Although metaphysicians disagree over the exact nature of constituents, for our purposes we might say that if C is a constituent of an event or process P, C exists where and when that event or process exists. Thus, for some process P, if C takes place prior to P's occurrence (even if in the location where P eventually occurs), or if C takes place apart from P's occurrence (even if during the time span of P), then C is not a constituent of P.

Harder to articulate, but crucial for the issues at hand, is the idea that some constituents of a process are central, or very important, in the sense that the process would break down, be incomplete, or become a different process, without the presence of these constituents. Thus, while beating the batter is a constituent event in the process of making a cake, we can imagine making a cake without beating the batter. Perhaps the resulting product would be lumpier than we'd like, but it would still be recognizable as a cake. On the other hand, *baking* the cake – another constituent in the cake-making process – seems to be a more important constituent. Removing this constituent from the cake-making process leaves one with something other than a cake. Similarly, World War I had many constituents, and imagining that it might have lacked one constituent, for instance the Battle of Gallipoli, is easier than imagining that it might have lacked others, for instance the Austro-Hungarian army. Because of the centrality of the Austro-Hungarian army in World War I, when one imagines World War I without it, a good case might be made that one is imagining something other than World War I.

The debate over Constitution turns on whether the body and world are *important* or *central* constituents in cognitive processes, such that cognition would break down, or be incomplete, or be something other than what it is, without their constituency. One way to conceptualize the constituents of a process is to imagine drawing a circle around those events, and only those events, that must be present when and where the process of interest is present.[1] Thus, although the Archduke's assassination may have sufficed to bring about World War I (may even have been *necessary* to the war's beginning), a circle drawn around the events that are present when and where the war occurs would not include the assassination. The event occurred *prior* to the events that constituted the war. Likewise, the circle containing only the constituents of diabetes would not contain the disease's genetic and environmental causes.

To be sure, intuitions play a large role in this distinction between cause and constituent. Where intuitions are uncertain, the distinction thus becomes blurry. For instance, consider the process of preparing a meal. You read recipes, gather ingredients, chop, sauté, blend, whisk, bake, broil, clean dishes, wipe countertops, set a table, and so on. Around which of these events do we draw the circle that divides the constituents of meal preparation from the events that lead up to or follow meal preparation? Making this question difficult is an apparent lack of precision regarding what it means to prepare a meal. Some might think that laying out the ingredients is part of a meal's preparation. Others might regard that task as merely a precursor to the actual preparation of the meal. Here we have a disagreement that does seem to be merely verbal. Whether collecting ingredients is a constituent of meal preparation, or something that you do prior to preparing the meal, simply depends on how one wishes to define the expression "preparation of a meal."

The lesson to take from this example is that the controversy over Constitution, if it is to avoid dwindling into linguistic insignificance, must confront questions over the meaning of *mental*, or *cognitive*, processes. Whether the body and world[2] may be constituents of cognition or merely causally related to cognition depends, first, on what we mean by cognition and, second, on whether the body and world fall within or outside the circle we draw around the constituents of cognition.

6.2 A Quick Refutation of Constitution? The Argument from Envatment

A simple, if not practical, test might seem easily to resolve the debate over Constitution. I have framed the issue in terms of *circle drawing*. Thus, we can ask whether, having drawn a circle around the brain, we have drawn a circle around all the constituents of cognition. Philosophers have long imagined a scenario that speaks to this question. Imagine a patient, Sylvia, whose body is failing but whose mental faculties remain intact. Her doctor recommends an experimental procedure that involves removing her brain from her decaying body and keeping it alive in a vat of nutrients. The afferent and efferent nerves to and from the brain will be connected to a computer that will create the sort of inputs that Sylvia's body would have ordinarily transmitted to her brain, and will receive the sort of outputs Sylvia's brain would have ordinarily transmitted to her body. If all goes well, Sylvia will live the remainder of her life as happily as she would have with an actual, healthy body. This brain-in-a-vat scenario suggests an argument that might seem to get at the heart of the Constitution question.

> Argument from Envatment
> 1   If processes outside the brain (e.g. in the body or world) are constituents of cognition then the brain alone does not suffice for cognition.
> 2   An envatted brain suffices for cognition.
> Therefore, processes outside the brain are not constituents of cognition.

In effect, the Argument from Envatment merely makes graphic the earlier discussion of drawing circles to identify constituents. The brain in a vat is separated from those parts of the body and the world that proponents of Constitution claim to be constituents of cognition. Hence, if the envatted brain is as cognitively able as an embodied brain, Constitution must be false – the brain alone constitutes the mind.

But perhaps this argument against Constitution is too quick. Clark (2008: 163–4) suggests the following embellishment to Sylvia's predicament.[3] Suppose that Sylvia's doctors become concerned that her disease will soon destroy parts of her visual cortex, e.g. V1, leaving her unable to see. Not to worry, the surgeons assure her, they can include in the computer a sub-routine that performs the processing that V1 currently performs. The sub-routine will receive inputs from the neurons that, in a healthy brain, transmit information to V1 and will output signals to those parts of the visual cortex that normally receive information from V1. In effect, a functional duplicate of Sylvia's V1 is installed in the computer which takes over visual processing the instant that Sylvia's neural V1 ceases to operate. In this case, the second premise of the Argument from Envatment is now false. Sylvia's envatted brain no longer, by itself, suffices for all of Sylvia's cognitive abilities because without the V1 sub-routine in the computer, Sylvia cannot see.

Undoubtedly, the thought experiment can be extended. Perhaps Sylvia's disease destroys the parts of her brain responsible for language comprehension, or memory, or speech, or attention, and so on, and in each case Sylvia's adept surgeons program sub-routines into the computer that take on the jobs that the damaged areas of Sylvia's brain once performed. This possibility reveals the larger problem with the Argument from Envatment. The Argument from Envatment addresses only a contingent fact about cognition – that the brain is, in actual cases, the sole constituent of the mind. From the perspective of Constitution, this is a mere accident. There is no reason to suppose that processes other than those taking place in the brain cannot be constituents of cognition; for the defining features of the constituents of cognition are information processing roles, and whether the mechanisms that play these roles are in the brain or external to it (in the body or beyond) is of no significance. Thus, there is no principled reason that cognition cannot extend into the body or the world.

Of course, supporters of Constitution believe that the brain by itself is not sufficient for cognition. In his response to the Argument from Envatment, Clark hopes to show that "vat intuitions, supposing they are reliable, are simply silent on which bits of the overall system are doing the essential work" (2008: 164). V1, in the scenario above, is outside the vat but nevertheless doing "essential work." Might it not be possible, then, that there exist constituents of cognition doing essential work that are outside the brain?

Possibility, however, is not enough. Fred Adams and Ken Aizawa, who sometimes present themselves as a lifesaving antibiotic fighting a battle against virulent strains of embodied cognition, are happy to accept what they call contingent intracranialism: "while transcranial cognition may be both a logical and a nomological possibility, no case has been made for its current existence" (2001: 43). The point is that supporters of Constitution must make a case that cognition actually extends beyond the brain if they are to convince standard cognitive scientists of the need to reconceive their subject matter. For this reason, Clark's response to the assertion that the brain alone suffices for cognition, depending as it does on probing the possible rather than the actual, will fail to impress those cognitive scientists who see their task as explaining actual cognitive systems rather than merely possible ones.

But defenders of Constitution have available another response to the Argument from Envatment. They might simply deny the second premise, insisting that an envatted brain does not suffice for cognition. There's more to thinking than brain processes. An evaluation of this claim and associated issues will take us through the remainder of this chapter.

6.3 Sensorimotor Theories of Perceptual Experience

The psychologist J. Kevin O'Regan, together with philosopher Alva Noë, has developed a theory of perceptual experience according to which the constituents of experience extend beyond the brain. The kind of experiences of most interest to O'Regan and Noë are *visual* experiences, e.g. the shape a circle looks to have through changes in perspective; the redness of an apple; the sense of seeing an entire cat rather than slices of cat when viewing the cat through a picket fence. Our brief examination of computational approaches to vision in chapter 1 indicated how a standard cognitive scientist would explain these sorts of experiences. The explanation begins with a description of the information available on the retina and proceeds to detail the algorithms that derive from this information a representation of shape (circle), or color (red), or kind (cat). The algorithm will "fill in" whatever the sparse inputs leave out, relying on rules or generalizations to compensate for the poverty of the stimuli. These processing stages from which the final visual experience emerges take place in the brain, and thus an envatted brain, stimulated in the right way, should have the same visual experiences as a normally embodied brain.

O'Regan and Noë reject this computational picture, adopting instead a neo-Gibsonian account that emphasizes the importance of action in perception. Consequently, they reject the computationalist's assumption that the brain alone suffices for visual experience and embrace a theory that extends the constituents of perception into the bodies of perceivers. If O'Regan and Noë are right, an envatted brain could not have visual experiences.[4] Below are some passages that clearly express O'Regan and Noë's opposition to the standard cognitivist's brain bias.

1   "[T]he experience of vision is actually *constituted* by a mode of exploring the environment" (2001: 946, their emphasis).

2   "[I]n seeing, specifying the brain state is not sufficient to determine the sensory experience, because we need to know how the visual apparatus and the environment are currently interacting. There can therefore be no one-to-one correspondence between visual experience and neural activations. Seeing is not constituted by activation of neural representations" (2001: 966).

3   "Just as mechanical activity in the engine of a car is not sufficient to guarantee driving activity (suppose the car is in a swamp, or suspended by a magnet), so neural activity alone is not sufficient to produce vision" (2001: 967).

4   "[W]e propose that experience does *not* derive from brain activity. Experience
    is just the activity in which the exploring of the environment consists. The
    experience lies in the doing" (2001: 968, their emphasis).

Likewise, Noë's further elaboration of the sensorimotor theory of perception (Noë 2004) yields the following:

5   "[O]ur ability to perceive not only depends on, but is constituted by, our
    possession of this sort of sensorimotor knowledge" (2004: 2).
6   "What perception is, however, is not a process in the brain, but a kind of
    skillful activity on the part of the animal as a whole" (2004: 2).
7   "Perceptual experience *just is* a mode of skillful exploration of the world"
    (2004: 194).

These claims about the constituents of perceptual experience, about
what perceptual experience *just is*, are of exactly the sort that might refute
the Argument from Envatment. If they're right, the second premise of the
Argument from Envatment must be wrong. But are they right?

O'Regan and Noë argue that perceptual experience derives from acquaint-
ance with sensorimotor contingencies (or dependencies). The basic idea is
this. Visual experience depends on the particular features of the visual apparatus as well as the features of the world to which this apparatus is sensitive.
An apparatus like *so*, when exposed to features such as *these*, will behave in
ways that can be lawfully described. These laws define the sensorimotor
contingencies unique to each sensory system. For instance, one feature of
the visual apparatus (among vertebrates) is a concave retina; and one feature
in the world that the visual apparatus can detect is shape (but not, e.g., odor
or sound). As the eyes move, or as a perceiver moves, or as shapes move
about a perceiver, the interactions between the visual apparatus and external
shapes will obey various regularities (akin to Gibson's *invariants*). These
regularities are sensorimotor contingencies. They are *sensory* contingencies
because they depend on the characteristics of the visual apparatus and the
properties in the world to which the apparatus is responding; they are *motor*
contingencies in the sense that they depend on the activities – eye movements, head movements, bodily movements – of muscles in the body.

As an example of a sensorimotor contingency, consider how a shape – a
straight line – transforms when projected on a concave retina. When at the
center of the eye's focus, the line produces an arc on the retina. But as you
shift your focus from the line to a point above the line, the curvature of the

line on the retina changes: "represented on a flattened-out retina, the line would now be curved" (O'Regan and Noë 2001: 941). Figure 6.1 illustrates the distortion of the line's projection on the retina as the line of sight moves from the line to a point above it.

In contrast, if your eyes move horizontally along a line rather than to a point above or below it, the projection on the retina does not change. This fact about how visual apparatuses with curved retinas interact with shapes like straight lines is one example of a sensorimotor contingency. There are, of course, many others. Every property to which a given visual apparatus is sensitive will interact with the visual apparatus in distinctive ways, thus distinguishing itself as visual property X, rather than Y or Z.

So far, O'Regan and Noë's account of perception should seem familiar. Gibson too, as we saw in chapter 3, explained perception in terms of invariances. As organisms move about their environment, lawful changes in the pencil-rays of light bombarding their light-sensitive organs specify, Gibson thought, the layout of surrounding surfaces. But O'Regan and Noë's next move departs from Gibson, who had little to say about qualitative experience. Visual experience itself, O'Regan and Noë contend, is the exercise of knowledge of sensorimotor contingencies. They remark approvingly on earlier work of MacKay (1967), adopting one of his examples:

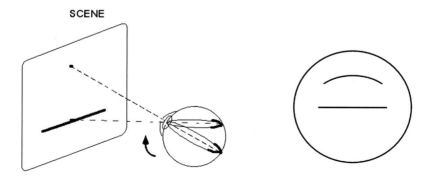

Figure 6.1 The figure on the left shows the line of sight shifting from a straight line to a point above it. On the right, the retina is depicted as a flat surface. The line transforms from straight to curved as the line of sight shifts to a point above it. Adapted from O'Regan and Noë (2001: 941).

You have the impression of seeing a bottle if there is knowledge in your nervous system concerning a certain web of contingencies. For example, you have knowledge of the fact that if you move your eyes up towards the neck of the bottle, the sensory stimulation will change in a way typical of what happens when a narrower region of the bottle comes into foveal vision; you have knowledge expressing the fact that if you move your eyes downwards, the sensory stimulation will change in a way typical of what happens when the white label is fixated by central vision.

(O'Regan and Noë 2001: 945)

In a similar vein, Myin and O'Regan (2009) describe tactile experiences as knowledge of the sensorimotor contingencies associated with particular tactile stimulations. For instance, suppose someone taps your leg. You have the feeling of being tapped here rather than there. What explains this experience? What makes it feel the way it does? "I can touch my finger to that location and create a similar feeling to the one that I am currently feeling. Furthermore, I can move my eyes to the location on my leg and see the person tapping, whereas if I move my eyes to other parts of my body, I do not see the person tapping" (2009: 192). The tapping feels as it does because you know that tapping yourself in the same spot will feel the same way, and you know that when you look at that spot you will see someone tapping it.

An obvious question about O'Regan and Noë's theory of perceptual experience concerns the nature of the knowledge perceivers have of sensorimotor contingencies. Clearly O'Regan and Noë do not intend this knowledge to be explicit. Few people are likely to know explicitly that a straight line will project an arc on a curved retina when focusing on a point above or below it. When O'Regan and Noë speak of knowledge of sensorimotor contingencies they have in mind something tacit. Experience with the objects in one's environment creates in the nervous system various expectations. Our nervous system comes to expect that a straight line will project a certain way on the retina, and that eye movements of this kind will create transformations in the line's projection of that kind. The experience of subjects who wear glasses with inverting lenses, or who learn to see with devices that translate optical information into vibratory stimulation to the back or tongue, is evidence that one can acquire knowledge of sensorimotor contingencies even if one is unable to articulate in what this knowledge consists.

In addition to being tacit, knowledge of sensorimotor contingencies is intended as a species of know-how, rather than as a kind of propositional knowledge. One has mastered knowledge of sensorimotor contingencies when one has acquired a set of skills, just as one has mastered knowledge of the violin when one has acquired the ability to play difficult concerti. The skills that display mastery of sensorimotor contingencies are those that uncover the regularities that suffice to specify features of the surrounding environment – in the case of visual perception, they are the movements and adjustments that harvest information particular to shape, color, texture, and other visual attributes.

A harder question facing O'Regan and Noë's theory concerns the meaning of their claim that experience *is* the exercise of sensorimotor knowledge. There is a stronger and weaker interpretation of this claim. On the weaker interpretation, exercise of sensorimotor knowledge consists only in the *potential* to perform those actions that define a class of sensorimotor contingencies. Thus, in the discussion of the experience of having one's leg tapped, Myin and O'Regan seem *not* to require that you actually tap yourself on the spot where you are being tapped, or that you look at the spot where you are being tapped. Rather, constituting an experience of being tapped at spot S is one's knowledge that if you did tap S, or if you did look at spot S, then you would have a similar feeling or would see a finger tapping. Likewise, the feeling one has of seeing a stationary object "consists in the knowledge that if you were to move your eye slightly leftwards, the object would shift one way on your retina" (O'Regan and Noë 2001: 949). The feeling does not seem to depend on having *actually* to move your eye leftwards. Thus, according to the weak interpretation, it is important only that one has, sometime in the past, acted on the world in ways that created knowledge of sensorimotor contingencies; perceptual experience *now* consists in the knowledge one has acquired from these previous actions.

On the stronger interpretation, the exercise of sensorimotor knowledge requires that one *actually* practice those actions that reveal sensorimotor contingencies. O'Regan and Noë on occasion suggest that the stronger interpretation is correct: "*Visual perception can now be understood as the activity of exploring the environment in ways mediated by knowledge of the relevant sensorimotor contingencies*" (2001: 943, their emphasis). And, again, "[u]nder the theory presented here, seeing involves testing the changes that occur through eye, body, and attention movements" (2001: 947). If this second interpretation is correct, then past experience with the environment does not, by itself, suffice for experience. Seeing, for instance, the line as straight requires not just knowing how the line will project on the retina as one's eyes move to a point above it, but requires actually moving one's eyes to a point above it.

Neither interpretation is without its problems. Aizawa (2007) argues that empirical evidence tells against the strong interpretation. He notes that victims of paralysis are nevertheless able to perceive, contrary to the implications of the strong interpretation. So, for instance, Aizawa recounts the testimony of a woman who experienced excruciating pain during a Caesarian section. The anesthesiologist had administered both anesthesia and a neuromuscular blockade. The neuromuscular blockade effectively paralyzed the woman, but the amount of anesthesia was inadequate to eliminate the pain. Due to her paralysis, the woman clearly could not cut herself where she was being cut, or look at the scalpel where it entered her belly, so if these are the kinds of sensorimotor contingencies that must be enacted in order to feel an incision, then, contrary to fact, the woman should have felt nothing.

These considerations tip in favor of the weaker interpretation, according to which it is not the actual exercise of actions that reveal sensorimotor contingencies that is important, but simply knowledge of these contingencies. Yet, that knowledge alone of sensorimotor contingencies is constitutive of perceptual experience makes a puzzle of O'Regan and Noë's efforts to explain away the perceptual experiences of those who are paralyzed (Noë 2004: 12) or whose eyes have been stabilized (O'Regan and Noë 2001: 947–8). Why be concerned with such cases if an ability to engage actively with the world in ways that illuminate sensorimotor contingencies is not necessary in the first place? Moreover, the weaker interpretation appears to be inconsistent with comments like those noted above (quotations 1, 4, 6, and 7) in which perceptual experience is equated with skillful activity. But perhaps a tougher challenge to the weaker interpretation comes again from the Argument from Envatment.

The burden that the sensorimotor theory of perception carries is to show that the brain alone is not constitutive of perceptual experience. The idea, we saw, is that perceptual experience is in some sense the product of the body's activities – motions of the eyes, head, and larger body. But if the weaker interpretation is correct, then perceptual experience consists in knowledge that can as well be located in an envatted brain as it can in a normally embodied brain. The sensorimotor theory of perception would count as an embodied theory only in the sense that it emphasizes the importance of the body in perception – a point with which a standard cognitive scientist might eagerly agree, or, if previously not appreciative of the body's significance, accept with feigned indifference as a helpful reminder.

Noë might respond to the foregoing by insisting that the knowledge constituting perceptual experience is not intended to be *propositional* knowledge (knowledge that such and such is the case), but is rather intended as know-how. Furthermore, know-how is not the sort of knowledge that a brain in a vat could have, because it requires a brain in a body in an environment to acquire the kinds of skills in which perceptual experience consists. Nothing short of a complete simulation of the body and its possible interactions with the environment could endow an envatted brain with the know-how that is essential to perceptual experience.[5]

However, even if Noë is right that know-how can never be represented propositionally (a controversial point – see Stanley and Williamson 2001), we might wonder why an envatted brain could not encode know-how. Remember that once envatted, Sylvia's brain still retains all the knowledge that she acquired when embodied and interacting with the environment. Were a new body constructed and Sylvia's brain placed within its head, it would, we can assume, interact as skillfully with the environment as her old body did. This establishes that know-how, however represented in the brain, is nevertheless within the brain, and so again the brain appears to contain all that is sufficient for perceptual experience.

In short, Aizawa's point that sensorimotor activity is not, in fact, necessary for perceptual experience forces on O'Regan and Noë a dilemma. Either their account of perceptual experience is empirically false, for it implies that paralytics cannot experience what they do in fact experience, or it fails to establish that the constituents of experience extend beyond the brain, for it limits the constituents of experience to knowledge which, presumably, is represented in the brain.

6.4 Constituents and Causes

Before leaving sensorimotor theories of perception, we should examine an objection that will recur in later discussions of Constitution. Both Ned Block (2005) and Aizawa (2007)[6] have charged Noë with missing a distinction between the *constituents* of visual experience and the *causes* of visual experience. Earlier, in §6.1, I described a difference between constituents and causes. If X is a central or important *constituent* of Y, then Y would fail or be something else without X's presence. In contrast, causes can be separated from their effects, even in those cases where the cause is necessary for the effect. If X is a *cause* of Y, as the Austrian Archduke's assassination is a cause of World War I, then, even if the war would not have started without the assassination, X is separable from Y in the sense that it happens before Y exists, or takes place in a location distinct from Y's. According to Block and Aizawa, the knowledge of sensorimotor contingencies that Noë identifies as constituents of perceptual experience is in fact merely a cause of perceptual experience.

In support of this charge, Aizawa invites us to consider two competing hypotheses:

(COH) Perceptual experiences are constituted, in part, by the exercise of sensorimotor skills.
(CAH) Perceptual experiences are caused, in part, by the exercise of sensorimotor skills.

(Aizawa 2007)

The issue now becomes one of deciding whether the evidence Noë cites in favor of COH might just as well support CAH.[7] If so, he has not provided a reason to prefer COH. Among Noë's evidence is the disruptive effect that inverting lenses have on perception, as well as experimental results that demonstrate the importance of action in the normal development of perceptual abilities. Regarding the first, Noë notes that when subjects first don goggles with lenses that invert the world so that scenes to the right appear to the left and vice versa, they show a deficit in their ability to adjust to objects that move along the horizontal axis. Over time, these difficulties ease until their perceptual facility is restored to what it was (or nearly so) prior to putting on the goggles. Noë explains this transition from poor to more normal perceptual ability as involving the acquisition of new sensorimotor skills. One must learn anew how to integrate one's sensations with one's actions, so that, for instance, one will come to use the left hand to grasp an object that appears to be moving in from the right. Having mastered this new set of skills, one regains normal perception. Noë's conclusion is that normal perceptual experience just is this new set of skills.

Similarly, Noë cites Held and Hein's (1963) classic experiment in which kittens are divided into two groups – those that pull a carriage around a room and those that ride in the carriage. Both groups of kittens are exposed to the same visual stimuli, but the riding kittens do not develop normal perceptual abilities. Noë's diagnosis is that the passive kittens failed to acquire the sensorimotor skills necessary for perceptual experience. Failure to integrate their visual experiences with movement in their own bodies caused visual deficits. Thus, perceptual experience consists in sensorimotor skills.

But, as Block and Aizawa are quick to note, the relationship of senso-rimotor contingencies to the results of experiments involving inverting lenses and passive kittens can as easily be conceived in terms of causes as constituents. "[W]hat they show," Block says, "is that sensorimotor contingencies have an *effect* on experience, not that experience is even partially *constituted* by ... bodily activity" (2005: 263). The point seems a natural one. Through his activities, the wearer of inverting lenses eventu-ally comes to experience the world as he did before, but this shows only that his actions and adjustments were a cause of the return to normal perceptual experience – not that the actions and adjustments *are* the expe-rience. Similarly, the passive kittens are prevented from activities that a normally developing perceptual system requires. The kittens' perceptual abilities are stunted *because* they were prevented from exercising sensori-motor skills. The burden now falls on Noë to explain why these accounts of the experimental results are inferior to one that identifies sensorimotor skills as constituents of perceptual experience.

The distinction between constituent and cause that I drew in §6.1 arrived with a caution. I observed that the distinction is only as precise as the concepts involved. Thus, when wondering about the *causes* of meal prepara-tion in contrast to the *constituents*, processes like reading recipes or collecting ingredients stand on uncertain ground. Whether gathering ingredients is a causal contributor to or a constituent of meal preparation depends on how one understands what it means to prepare a meal. Perhaps Noë believes that the meaning of perceptual experience makes natural the adoption of senso-rimotor skills as constituents of experience. This is a view that, as Block observes, a behavioristically inclined psychologist might find appealing (2005: 262). For a behaviorist (of a certain sort), there's nothing more to experience than the exercise of various skills. This suggests one path Noë might take in response to Aizawa and Block – a defense of a particular conception of perceptual experience, according to which sensorimotor skills are more plausibly conceived as constituents than causes. This path too is not without hazards. Presumably, Noë does not wish to reduce his sensorimotor theory to a conceptual truth. The motivation for identifying sensorimotor skills as constituents of experience must rest on, e.g., the fruitfulness and explanatory power of doing so rather than on a stipulation. Further work in this direction offers perhaps the best hope for answering criticisms like those Block and Aizawa make.

Issues concerning the line between constituent and cause vex other disputes over Constitution, but, unlike Noë, whose work has shown an insensitivity to the distinction,[8] other defenders of Constitution have armed themselves with responses, as we shall now see.

6.5 More Than Just a Gesture?

Here are some interesting facts about the human tendency to gesture while speaking. Gesture is a cultural universal – everybody does it, although some, for example Southern Europeans, may do it more extravagantly than others. People gesture even when their interlocutors, who may be in another room, or on a phone half-way around the world, or sharing space in a dark tunnel, cannot possibly see their gestures. The frequency and variety of gestures depends on the ideas the gesturer wishes to communicate. Communicating a solution to a problem or trying to convey various choices tends to elicit more gesturing than other communicative tasks. Gesturing often accompanies speech, but it might appear on its own – even when the gesturer is alone – especially when one is attempting to solve problems that require spatial reasoning.

Many psychologists who study gesture see these facts as evidence that gesture is something more than a useful tool for clarifying communicative intentions, as the tendency to speak more slowly or loudly to one who has not quite mastered a language might be. If gesture's role were purely communicative, we would not do it if we were blind, we would not do it from behind; we would not do it on the phone, we would not, could not all alone. The alternative proposal is that gestures contribute in some way to the processes of thinking. Experimental evidence suggests that this is so.

For instance, Rauscher, Krauss, and Chen (1996) asked subjects to describe situations involving spatial content. The speech of subjects who were prevented from gesturing showed dysfluencies: it is slower than normal and filled with pauses within rather than between grammatical clauses. Rauscher, et al. hypothesize that gesturing facilitates lexical access, so that when subjects cannot gesture they have more difficulty "finding the words" to describe spatial situations. Significantly, the difference in subjects' performance cannot be attributed to the effort that subjects in the no-gesture group must exert to keep themselves from gesturing, for subjects in this group surprisingly showed *greater* fluency than subjects in the free-gesture group when speaking about non-spatial situations.

In another study, Ehrlich, Levine, and Goldin-Meadow (2006) investigated sex differences in spatial reasoning abilities in groups of girls and boys. Males' spatial reasoning appears to be superior to females' from an early age. In addition to replicating this finding, Ehrlich, et al. also found that five-year-old boys tend to gesture more frequently than girls of the same age when engaged in a spatial rotation task. Boys performed more gestures than girls when describing a solution to the task and also used more gestures when not speaking. Boys were also more likely than girls to use gestures that describe one strategy for spatial rotation while simultaneously using speech to describe another, suggesting that gestures were expressing one way of thinking about the problem while speech was expressing another.

Experiments like those above, as well as many others (Goldin-Meadow 2003 and McNeill 2005 contain many fascinating studies) make a very strong case that gesturing does indeed have a function beyond the merely communicative. Gesture, in at least some cases, seems bound to thought. The question we must now consider is what this shows about Constitution. Even if gesture plays *some* role in cognition, this does not tell us *what* role it plays: it does not settle the issue whether gesture is a *constituent* of cognition or a *causal contributor* to cognition. It does not settle whether cognition is *embodied*.

In chapter 3 I described a number of points that Andy Clark thinks characterize embodied cognition. Among them was the idea of information self-structuring. Cognizers will use their bodies or features of the world to structure information, thereby relieving the brain of a burden that it would otherwise need to assume. Gesture does indeed seem to play this role. In Ehrlich, et al.'s study, for instance, gestures provide a tool for representing spatial relationships. It is reasonable to suppose that boys' performance in spatial reasoning tasks is better than girls' in part because they avail themselves of spatial information contained in their gestures while girls, who gesture less frequently, do not. As Goldin-Meadow has observed, the use of gesture "expands the set of representational tools available to speakers and listeners. It can redundantly reflect information represented through verbal formats or it can augment that information" (2003: 186).

But, in light of our earlier discussion of sensorimotor theories of perception, we must be especially sensitive to the possibility that the use of gesture to structure information is as well or better described as a means for enabling or enhancing cognition than as a genuine constituent of cognition. For instance, Barbara Tversky describes a study in which two groups of subjects were asked to solve a variety of problems. One group was provided with pencil and paper while the other was not. Interestingly, the problems that elicited gestures in the group without pencil and paper were just those that the second group used pencil and paper to solve. Tversky takes the finding to "suggest that gestures were used to off-load and organize spatial working memory when internal capacity was taxed," (2009: 210) just as one would use pencil and paper for the same reason. If gesture's role is comparable to that of paper and pencil, then an argument that gestures are a constituent of cognition rather than simply an aid to cognition would entail as well that paper and pencil are constituents of cognition. For some, this would reduce the argument to absurdity (but, as we shall soon see, not for others). But perhaps gestures do more than serve as an external representational store. As Clark conceives of information self-structuring, there is more to it than just that.

6.6 Coupling and Constitution

Clark appreciates that embodied cognition, if it is truly to distinguish itself from the standard conception of cognition that limits cognitive processes to computational events within the brain, must motivate Constitution – must justify the claim that parts of the extracranial body are parts of the cognitive process. Revisiting the Argument from Envatment (§6.2) will help us to understand Clark's defense of Constitution. Suppose someone were to claim that, for all the studies of gesture have shown, a brain in a vat could enjoy the benefits of gesturing if a suitably programmed computer relayed simulated gestures to the brain. This possibility would seem to count against Constitution. If a brain all on its own, provided with information from gestures, can perform spatial reasoning tasks, then gestures apparently do nothing more than contribute to the cognitive activity taking place in the brain. They are not constituents of this activity. Clark denies this, remarking that "[i]t does not follow from this that the gestures play only a causal role and do not help to constitute the machinery of cognition" (2008: 130). The reason this does not follow mimics the reasoning in Clark's earlier response to the Argument from Envatment. The defective portion of Sylvia's visual cortex that is now replicated in the off-board computer to which Sylvia's envatted brain is attached is a constituent in Sylvia's perceptual system. Similarly, gestures ought to count as constituents of cognitive routines that underlie spatial reasoning because, like the computational instantiation of V1, gestures are integrated with neural states in a manner that makes them constituents of cognition.

Of course, we should like to know what this manner of integration with neural states is in virtue of which gestures are a constituent of cognition. This question returns us to the feature of self-structuring information that so impresses Clark. Consider first an example from a different context (Clark 2008: 131). The engines of some automobiles are turbo-driven. These engines produce exhaust that spins a turbine, which in turn spins an air pump that then compresses the air that enters the engine's cylinders. Because compression allows more air to enter the cylinders than would otherwise be possible, the explosions in the cylinder are more powerful than they otherwise would be. Consequently, the engine produces more power, creating more exhaust, spinning the turbine even faster, and so on. The turbo-driven engine is another example of the sort of system that Watt's centrifugal governor illustrated: a dynamical system in which the components are *coupled*. The behavior of each part of the system is a function of the behavior of the other parts.

Clark relies on the idea of coupling to defend the claim that gestures are constituents of cognition. But, as he recognizes, there must be more to constitution than coupling. Adams and Aizawa (forthcoming) press this point. Mocking (good-naturedly) Clark, they write:

> Question: Why did the pencil think that 2 + 2 = 4?
> Clark's Answer: Because it was coupled to the mathematician (forthcoming).

There are several points Adams and Aizawa wish to draw from this example, but for now we must focus on the challenge it presents to the possibility that gestures are a constituent of cognition. When should coupled components count as causal contributors to a process and when as constituents?

Recall Huygen's discovery that pendulums hanging from a common wooden beam would synchronize their swings (either in-phase or anti-phase). The pendulums are coupled. The equation that describes the period of one pendulum must contain a term describing the behavior of the other. Still, this does not seem to be a reason to think that one pendulum is a constituent of another. We might think of one pendulum as producing an input that is fed to the other, which then produces an output that is fed as input into the first. The two pendulums thus *affect* each other's behavior, but they remain distinct. If this is all there ever is to coupling, then we should similarly conclude that gestures may affect the cognitive processing that takes place in the brain, but there is no need to accept gestures as constituents of the cognitive process.

But, Clark thinks, the turbo-driven engine, like the system of which gestures are a part, displays a special sort of coupling. "There is a crucially important complication," Clark says, that marks some coupled cognitive systems as *extended*:

> These are the cases when we confront a recognizably cognitive process, running in some agent, that creates outputs (speech, gesture, expressive movements, written words) that, recycled as inputs, drive the cognitive process along. In such cases, any intuitive ban on counting inputs as parts of mechanisms seems wrong.
>
> (2008: 131)

Like the exhaust fumes that the turbo-driven engine creates to enhance its own power, the spatial reasoning system *uses* the very gestures it creates *in order to* improve its own operations. Gestures, as Clark and many psychologists who study them believe, are the spatial reasoning system's invention for doing spatial reasoning. Accordingly, they earn their status as actual *constituents* of spatial reasoning, being more than simply external, if still useful, influences on processes occurring exclusively within the skull.

In Clark's analysis of gestures we find a clearer picture of the failing he sees in the Argument from Envatment. Suppose one were to hold doggedly to that argument, pointing out that the gestures the spatial reasoning system produces are of no value unless they have some effect on the brain, and so one can still draw a circle around the brain when identifying the constituents of spatial reasoning. This observation is made with the intent to demote gestures once again from constituents of spatial reasoning to mere influences on spatial reasoning processes taking place within the brain.

But, from Clark's perspective, this re-assertion of the brain's primacy reflects nothing more than an unwarranted bias. Why draw the circle around the brain? Why not, it is fair to wonder, draw the circle around one thousand neurons of, let's say, the million involved in spatial reasoning tasks? Having drawn the circle around these thousand, one can then insist that the other 999,000 neurons involved in spatial reasoning are merely influences on those thousand neurons that are the *real* constituents of spatial reasoning. But this surely is an arbitrary stipulation. Why these thousand? Why one thousand rather than one hundred thousand? Clark has something to say about where to draw the line. Because gestures are coupled to processes in the brain as exhaust fumes are coupled to other processes in the turbo-driven engine – as effects created for the purpose of serving as inputs to the very system that produces them – they ought to count as parts of the system. Whether one agrees that this is a *good* reason for distinguishing constituents from causes is another matter. But it is a reason, and it places the burden on proponents of the Argument from Envatment to say why constituents of cognition cannot reside outside the brain.

In our earlier discussion of the Argument from Envatment (§6.2) I noted Adams and Aizawa's position of *contingent intracranialism*. Adams and Aizawa believe that Constitution is possible – cognition *may* extend beyond the cranium – but that in fact it does not. This response was effective against Clark's imaginary scenario involving a brain in the vat that relies on an off-board computer for some elements of its cognitive processing. But with gestures, if Clark's analysis is correct, we have an example of cognitive extension that is not just possible but actual. Gestures do cognitive work – they represent, e.g., spatial relations – in the context of a system that produces them precisely for their representational capacities. If Adams and Aizawa agree that Constitution is possible but not actual, work on gesture requires them to explain why Constitution remains, still, only a possibility. We shall soon turn to their arguments.

6.7 Extending Cognition Further

Having examined cases of Constitution that involve the body, the possibility of Constitution involving attributes of the world beyond the body is easier to understand. Although body-involving Constitution and world-involving Constitution often receive justification through the same lines of reasoning, it is the latter that has generated the brightest fireworks in discussions of embodied cognition. Many critics who, albeit begrudgingly, accept the idea that parts of the body might be constituents of cognition seem to find themselves pushed too far when asked to accept that cognition might extend into the world. Yet, proponents of Constitution seem to delight in pushing. Just after defending gestures as constituents of cognition, Clark takes the next step: "[s]omething very similar," he says,

> may, as frequently remarked, occur when we are busy writing and thinking at the same time. It is not always that fully formed thoughts get committed to paper. Rather, the paper provides a medium in which, this time via some kind of coupled neural-scribbling-reading unfolding, we are enabled to explore ways of thinking that might otherwise be unavailable to us.
>
> (2008: 126)

From brain, to paper, back to brain, thence again to paper – the result being a product that the brain alone could not produce. But, Clark would insist, this process shows more than the brain's mere dependency on the scribbled thoughts. The point is not simply that the brain could not cognize, or cognize as well, without the assistance of paper and pencil. The brain requires many things in order to function well: blood, hormones, oxygen, and so on. Distinguishing the printed words from factors like these is the fact that the brain produces them in order to enhance its ability to, say, produce a philosophy paper. The words, are a "self-generated external structure on thought and reason" (Clark 2008: 126), and thus, Clark concludes, a very part of thought and reason.

This coupling argument for extended cognition – for cognition that extends beyond the body – is just one of several that, although similar in spirit, are worth separating. There is another argument for extended cognition that depends on what has come to be called the *parity principle*. There is also an argument that deploys a conception of *wide computationalism*. For each of these positive arguments there are counterarguments. There are also broader critiques of extended cognition that question its utility, or seek to reduce some of its consequences to absurdity. These issues will occupy us in the remaining sections of this chapter.

6.8 The Coupling-Constitution Fallacy

Adams and Aizawa (2008; 2009; forthcoming) have argued that Clark and other defenders of extended cognition (e.g. Noë 2004; Wilson 2004) commit what they call the *coupling-constitution fallacy*. The fallacy, they claim, is evident in two types of coupling arguments that they distinguish. In the first, *simple* coupling arguments, "all that is invoked in arguing for an extended cognitive process is a causal connection or looping between the cognizing organism and the environment" (2009: 81). As an example, Adams and Aizawa mention a famous example from Clark and Chalmers (1998): "[i]f you are coupled to your pocket notebook in the sense of always having it readily available, use it a lot, trust it implicitly, and so forth, then Clark infers that the pocket notebook constitutes a part of your memory store" (forthcoming). In contrast to *simple* coupling arguments are those that introduce the notion of a system. Like simple coupling arguments, *system* coupling arguments emphasize causal connections between the brain, body, and world but then take the intermediate step of describing these causal relata as parts of a cognitive system, from there moving to the conclusion that cognition extends into the body and world. Presumably, the earlier discussion of gesturing depends on a system coupling argument, for gestures are conceived as part of a spatial reasoning system that includes processes in the brain as well.

In either form, coupling arguments commit the coupling-constitution fallacy. Schematically, the fallacy is this: "The pattern of reasoning here involves moving from the observation that process X is in some way causally connected (coupled) to a process Y of type φ to the conclusion that X is part of a process of type φ" (Adams and Aizawa 2009: 81). More vividly, Adams and Aizawa illustrate the fallacy with this example: "[i]t is the interaction of the spinning bowling ball with the surface of the alley that leads to all the pins falling. Still, the process of the ball's spinning does not extend into the surface of the alley or the pins" (2009: 83). No less, Adams and Aizawa insist, does cognition extend into gesturing hands or scribbling pencils. Hands, pencil, and paper may serve as props useful to cognition, may, even, be parts of a system that includes processes within the brain, but this no more makes them cognitive than does a spinning ball make the surface on which it is spinning itself spin.

The fallacy Adams and Aizawa identify is doubtless real, but whether defenders of Constitution are its perpetrators is less clear. One response that should by now be obvious is to distinguish between kinds of dependency relations. Clark, we saw, has more to say about the coupling relationship that distinguishes causes from constituents than Adams and Aizawa seem to appreciate. Of course the bowling ball's spinning does not extend into the surface of the alley or the pins it knocks down. This is true even though, assume, the ball could not spin unless on a surface, or could not knock down the pins unless spinning. But this is not a system that creates its own inputs for the purpose of enhancing a particular capacity. If the bowler deliberately causes the ball to spin, and its spinning then feeds back into the bowler, thereby enhancing future bowling, which in turn leads to faster spinning, and so on then the spinning process does indeed seem to be a constituent of a system for knocking down the pins. However, nothing like this is happening when the bowler bowls.

But consideration of this point introduces a second response to the coupling-constitution fallacy. Adams and Aizawa often interpret Constitution as the claim that the constituents of cognitive processes are themselves engaged in cognitive processes.[9] This explains the fun we earlier (§6.6) saw them having with Clark's alleged position:

Question: Why did the pencil think that 2 + 2 = 4?
Clark's Answer: Because it was coupled to the mathematician (forthcoming).

But Clark is not committed to the claim that parts of a cognitive system or process must themselves be *doing* cognitive processing. Of course the pencil coupled to a mathematician cannot think, and of course cognitive processing is not taking place in gesturing hands or on the pencil and paper on which one is scribbling half-baked ideas. We might describe Adams and Aizawa's mistake here as the process-constituent fallacy (PCF):

Process-Constituent Fallacy: the assumption that those who defend X as a constituent of process Y must believe that process Y occurs in X.

But if the process-constituent fallacy is a fallacy, how *are* we to understand the claims that proponents of Constitution make about the constituents of cognitive processes?

To be fair, advocates of Constitution do on occasion make remarks that might tempt one to see PCF as no fallacy at all. For instance, Clark has claimed that "[h]uman cognitive processing (sometimes) literally extends into the environment surrounding the organism" (2008: 139). Moreover, we saw that in his initial response to the Argument from Envatment he suggests the possibility that processes that ordinarily take place in the brain might occur in a computer, suggesting (perhaps) that Constitution requires that the external constituents of cognition actually perform cognitive processes. Rob Wilson too makes remarks that perhaps encourage one to see merit in Adams and Aizawa's allegation, as when he describes how a player solves a board game problem, saying "the thinking, the cognitive part of solving the problem, is not squirreled away inside us, wedged between the looking and moving, but developed and made possible through these interactions with the board" (2004: 194).

However, these remarks are at best ambiguous, and given the relative obviousness of the coupling-constitution fallacy, the charitable course is to look for some non-fallacious interpretation of them. An analogy to the circulatory system may offer some help (Shapiro 2009). Veins, arteries, and capillaries are, I submit, indisputably constituents of the circulatory system. But does the process of circulation take place within them? The question is ambiguous. If it is asking whether, were we to remove a given vein, circulation would be happening in that vein, then the answer is "no." Similarly, if

Clark were to assert that cognition is taking place in gestures, all on their own, then he would surely be mistaken. But if, on the other hand, the question is asking whether the events taking place within the vein are part of the process of circulation, the answer seems clearly to be "yes." To paraphrase Wilson's earlier remark, with relevant substitutions, circulation is not squirreled away in the heart, but made possible through the heart's interactions with the veins, arteries, and capillaries. I do not see why this claim is false, nor why it must commit one to the view that circulation occurs within each vein, artery, and capillary belonging to the circulatory system. Claims of Constitution should be understood in this same way. Cognition need not be "going on" in non-neural constituents of cognitive processes for Constitution to make sense. Rather, these constituents must, like veins in the circulatory system, be integrated with other parts of a cognitive system in a way that certifies them as constituents of the system.

The allegation of a coupling-constitution fallacy falls short as a criticism of Constitution insofar as it neglects to distinguish various forms of coupling, some of which may make more plausible the idea that coupled causes of cognitive systems are more than just that – are in fact constituents of these systems. Adams and Aizawa's criticism also seems unfair, insofar as it attributes to many defenders of Constitution a view that, although perhaps suggested in some careless or ambiguous remarks, is on its surface implausible. Properly understood, there are arguments for Constitution that depend on coupling claims but that do not appear to commit the coupling-constitution fallacy.[10]

6.9 A Parity Argument for Constitution

In an article that first introduced most philosophers to the idea of extended cognition, Clark and Chalmers (1998) make a case for Constitution on the basis of a parity argument. Perhaps the best known parity argument concerns a duck: If it walks like a duck, quacks like a duck, and flies like a duck, it is a duck. The role of parity in this argument is obvious: if something is equal to a duck in all relevant respects, it is a duck.

Now let's see how a parity argument might be recruited for the purpose of establishing Constitution. The following is perhaps the most famous (and notorious) of all illustrations of extended cognition. Inga has normal capacities for memory. She hears about an art exhibit that she'd like to see at the Museum of Modern Art (MoMA), pauses a second to recall that the museum is located on 53rd St., and off she goes. Notice that before bringing the museum's location to mind, there is a sense in which Inga still *believed* that the museum was on 53rd St. Philosophers describe beliefs of this sort, present but not yet *consciously* present, as *non-occurrent*. Only when actively attending to the belief does it become occurrent.

Now consider Otto, who suffers from Alzheimer's disease. When Otto hears about the exhibit at MoMA and forms an intention to attend, he cannot, like Inga, consult his memory to recover the museum's address. The disease has, in effect, erased it or rendered it inaccessible. However, Otto compensates for this deficit through use of a notebook in which he has written much of the information that at one time he relied on his normal memory to recover. Now when Otto must "remember" some fact, such as MoMA's address, he opens his notebook and finds what he needs. "For Otto," Clark and Chalmers say, "his notebook plays the role usually played by a biological memory" (Clark 2008: 227). The conclusion of this thought experiment is that within Otto's notebook are his non-occurrent beliefs.

Helpfully, Clark and Chalmers sketch those conditions that, they believe, the notebook entries must meet if they are to play the same role as Inga's non-occurrent beliefs (2008: 231). As with the non-occurrent beliefs in Inga's memory, Otto's notebook entries are (i) always available to him. He never leaves home without his notebook, and so its contents are always there for him. Also, (ii) the information in the notebook is easily available. Otto has organized it so that, suppose, he's no slower than Inga in turning its non-occurrent contents into occurrent beliefs. Moreover, (iii) Otto automatically endorses the information in his notebook, just as we rarely question the truth of our own recollections. Finally, (iv) the contents of the notebook have been endorsed by Otto in the past and are in the notebook for this reason.[11]

Importantly, although Clark and Chalmers think that these conditions are characteristic of memories, and so should be true of the notebook's entries if the case for their mental status is to be compelling, they are not intended to be exceptionless. Perhaps Otto has spilled some ice-cream on a page of his notebook and it now sticks to another page, making its contents more difficult to access or harder to read than the contents of other pages. This is okay. Inga may show similar difficulties in accessing or reconstructing some of her memories (but not because she spilled ice-cream on them). Likewise, maybe Otto enjoys swimming, but when he's in the pool his notebook remains in the locker room, out of harm's way. While swimming, he's unable to remember various facts. But, of course, Inga may go through similar periods of temporary memory loss, as when she's sleeping, or stoned, or meditating. Perhaps Otto reads an entry that strikes him as bizarre: "Can MoMA really be on 533rd St.?" Inga too may on occasion question her memory. These examples show that the parallel between Otto's relationship to his notebook and Inga's relation to her memory is fairly robust, able to withstand several obvious prima facie discrepancies.

The discussion of Otto and Inga is intended, of course, to establish a parity between the contents of Otto's notebook and Inga's memory. Once established, it is an easy matter to show that mental states – constituents of cognitive processes – can exist outside the head. All that's necessary to take premise to conclusion is what has come to be called the *parity principle*:

> Parity Principle: If, as we confront some task, a part of the world functions as a process which, were it done in the head, we would have no hesitation in recognizing as part of the cognitive process, then that part of the world is ... part of the cognitive process.
>
> (Clark 2008: 222)[12]

The content's of Otto's notebook are non-occurrent beliefs because they have parity with the non-occurrent beliefs of an ordinary human being.

6.10 Against Parity – Meeting the Marks of the Cognitive

Critics have had a variety of reactions to the tale of Otto and Inga and, more generally, the conception of cognition that it is used to promote. In this section we will examine two efforts to chip away at the alleged parity between Otto and Inga. Both efforts assume that cognition is a *natural kind* of some sort and so, like other kinds, has conditions for membership. Something counts as gold, for example, if (and only if) it has an atomic number of seventy-nine. However, the kind *gold* is perhaps an exceptional case insofar as it is possible to define it with strict necessary and sufficient conditions. More commonly, kind-membership involves the satisfaction of some subset of a cluster of conditions. Thus, *predator* is a kind, but we shouldn't expect that all and only predators have sharp teeth or long claws. There is a cluster of properties that we commonly associate with predators, and an animal can qualify as a predator if it possesses enough properties within this cluster.

Adams and Aizawa have claimed that supporters of Constitution fail to provide a mark of the cognitive (2001; 2008; Adams forthcoming). This means that their claim to find cognition outside the skull is immediately suspect. How do they know that cognition extends if they haven't bothered to figure out how to recognize instances of cognition? Furthermore, Adams and Aizawa offer two marks of the cognitive that they believe to be reasonable, and argue, consistently with their contingent intracranialism, that examples of extended cognition lack these marks. The result, Adams and Aizawa contend, is that defenders of Constitution have nothing positive to say about why their examples of extended cognition are genuinely cognitive, and, just as gravely, find themselves having to deny that Adams and Aizawa's marks of the cognitive are indeed plausible.

Before turning to discussion of these marks, we need to assess in greater detail the nature of this challenge. The motivation for requiring marks of the cognitive seems to be this. Suppose one were studying viruses in order to discover whether they are living entities or merely packets of self-replicating chemicals. Clearly, any conclusion would be impossible without some prior theory of what it takes to be alive. Without marks of the living in hand, the virologist is in no position to judge whether viruses are alive. Likewise, Adams and Aizawa believe that claims of extended cognition are fruitless prior to establishing marks of the cognitive. Whether gestures, for instance, or the entries in Otto's notebook, are cognitive depends on whether they bear the marks of the cognitive. But without having articulated what these marks are, who's to say?

All this sounds quite compelling, but on further reflection the case is not so clear cut. One reason to question the need for marks of the cognitive is that, as I argued in §6.8, supporters of Constitution are not claiming, as Adams and Aizawa allege, that cognition is *going on in*, for example, a person's gestures or Otto's notebook. If there is not a cognitive process occurring in Otto's notebook, why must Clark and Chalmers tell us how to recognize a cognitive process? Rather, Clark and Chalmers' claim is that the entries in Otto's notebook are *constituents* in a cognitive process. Perhaps Clark and Chalmers never saw the need to define marks of the cognitive because they thought uncontroversial the assumption that memory is a cognitive process. Likewise, *having granted* that the process that involves moving blood around the body is a circulation process, there is no need to define marks of circulation to determine whether veins are constituents of this process. The nature of the process is assumed; the question is about its constituents. In short, it is one thing to ask what makes some process cognitive; another to ask what makes something a constituent of a cognitive process. Insofar as it is possible to answer the second question without answering the first, defenders of Constitution might rebuff Adams and Aizawa's demand for marks of the cognitive.

A related point emerges from more careful scrutiny of the Parity Principle. The principle is stated in a manner that quite deliberately sidesteps any need to articulate marks of the cognitive. The condition it lays upon external constituents of cognition is simply that they would be recognized as parts of a cognitive system if the functional role they played were replicated in parts of the brain. This leaves open how one might identify parts of the brain as constituents of a cognitive system, assuming simply that whatever conditions these parts of the brain meet in virtue of being constituents of a cognitive system, external features can just as well meet these conditions.

To see this last point more clearly, consider these analogous statements of the parity principle:

> Herring Parity: If a part of the world functions as an organism which, were it in an ocean, we would have no hesitation in recognizing it as a herring, then that part of the world is (so we claim) a herring; or
>
> Olive Parity: If a part of the world functions as a food which, were it in our mouths, we would have no hesitation in recognizing it as an olive, then that part of the world is (so we claim) an olive.

These principles describe a very sensible means by which to identify herring and olives despite not providing criteria of herring-hood or olive-hood. To be sure, they assume that one is already in a position to recognize herrings or to recognize olives, but, Clark and Chalmers suppose, so too are cognitive scientists familiar enough with cognitive processes to recognize one when they see it. Marks of the cognitive would surely be useful were one unsure whether the process under investigation were cognitive, but when this is not an issue, as it should not be in the case, for instance, of memory or spatial reasoning, demanding their characterization might fairly be dismissed as a red herring (or a red olive).

6.10.1 Mark I: Intrinsic Content

By now you should be familiar with various issues concerning how parts of the brain come to represent, or stand for, things outside the brain. We looked at one theory in §5.9 – Fred Dretske's – according to which a neural state comes to represent, for instance, a martini, when the state reliably correlates with martinis and is used within a cognitive system *because* it reliably correlates with martinis. Dretske's is just one theory of content – there are others (Cummins 1996; Fodor 1990: Millikan 1984).The focus of these theories is to analyze *intrinsic* (or *original*, or *non-derived*) representational content.

The word *intrinsic* is meant to call attention to the fact that the representational states in organisms' nervous systems have their content *on their own*. The contrast is with representational states that have only *extrinsic* (or non-original, or derived) content. Tie a yellow ribbon 'round the old oak tree if you still love me. Honk if you like vegemite. Put the towel on the floor if you want it washed. These sentences *stipulate* how to represent some fact. If a yellow ribbon means that you still love me, this is because of a compact created between the two of us: "Hey – I'm not sure that you still love me. If you do, how about tying a yellow ribbon around a tree so that I'll know?" The meaning of the yellow ribbon *derives* from a convention to use it to mean what it does. Words are other examples of representations that have derived content. "Cardinal" does not naturally refer to cardinals, but does so only because of conventions established within our linguistic practices.

On the other hand, our perceptual states, thoughts, and concepts do not derive their meaning through a compact or set of conventions. My thoughts about cardinals do not refer to cardinals because convention dictates that neurons of the sort that realize the thought should refer to cardinals. How states of the brain might come to refer to cardinals is the business of a theory of content like the one which Dretske proposes. Much less mysterious is how yellow ribbons, honking horns, towels, and words come to represent.

Adams and Aizawa (2001; 2008; forthcoming) believe that the distinction between intrinsic and extrinsic content parallels that between the cognitive and the non-cognitive: "[a] first essential condition on the cognitive is that cognitive states must involve intrinsic, non-derived content" (2001: 48). This way of stating the condition may appear salubrious, for it avoids a line of objection I mentioned above.

As we saw, Adams and Aizawa on occasion demand conditions for identifying cognitive *processes* rather than cognitive states ("One needs a theory of what makes a process a cognitive process, rather than a non-cognitive process. One needs a theory of the 'mark of the cognitive'" (forthcoming)). This opens them to the criticism that they have misunderstood Constitution, which is a thesis about the location of the *constituents* of cognitive processes. The question to ask is whether constituents of a cognitive process appear outside the brain; not whether a cognitive process appears outside the brain.[13] Because Adams and Aizawa are now placing a demand on the nature of cognitive *states* rather than cognitive *processes*, their request can be reasonably interpreted as one concerning constituents of cognitive processes. The constituents of cognitive processes, they claim, must involve intrinsic content.

Obviously, if Adams and Aizawa are right that the constituents of cognitive processes must involve intrinsic content, then Otto's notebook does not, after all, house his non-occurrent beliefs, for the English sentences contained within possess only extrinsic content. Moreover, Adams and Aizawa suspect that neural states alone are the right stuff for intrinsic content, and thus the circle that surrounds the constituents of cognition will surround only the brain.[14]

Clark (forthcoming) has raised a number of questions about using intrinsic content as a mark of the cognitive, and Adams and Aizawa (forthcoming) have responded. The focal point of the debate has seemed to turn on a question of quantity: how much intrinsic content must a process contain before it is to count as cognitive?[15] In an effort to clarify their position, Adams and Aizawa settle on the following: "[c]learly, we mean that if you have a process that involves no intrinsic content, then the condition rules that the process is non-cognitive" (forthcoming). But this clarification, unfortunately, shifts talk once again away from cognitive *constituents* and towards cognitive *processes*.

To see the effect of this shift, consider how one might defend Clark and Chalmers' analysis of Otto against the requirement for intrinsic content. One can grant that the sentences in Otto's notebook do not have intrinsic content, but this does not entail that the process in which these sentences are constituents involves *no* intrinsic content. Presumably, the sentences in the notebook must, in order to become integrated with Otto's *internal* cognitive states, become encoded in the brain. We can suppose, along with Adams and Aizawa, that the representations in the brain do have intrinsic content. Thus, the notebook entry that reads "MoMA is on 53rd St.," is a constituent in a *cognitive* process that produces a neural state with the *intrinsic* content "MoMA is on 53rd St.," which in turn is a constituent in a cognitive process that produces the decision to take a train to 53rd St.[16] Given this description of events, Adams and Aizawa's requirement seems to have been met: the notebook entries are part of a process in which there is some intrinsic content.

Because Adams and Aizawa do not argue that *every* constituent of a cognitive process must have intrinsic content (indeed, they deny this in Adams and Aizawa 2001), their first mark of the cognitive may well in fact be consistent with Constitution. Furthermore, advocates of Constitution might well *embrace* the condition as a useful restriction on what is to count as a cognitive process. If Adams and Aizawa are correct that cognitive processes must involve intrinsic content, they can explain the intuition that some representational processes are cognitive and others, for instance those within a computer or DVD player, are not. Proponents of Constitution should agree, for fear of trivializing their own view, that there must be *some* representational processes that do not qualify as cognitive. Perhaps the difference between the cognitive and the non-cognitive is as Adams and Aizawa suggest: the former involves states with intrinsic content whereas the latter does not.

6.10.2 Mark II: Causal Processes

Distinguishing the subject matters of many sciences are the unique causal regularities they display. Electrical engineers study phenomena that obey Ohm's Law and Kirchoff's laws of current and voltage. Population geneticists study kinds that observe various genetic and epigenetic laws. Plasma physicists are interested in processes in which ionization occurs. One might expect no less from the subject matter of cognitive science. Causal processes within the brain have their own special flavor in virtue of which they constitute an object amenable to scientific investigation. This special flavor, Adams and Aizawa contend, is the second mark of the cognitive: "We maintain that the weight of empirical evidence supports the view that there are processes that a) are plausibly construed to be cognitive b) occur within the brain, c) do not occur outside of the brain and d) do not cross the bounds of the brain" (forthcoming). This claim becomes the first premise in an objection to Constitution that I shall call the *Motley Crew Argument*:

Motley Crew Argument
1   There are cognitive processes wholly in the brain that are distinct from processes crossing the bounds of the brain.
2   Processes within the brain are well-defined, in the sense that they can be an object of scientific investigation, whereas processes that cross the bounds of the brain are not well-defined – are a motley crew – and so cannot be an object of scientific investigation.
Therefore, cognitive science should limit its investigations to processes within the brain.

The Motley Crew Argument poses an interesting challenge to Constitution that we must now consider carefully.

The first premise of the argument is surely correct in at least an obvious sense. Cognitive processes in the brain involve neurons, and neural activity includes a variety of chemical and electrical events that doubtless do not take place outside the brain. More controversially, the first premise claims that the properties which are, in some sense, *defining features* of cognitive processes do not cross the brain/world boundary. The second premise now becomes important, for without it the first premise has no force against proponents of Constitution. Those committed to Constitution think that cognitive processes do span brain, body, and world, and so they would reject an interpretation of the first premise that simply denies this.

The second premise rests on suspicions that a system including the brain *plus* pieces of the world is a foul hybrid – a nasty mess that is not amenable to scientific scrutiny. There are at least two reasons why this might be so. Adams and Aizawa provide the first. They point out that the external props on which extended cognitive systems depend do not themselves constitute a well-formed kind. They do not exhibit a uniformity in causal processes that would suffice to bring them under the umbrella of a single science:

> Tools do not constitute a natural kind; tools are, after all, artifacts. It is for this reason that a would-be brain-tool science would have to cover more than just a multiplicity of causal processes. It would have to cover a genuine motley. A brain-tool science would not have to cover a mere disjunction of things; it would have to cover an open disjunction.
>
> (Adams and Aizawa, forthcoming)

On Adams and Aizawa's view, a science of extended cognition is at least a practical nightmare and perhaps even impossible. The external portions of the brain-tool system could consist in anything, and so the job of understanding such systems would have to draw on whatever sciences are necessary for explaining the behavior of these external bits. This would place the study of cognition outside the reach of cognitive science.

A second justification for the second premise comes from Rob Rupert (2004), who observes that when the outside world is made to do tasks that the brain might otherwise do, they are done very differently. The storage of non-occurrent beliefs in Otto's notebook, for instance, involves different sorts of processes from the storage of non-occurrent beliefs in Inga's memory. This is obvious when one considers that, for instance, when Inga learns that MoMA has temporarily moved to Queens, it is an easy matter for her to update her beliefs about MoMA (so easy she doesn't even know how she does it). Otto, however, might end up having to erase or re-organize a number of entries concerning MoMA, e.g. non-occurrent beliefs about the best way to get there, nice places to stop along the way, the length of time the journey typically takes, and so on.[17] In short, Rupert claims that "the external portions of extended 'memory' states (processes) differ so greatly from internal memories (the process of remembering) that they should be treated as distinct kinds" (2004: 19). The differences in causal processes occurring within and without the brain entail that no single science can possibly study a system that includes both. One might add, following Adams and Aizawa's lead, that if the external bits of extended cognitive systems could be trusted to be of a single kind, then perhaps matters would not be so desperate, but because they might be of virtually *any* kind, the prospects of developing a single science of extended systems are dim.

Rob Wilson's idea of *wide computationalism* (Wilson 1994; 2004) suggests a response to these worries about the motley nature of extended cognitive systems. Wilson, whose arguments for Constitution were developed independently of Clark's, retains the computational conception of cognition that, we have seen, is a central dogma of standard cognitive science. In a twist, however, he argues that computationalism by itself is silent regarding the location of the computations that comprise cognitive processing. Thus, when devising algorithms for visual processing, computational vision theorists will describe representational states that carry information about, e.g., shading, and will then describe computations that modify these representations in order to extract information about, e.g., shape. At this stage in the computational theory, the theorist needn't commit to where or how these computations actually occur. Of course, the assumption is that they happen in the brain, and if it can be shown that the proposed algorithms are impossible to implement in a human nervous system, then this would count as a serious objection if the project were one of discovering how human beings see. But, as far as the computational theory itself is concerned, there is no constraint on the location of the representational states involved. The identifying features of these states are the information they carry and their role within a larger computational system.

Because descriptions of computation abstract away from the wheres and hows of implementation, there is, Wilson argues, no motivation for insisting that the constituents of *cognitive* computational systems must be cranially bound. Figure 6.2 illustrates two cognitive systems, the first of

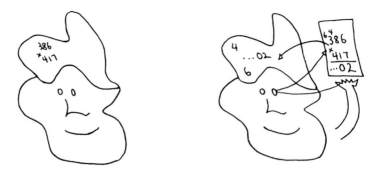

Figure 6.2 Self-portrait of Rob Wilson in which the computational process of multiplying two numbers involves constituents within the head (left) and both within and outside the head (right). From Wilson (2004: 165–6).

which contains all of its computational constituents within the subject's brain, and the second of which permits some computational constituents to exist outside the subject's brain.

The head on the right is "off-loading" some of the constituents of the multiplication process onto a piece of paper. The fact that the numerical representations involved in the process are, in the picture on the left, encoded purely neurally, and, on the right, encoded (in part) on paper, does not, Wilson claims, mark an interesting difference from the perspective of a computational theory of the process.

The idea that computational cognitive processes are locationally unconstrained, leads directly to an argument for wide computationalism – the idea that "at least some of the computational systems that drive cognition reach beyond the limits of the organismic boundary" (2004: 165).

Argument for Wide Computationalism[18]
1   Cognitive processes are computational.
2   If the computational processes that comprise some cognitive systems have constituents outside the head, then these cognitive systems extend outside the head.
3   The computational processes that comprise some cognitive systems do have constituents outside the head.
Therefore, some cognitive systems extend beyond the head.

This argument differs interestingly from the coupling argument for Constitution that we saw Clark offering in §6.6. Whereas Clark tends to think of extended cognitive systems as those that involve self-generated inputs, Wilson's conception appears broader. Computation is, after all, a fairly loose notion. If you use the fact that the Mediterranean's waves lap the shore every two seconds to help figure out how long you've lain on the beach, then the constituents of your cognitive processing extend quite far indeed. Wilson may not find this discomfiting. Or, as his discussion of the especially tight integration between the chimp Kanzi and the keyboard he uses for rudimentary communication intimates, he might, like Clark, seek to define a special sort of computational relationship in order to exclude some instances of cognitive extension (Wilson 2004: Ch. Eight; Wilson and Clark 2009: 67).

For present purposes, our interest in wide computationalism is for the answer it suggests to the Motley Crew Argument. This argument assumes that brain-world systems are scientifically inaccessible because the portions of the world to which the brain might be connected constitute a motley crew, or operate on principles entirely distinct from those that govern processes within the brain. But on the understanding of computationalism on which wide computationalism rests, the *physical* diversity of things to which the brain is connected is irrelevant. Solving a multiplication problem in the head and solving a multiplication problem with pencil and paper might involve the same computational processes, or might (as is more likely) involve different computational processes, but in both cases the computational description of the processes involved abstracts away from the nature of the material (neural, paper, graphite) in which the computational processes are implemented. The computational processes thus may be purely internal, or may encompass both internal and external constituents. Because the distinction between inner and outer makes no appearance in a computational description of cognitive processes, the fears Adams, Aizawa, and Rupert express about the unruliness of extended cognitive hybrids dissipate. The crew may be motley from the perspective of, say, physics, but its members are well-behaved when addressed computationally.

6.11 Extended v. Embedded

Philosopher Rob Rupert has challenged supporters of Constitution to explain why cognitive science should adopt their radical view of cognition in favor of one that is both more in line with common sense and as explanatorily adequate. The view Rupert has in mind is what he calls the *Hypothesis of Embedded Cognition* (HEMC):

> Hypothesis of Embedded Cognition: cognitive processes depend *very* heavily, in hitherto unexpected ways, on organismically external props and devices and on the structure of the external environment in which cognition takes place.
>
> (2004: 5, his emphasis)

Rupert thinks that HEMC is itself something of a departure from standard cognitive science, but is not nearly so extreme as what he calls the *Hypothesis of Extended Cognition* (HEC). Where HEC sees the organism and the pieces of the world it uses in cognizing as a single, unified system, HEMC sees the organism as embedded in an environment in a manner that enables it to exploit resources that vastly simplify or reduce the cognitive load its brain would otherwise have to bear. HEMC agrees with HEC that standard cognitive science is inadequate. Adopting HEMC "significantly affects our estimation of what goes on inside the thinking subject – for example, which computations she must perform using her own neural resources in order to exercise a given cognitive ability" (Rupert 2004: 5). But it maintains with standard cognitive science a commitment to the brain as the locus of cognition. The constituents of cognition remain within the skull, according to HEMC, although the cognitive uses to which the embedded organism puts features of its environment are far more dramatic and extensive than standard cognitive science ever imagined.

As Rupert sees matters, HEC carries the burden of proof because "HEMC is significantly less radical than HEC" (2004: 7). After all, acceptance of HEC would "significantly change our conception of persons" (2004: 2). Clark and Chalmers' discussion of Otto makes this plain. Our ordinary conception of persons does not allow non-occurrent beliefs to appear in a notebook. Nor does HEMC. Perhaps standard cognitive science errs in under-appreciating the extent to which computational and representational work can be offloaded into the environment, but it is correct, supporters of HEMC believe, to insist that cognitive states like beliefs are in the head. Given HEC's radical revisionism, *and* given that it would seem to have no explanatory benefits over HEMC, a reasonable conservatism speaks in favor of the latter hypothesis.

I mentioned at the start of this chapter that the dispute over Constitution at times threatens to dissolve into nothing more than a linguistic issue. One might interpret Rupert's introduction of HEMC as a device for making

this point. Devotees of HEC paint themselves as the rebellious next genera-
tion, but in fact they are not as different from their parents as they think.
Everything said in HEC-speak can be easily, although less dramatically, translated into HEMC-speak. Revolution schmevolution.

An analogy makes even clearer why one might suspect that there's
nothing more to the dispute over Constitution than a decision about how
to use words. Suppose you and your friend decide to spend an afternoon at
the playground. You're both see-saw enthusiasts. The problem is that your
friend weighs five pounds more than you and this means you are always up
in the air. You've come prepared. You are wearing your father's heavy boots
which add five pounds to your weight. Your friend, who's grown tired of
bruising her backside, is pleased but surprised. You say "I now weigh the
same as you." Your friend responds, "No – you weigh the same as you did
yesterday, but you and your father's boots together weigh the same as me."[19]
The dispute is silly. The sentence "I weigh X pounds" is ambiguous between
"Unclothed, I weigh X pounds" and "Clothed, I weigh X pounds." Saying
which you mean leaves nothing more to be said.

One might hope for a similar resolution between supporters of HEC and
HEMC. HEC-ers say "Cognition extends beyond the brain into the world."
HEMC-ers reply "Cognition does not extend beyond the brain, but your
brain and bits of the world together produce cognition." This dispute
differs from the one about the see-saw only insofar as there is a standard
conception of cognition to which appeals can be made. The "I" in "I weigh
X pounds" may, with no offense to common sense, refer to an individual
clothed or not (hence the question: "Is that with or without clothing?").
But the word "cognition" is not so licentious. Saying that some of Otto's
cognitive states are in a notebook is *bizarre*.

Clark offers two responses to Rupert's challenge. The first seeks to temper
the initial strangeness of extended cognition. The second rejects Rupert's
claim that HEMC explanations are always as good as HEC explanations.
Regarding the first point, Clark draws a distinction between processes that
are organism *bound* and processes that are organism *centered*. An organism-
bound process has no constituents beyond the boundaries of the organism.
Blood filtration is ordinarily organism-bound, but in cases of renal failure
parts of the filtration process might take place outside the bounds of the
organism. Organism-*centered* processes are those in which the organism plays
the central role; is, in Clark's words, "in the driver's seat" (2008: 122).
While all organism-bound processes must as well be organism-centered,
many organism-centered processes are not organism bound. The processes

of sawing wood or smoking a cigarette are not organism bound, because they involve constituents outside the boundaries of the organism. In each case, however, the organism is the central component of the process. The organism uses the saw to cut the wood rather than the saw using the organism. The organism draws smoke from the cigarette; the cigarette does not push smoke into the organism.

Consistent with HEC, "the brain surely plays a very special role" (Clark 2008: 122). Through the brain's efforts the environment is structured for the brain's efforts. The brain decides which resources in the environment are worth recruiting, manipulates those that are not in order to make them so, creates channels of information flow that loop through the environment, and in many other ways creates for itself a menagerie of cognitive enhancements. Thus, although HEC does indeed extend minds beyond the organism's boundaries, not so clearly does it, as Rupert charges, "significantly change our conception of persons" (2004: 2). The organism remains the seat of reason.

Clark's second rejoinder to Rupert denies that HEMC explanations of cognition are in fact adequate. HEMC, not HEC, is ad hoc, drawing a gratuitous distinction between internal and external that has nothing but staid and crusty conceptions of the mind to recommend it. The distinction is gratuitous because, as we saw in our discussion of wide computationalism (§6.10), computational characterizations of cognition *know no boundaries*. As Clark puts it, the brain is "'cognitively impartial': It does not care how and where key operations are performed" (2008: 136).

Turning Rupert's objection on its head, Clark accuses HEMC of insisting on an artificial boundary between the neural and the non-neural, and thus running the risk of misunderstanding, or misdescribing, the cognitive phenomena of interest. As an example of this danger, Wilson and Clark describe a cognitive system consisting of "pen, paper, graphics programs, and a trained mathematical brain" (Wilson and Clark 2009: 73). The interactions among these constituents, suppose, are tangled, nested, and complex. "As a result, there may be no viable means of understanding the behavior and potential of the extended cognitive ensembles by piecemeal decomposition and additive reassembly" (Wilson and Clark 2009: 73). The situation, and their diagnosis of it, here mirrors Beer's discussion of his simulated agent (§5.6). Just as the agent's catching behavior emerges from interactions among the agent's nervous system, body, and falling object, so too the solutions at which the mathematically trained brain arrives derive from its interactions with pen, paper, and graphics programs. If HEMC is the wrong perspective for understanding the behavior of Beer's simulated agent, it is no less wrong for understanding many instances of organism-centered, but not -bounded, cognition. HEC is thus superior to HEMC insofar as it has available to it explanations of cognition that a brain bias would render unacceptable.

6.12 Whose Action is it Anyway?

Before closing this chapter, a final and especially creative objection to Constitution requires our examination.[20] The philosopher Brie Gertler notes a connection between non-occurrent (or what she and Clark and Chalmers sometimes call *standing*) beliefs and action. Many actions (perhaps all) are the product of combinations of non-occurrent and occurrent beliefs. When I form a desire to brush my teeth, I go to the bathroom where I keep my toothbrush. My belief about the location of my toothbrush is *non-occurrent*. I never bother to bring it to conscious light. For example, I never say to myself, unless, for some reason, I cannot find my toothbrush, "Where is my toothbrush?" The occurrent desire to brush my teeth meshes seamlessly with my non-occurrent belief about my toothbrush's location to cause me to walk toward my bathroom.

Clark and Chalmers offer the same analysis of Otto's and Inga's actions. Both have an occurrent desire to see an exhibit at MoMA. Both have non-occurrent beliefs that MoMA is on 53rd St. Both take actions that eventuate in their arrival at MoMA an hour later. That Inga's non-occurrent beliefs are stored in her brain, and Otto's are written in his notebook, is, Clark and Chalmers think, only a skin-deep difference between the two. Ignore the skin and there are no differences between Otto's and Inga's non-occurrent beliefs about MoMA's location.

Gertler is willing to grant both that Otto's notebook contains his non-occurrent beliefs and that non-occurrent beliefs play the role in the production of actions that Clark and Chalmers ascribe to them. But, Gertler continues, Otto's notebook might be just the tip of the cognitive iceberg. Suppose an ingenious roboticist has figured out how to download Otto's non-occurrent beliefs onto a computer chip. Moreover, after lengthy interviews with Otto, the roboticist programs another chip with Otto's non-occurrent desires: "he records the desire to make banana bread on Tuesday; the belief that banana bread requires bananas; the belief that the corner grocery store is a good source for bananas" (Gertler 2007: 196).[21] The real genius of the roboticist, however, is in the robot he has constructed. The robot is designed to combine Otto's non-occurrent beliefs and desires with which it is programmed in order to produce those actions that they together entail. And so, Otto awakes late Tuesday morning (the exhibit at

MoMA the previous evening had worn him out) to the smell of freshly baked banana bread.

The question this bit of fantasy raises is this: Who made the bread? Gertler argues that Clark and Chalmers must say that Otto made the bread. After all, it is his desire to make the bread on Tuesday and his belief about what ingredients to use and where to buy them that cause the actions that produced the banana bread. If non-occurrent beliefs and desires are capable of producing actions, and if the agent who acts is the agent whose beliefs and desires cause the action, then, while sound asleep, Otto was also busy making bread.

But things get worse (or, at any rate, weirder). Giddy with his success, the roboticist creates an army of Otto-surrogates which are capable of communicating with each other to the extent necessary to prevent the duplication of actions:

> Some take a slow boat to China; others descend on a neighborhood in Texas and ring all the doorbells at once; others compete in karaoke contests in Tokyo. When we say that all of these activities are Otto's actions, we are not simply saying that he is somehow responsible for them, or that he did something in the past that causally contributed to them. We are saying that he is, quite literally, performing each of these actions: he is enormously busy (though tireless) and, unlike Superman, he can be in two places at once.
>
> (Gertler 2007: 197)

That the possibility of this consequence is, Gertler thinks, unacceptable shows that the argument for extended cognition has somewhere gone wrong.

Gertler's own solution is to reject Clark and Chalmers' claim that Otto's extended non-occurrent beliefs are genuinely *mental*. That is, she accepts, along with Clark and Chalmers, the coherence of the possibility of extended non-occurrent beliefs, but she denies that these beliefs are properly construed as parts of Otto's mind. The result is a *narrowing* of the mind to those cognitive states that are occurrent, or conscious. This narrowing gives a reason to resist the absurdity that Otto may be acting in a hundred different locations at once. The robot's actions are not Otto's actions, because they are not caused by Otto's mental states. On the other hand, one might see this response as trading one absurdity for another: that Otto's mind consists only in those states of which he is presently conscious. This view calls into question ordinary conceptions of psychological unity, according to which an individual's identity requires the persistence of at least some mental states. In dismissing non-occurrent states as non-mental, Gertler needs some other account of psychological unity. Otherwise, for instance, every morning one would awake as a new person.[22]

Interestingly, Clark does not push hard against Gertler's argument. He acknowledges that recognition of extended minds carries with it "vexing questions about personal identity and the nature of the self" (2008: 161), but chooses to leave for another time their examination. However, I think one might do more to allay Gertler's concerns, if not resolve them. The point to note is that the puzzles extended cognition raises for concepts of personal identity and agency seem no more pernicious than puzzles that afflict non-extended minds.[23] These puzzles have intrigued philosophers for thousands of years, and if the possibility of extended minds adds a few mysteries, perhaps it might resolve a few others.

6.13 Summary

In this chapter we have surveyed a number of arguments for Constitution and considered a variety of objections. Many of the disputes center on a distinction between causal influences on cognition and constituents of cognition. Sensorimotor theories of perception, as developed so far, have tended not to heed this distinction, with the result that they have not made good on their claim that cognition is a form of bodily activity. On the other hand, other supporters of Constitution, especially Clark and Wilson, have tackled head-on the need to distinguish cause from constituent. For Clark, Constitution is most evident in systems involving loops of self-generated inputs that extend beyond the brain. Some of these inputs may be parts of the body, as in the case of gestures, others parts of the world, as with the scribblings one generates when composing a complex essay. Wilson, on the other hand, emphasizes the impartiality of computational descriptions of cognitive processes. Such descriptions have nothing to say about the location of the constituents of algorithmic processes, opening the door to the possibility that cognitive processes incorporate parts of the world.

Objections to Constitution point to a need for various clarifications. The hypothesis is most plausible when understood as claiming that the constituents of cognitive processes extend beyond the brain rather than as claiming that cognitive processes themselves take place outside the brain. Many of Adams and Aizawa's criticisms of Constitution lose their bite when one insists on this distinction. Similarly, there is confusion over how to understand parity arguments for Constitution. Critics have labored to show that extended cognitive systems differ importantly from brain-constrained cognitive systems – they lack marks of the cognitive. However, parity arguments needn't carry the burden of showing that extended systems meet marks of the cognitive. They seek to show only that those things we would be willing to recognize as *constituents* of a cognitive system might as well be outside the brain as inside. That the system is cognitive in the first place is offered as a given. Finally, also important for understanding Constitution is a proper characterization of the role that external constituents play in cognitive systems. Whether cognitive systems can be at once extended and legitimate objects of scientific investigation depends on whether there is a scientific framework in which they are proper kinds. Wilson's wide computationalism suggests such a possibility, trading on the fact that extended cognitive systems that look like messy hybrids from one perspective can look like tightly unified systems from a computational perspective.

The dialectic between those for and against Constitution remains, however, largely within the confines of standard cognitive science. Constitution might readily be viewed as applying in new ways the methodology and conceptual commitments of standard cognitive science. This is most evident in the argument for Constitution that emerges from Wilson's defense of wide computationalism. Wilson does not seek to overturn or replace the central computational core of cognitive science – rather, he wishes only to push it further, revealing how it might actually enhance our understanding of systems in which brain, body, and world are knotted together. Whereas the standard cognitive scientist might approach the knot with scissors in hand, hoping to untangle it by cutting it into its separate strands, Wilson, Clark, and other supporters of Constitution see the knot not as tangled mess, but as an integrated and irresistibly interesting whole.

6.14 Suggested Reading

Adams, F. and Aizawa, K. (2008). *The Bounds of Cognition* (Malden: Blackwell Publishing).

Adams, F. and Aizawa, K. (2009). "Why the Mind is Still in the Head," in P. Robbins and M. Aydede (eds.) *Cambridge Handbook of Situated Cognition* (Cambridge: Cambridge University Press, pp. 78–95).

Clark, A. (2008). *Supersizing the Mind: Embodiment, Action, and Cognitive Extension* (Oxford: Oxford University Press).

Clark, A. and Chalmers, D. (1998). "The Extended Mind," *Analysis* 58: 7–19.

Noë, A. (2004). *Action in Perception* (Cambridge: MIT Press).

Wilson, R. (1994). "Wide Computationalism," *Mind* 103: 351–72.

Wilson, R. (2004). *Boundaries of the Mind. The Individual in the Fragile Sciences: Cognition* (Cambridge: Cambridge University Press).

7

CONCLUDING THOUGHTS

7.1 Back to the Decision Tree

In the Introduction I presented a decision tree as a way to analyze the challenge that embodied cognition presents to standard cognitive science. Here, again, is the complete tree:

> Do embodied cognition and standard cognitive science have the same subject matter?
> If yes: Do they offer competing explanations of this subject matter?
> If yes: Scientists should adopt the better explanation.
> If no: The explanations are redundant or complementary in some sense, and scientists should feel free to pursue either.
> If no: Are the distinct subject matters worth pursuing?
> If yes: All is well — embodied cognition and standard cognitive science both have their uses.
> If no: Either embodied cognition and standard cognitive science should be abandoned.

Having behind us now a detailed account of three prominent lines of research within embodied cognition, we can attempt to prune the tree, lopping off the branches that do not apply and following those that do.

The first question we confront, concerning the subject matters of embodied cognition and standard cognitive science, turns out not to be so difficult. The answer depends on whether research in pursuit of Conceptualization, Replacement, and Constitution shares a common subject matter. Of course, depending on how loosely one describes subject matters, it is an easy matter either to distinguish or to unify various bodies of research. However, I believe that it is natural to see the subject matters of Conceptualization, Replacement, and Constitution as, for the most part, the same. Choose a cognitive capacity – perception, categorization, language comprehension – and proponents of Conceptualization, Replacement, and Constitution will have something to say about it, or will be hoping to have something to say about it. Distinguishing the three hypotheses is not what is studied, but how it is studied, or, more precisely, how the body's significance in its investigation is envisioned.

If this is correct, then the answer to the first question in the decision tree is "yes." Embodied cognition theorists, whether focused on Conceptualization, Replacement, or Constitution, seek to understand cognitive capacities and, of course, so do standard cognitive scientists. This is a happy result, because it means that the amount of effort that embodied cognition theorists have invested in showing standard cognitive science to be lacking, or misguided, and the labor standard cognitive scientists have undertaken to mount counter-attacks, have not been for nothing. Embodied cognition theorists and standard cognitive scientists are pulling on the ends of the same rope.

We can now lop off the second branch of the tree and climb the first. Do embodied cognition theorists and standard cognitive scientists offer competing explanations of their subject matter? This is the question that brings into relief the differences between Conceptualization, Replacement, and Constitution. Because each assigns to the body a different role in cognition, resulting in different explanations of cognition, the answer to this question requires treating Conceptualization, Replacement, and Constitution separately.

7.2 Conceptualization and Standard Cognitive Science

The goal of Conceptualization is to show that bodies determine, limit, or constrain how an organism conceives its world. If an apple appears red to a human being, according to Varela, Thompson, and Rosch, this is because the human being is equipped with perceptual equipment that *makes* the apple look red – nothing about the real color of the apple, or whether it even really has a color, follows. Other organisms, with other kinds of sensory equipment, may see the apple as having a different color. How the color of the apple is conceived depends on features of an organism's body (in this case, the organism's visual apparatus).

More spectacularly, according to Lakoff and Johnson, how an organism categorizes kinds in the world – how it carves nature's joints – depends on features of the body as banal as whether it walks upright or on all fours, whether its sensory organs face forward or toward the sides, whether its movements are in the direction of its sensory organs or in an orthogonal direction. Because categorization is a fundamental cognitive ability, one would expect that as organisms differ in how they categorize, they would differ as well in all those cognitive capacities that depend on categorization: reasoning, language comprehension, recall, and so on.

Glenberg, et al. have studied some effects one might expect if Conceptualization were true. Judgments of sentences as sensible or not, according to Glenberg's Indexical Hypothesis, depend on whether the actions the sentences describe are ones that are possible for an organism with a body like *so* to take. Thus, if the indexical hypothesis is true, we should expect that language comprehension is grounded in features of the organism's body. A sentence may mean one thing to organism X, another to organism Y, nothing at all to organism Z, depending on what their respective bodies bring to their abilities to process language.

The phenomena we have seen supporters of Conceptualization discuss – color perception, categorization, language comprehension – are all squarely within the domain of standard cognitive science. The question is whether the explanations Conceptualization offers for these phenomena compete with those that standard cognitive scientists would make. In answering this question, distinguishing *data* from *interpretations of data* becomes very important.

Among the *data* Varela, Thompson, and Rosch discuss are differences in color perception that correlate with differences in visual systems. Their *interpretation* of these data is that organisms make their worlds: there is no pregiven world that an organism discovers. Hence, "we will not be able to explain color if we seek to locate it in a world independent of our perceptual capacities. Instead, we must locate color in the perceived or experiential world that is brought forth from our history of structural coupling" (1991: 165). Similarly, Glenberg, et al.'s *data* are the effects of sentence meaning on response times, i.e. the action-sentence compatibility effect. The *interpretation* of the data involves the idea that subjects extract affordances from the meanings of the words in sentences and then attempt to mesh these with each other in a way that makes sense, yielding a judgment about the sensibility of the sentence.

The question whether Conceptualization competes with standard cognitive science is the question whether the *interpretations* of the data are in competition. Apparently they are. It is no part of standard cognitive science that, as Varela, Thompson, and Rosch insist, organisms bring forth a world. Indeed, work in computational theories of vision takes for granted a world "independent of our perceptual capacities." This is a world of edges, shapes, surfaces, shading, and texture. It is the very independence of the world from our conception of it that makes possible the construction of algorithms that derive depth information from disparity. Recall that Marr and Poggio's depth from disparity algorithm (§1.6) solved the problem of false targets by assuming facts about the world, i.e. that each point on the retina corresponds to one point in the world, and that surfaces tend to be smooth rather than discontinuous. Because computational theories of vision could not succeed without such assumptions, it competes with Varela, Thompson, and Rosch's view of cognitive science.

Similarly, Lakoff and Johnson, and Glenberg find standard cognitive science at fault for relying on an apparatus of amodal symbols and algorithms. Such symbols, they contend, cannot be meaningful, and so cannot acquire the representational function that standard cognitive science assigns to them. Cognitive science must therefore look for meaning elsewhere, e.g., in the properties of the body and the unique styles of worldly interaction that particular kinds of body afford.

These comments suffice, I hope, to show that Conceptualization and standard cognitive science do genuinely differ over how to explain various data involving perceptual and linguistic phenomena. This takes us to the next branch in the decision tree. If the explanations compete, scientists should of course opt for the better explanation. But which is better?

Philosophers of science have identified a number of considerations that are relevant to theory evaluation – simplicity, testability, fruitfulness, conservatism, power to unify, and so on. Understanding the nuances of these attributes is often impossible except within the context of particular sciences, and even then matters are not always as clear as one would hope. However, as I indicated in chapter 4, there are reasons to prefer the explanations of standard cognitive science to those that supporters of Conceptualization offer. First, Varela, Thompson, and Rosch's conclusion that there is no pregiven world simply does not follow from the fact that perception of the world is possible in virtue of sensory systems that determine, for instance, whether an apple appears to be red or some other color. Hence, rejection of a pregiven world should not, as Varela, Thompson, and Rosch argue, play a fundamental role in explanations of cognition.

Of more interest is Lakoff and Johnson, and Glenberg's charge that computational explanations of cognition, because they rely on symbolic representations that are not grounded in the body, cannot succeed, or, at any rate, cannot succeed in explaining the full range of cognitive phenomena. I argued in chapter 4 that this objection to standard cognitive science is wrong on two counts. First, even if Glenberg is correct that that understanding depends on the re-creation of symbols that occurred initially in perceptual systems, and that such symbols are modal, i.e. coded as being of one mode of perception or another, he has not shown that amodal symbols of the sort to which standard cognitive scientists typically appeal cannot similarly trace back to perceptual origins. If understanding a symbol requires tracing it back to its perceptual origins, then standard cognitive scientists should allow that amodal symbols have, no less than modal symbols, a connection to these origins. There is no apparent reason why amodal symbols cannot do so.

But second, the data that impress proponents of Conceptualization might as well, or better, be accounted for within the framework of standard cognitive science. As I illustrated with my discussion of interaural time differences (§4.5.2), there is nothing to prevent standard cognitive science from recognizing features of the body that, perhaps surprisingly, turn out to play a significant role in cognitive processing. Thus, given that the distance between the ears is a factor in sound localization, a computational explanation of sound localization must represent this distance in its algorithms. Similarly, the results Glenberg found with his action-sentence compatibility paradigm have a ready explanation in familiar terms: a representation of sentence meaning primes a motor response which conflicts with the motor response that the experimental instructions require.

These points now allow us to view the dispute between Conceptualization and standard cognitive science from the perspective of some of the theoretical virtues I mentioned above. One reason to prefer the standard explanations to the Conceptualization explanations is that they *conserve* explanatory concepts that have a proven track record. While one might, for reasons we saw in chapter 2, question whether standard cognitive science is the only game in town, one should not question whether it has had its share of successes. Standard cognitive science has deepened our understanding of the mind to an extent unprecedented in previous scientific efforts to do the same. Thus, retaining its conceptual apparatus, when possible, seems reasonable.

Similarly, insofar as the explanatory tools of Conceptualization are still developing, whether they can apply equally well across the range of cognitive phenomena is, at this point, anyone's guess. In contrast, standard cognitive science has shown its power to unify under the same explanatory framework phenomena as diverse as perception, attention, memory, language, problem solving, categorization, and so on. Each of these subjects has been the target of explanations in terms of computations involving rules and representations. Indeed, that they have been so is one reason to conceive of them as cognitive in the first place. Given the uncertain status of some of the ideas to which Conceptualization appeals (e.g. affordances, meshing, world-making, basic concepts), any confidence about the range of its explanatory power would be premature.

This last point raises another reason to favor standard cognitive science. The interpretations of data that Conceptualization offers are sometimes not testable. We saw this clearly in Lakoff and Johnson's speculation that spherical beings in weightless environments will conceive the world differently from beings like ourselves. This claim makes clear the commitments of Conceptualization, but also betrays the difficulties entailed in testing it. To discover whether the body really does limit conceptions of the world in the sense that Conceptualization implies may require that we test the conceptual abilities of differently embodied organisms. Perhaps further work on canonical and mirror neurons will create progress in this direction. For now, however, standard cognitive science has the edge over Conceptualization on the matter of the testability of its claims.

In conclusion, Conceptualization and standard cognitive science do offer competing explanations of cognition. The winner of this competition seems to be standard cognitive science. Conceptualization fails to make a case against symbolic representation, and so finds no strength in another's weakness. Of greater import, the experimental results on which Conceptualization rests can as well be explained by standard cognitive science, making one wonder why the tried and true should be abandoned in favor of something less certain.

7.3 Replacement and Standard Cognitive Science

The goal of Replacement is to show that the methods and concepts of standard cognitive science should be abandoned in favor of new methods and conceptual foundations. Replacement's challenge to standard cognitive science cannot be as easily assessed as Conceptualization's. Certainly those advocating Replacement see themselves in competition with standard cognitive science. Replacement explanations tend to deploy the mathematical apparatus of dynamical systems theory or envision cognition as emerging from the non-additive interactions of simple, mindless, sense-act modules. Emphasis is on interactions among a nervous system, a body, and properties of the world. Because Replacement views organisms as always in contact with the world, there is no need to re-present the world. Also, because the interactions from which cognition emerges are continuous, with the timing of events playing a crucial role, a computational description of them cannot possibly be adequate.

In response to these points, I think that standard cognitive science must concede that, with respect to some phenomena – perseverative behavior in infants, categorical perception in Randy Beer's agent, navigation in Rodney Brooks's creatures – there may exist better explanations than those that draw on the conceptual resources of standard cognitive science. This does not mean that these phenomena turn out not to be cognitive in the first place. Such a response suggests that, by stipulation, any explanation of cognition that is inconsistent with the commitments of standard cognitive science cannot, in fact, be an explanation of *cognition*. Rather, it means that standard cognitive science may turn out not to offer the best explanatory framework for understanding all varieties of cognition.

We saw another instance of this in chapter 2 when we examined ecological psychology, connectionism, and Hatfield's noncognitive computationalism. Common to these programs is the conviction that standard cognitive science is not the only game in town. There exist alternative perspectives to the rules and representations routine of standard cognitive science. For at least some cognitive capacities, e.g., perception and tasks that involve pattern matching, explanations that make no appeal to symbolic representations might be preferable to those that do.

But furthermore, just as the limitations of ecological psychology and connectionism are uncertain, so too the reach of Replacement-style explanations is unknown. As Clark and Toribio argued, there appear to be representation-hungry problems, problems requiring counterfactual reasoning or abstraction, that are by their very nature out of bounds to explanations that do not utilize representations. If this is correct, then Replacement can at best claim rights to only a portion of standard cognitive science's domain.

Standard cognitive scientists needn't receive Replacement successes with despair. Rather, Replacement-style explanations should be welcomed as a new piece of equipment in the cognitive scientist's tool box, broadening cognitive science's span to otherwise intractable phenomena in some cases, perhaps augmenting existing explanations in other cases. Replacement-style explanations may even have a role to play in the explanation of representation-hungry problems. The idea would be that the organism's dynamic interactions with its environment simplify the problem's representational needs, so that although the problem remains representation-hungry, it is no longer representation-*starving*.

Research within embodied cognition that has Replacement as its goal has brighter prospects than Conceptualization. Both claim to compete with standard cognitive science, but the former more so than the latter can plausibly claim victories in this competition. Still, the victories are limited. Work in Replacement does not yet hold forth the promise of full-scale conquest, leaving standard cognitive scientists with the happy result that they now have in their grasp a greater number of explanatory strategies to use in their investigations of cognition.

7.4 Constitution and Standard Cognitive Science

Unlike Conceptualization and Replacement, Constitution, I submit, should not be construed as competing with standard cognitive science. This may seem surprising. After all, some who promote Constitution, for instance O'Regan and Noë, see themselves as challenging orthodoxy. Moreover, some who criticize Constitution, for instance Adams, Aizawa, and Rupert, believe that embodied or extended systems lack marks of the cognitive, or are unsuited to scientific investigation.

However, we saw that the more radical commitments of O'Regan and Noë, especially the suggestion that perceptual experience is a form of skillful activity, constituted by the exercise of sensorimotor contingencies, are poorly motivated. A more reasonable interpretation of their claim is that perceptual experience depends on *knowledge* of sensorimotor contingencies, where this knowledge, just as standard cognitive science would expect, is represented in the brain.

Furthermore, the complaints of Adams, Aizawa, and Rupert miss their mark. They too often portray Constitution as a claim about whether cognitive *processes* can extend beyond the brain rather than whether the *constituents* of these processes might extend beyond the brain. As well, they underestimate the generality of computational descriptions, drawing a misguided distinction between constituents of computational processes within the brain and without. Properly understood, Wilson and Clark argue, standard cognitive science is committed to no such distinction.

As Clark and Wilson understand Constitution, it is an *extension* of standard cognitive science, one that the practitioners of standard cognitive science did not anticipate, but one that proper appreciation of the organism's recruitment of extracranial resources renders necessary for understanding cognition.[1] In one sense, then, Constitution is nothing new. This is clearest in Wilson's conception of wide computationalism, which clings to the computational obligations that are central to standard cognitive science while revealing how parts of an organism's body or world might meet these obligations no less adequately than parts of the brain. Clark too is transparent in his belief that the study of cognition should continue to avail itself of the explanatory strategies that standard cognitive science has deployed with great success, although he is quick to acknowledge the value that alliances with connectionism and dynamical systems theory will have in a more complete understanding of cognition. As Adams and Aizawa have noted, whether the constituents of cognition extend beyond the brain is a contingent matter. That they do, Clark and Wilson reply, means not that the methods and concepts of standard cognitive science must be rejected, but only re-fitted.

As I have been interpreting the idea of competing explanations, Constitution and standard cognitive science are not in competition because one can pursue Constitution with the assistance of explanatory concepts that are central to standard cognitive science. This could not be said of Conceptualization and Replacement. However, that Constitution and standard cognitive science agree to a large extent about how to explain cognition is not to say that Constitution doesn't compete with standard cognitive science in other respects. There is competition with respect to what should be *included* in explanations of cognition. Hobbling standard cognitive science, Constitution proponents aver, is its brain-centrism − its assumption that the constituents of cognition must fit within the boundaries of the cranium. Because standard cognitive science is unwilling to *extend* its explanations to incorporate non-neural resources, it will often fail to see the fuller picture of what makes cognition possible, or will be blind to cognition's remarkable ability to self-structure its surrounding environs.

Reverting to our decision tree, we see now that Constitution and standard cognitive science do not offer competing explanations of cognition in the sense of drawing on distinct conceptual frameworks. Because they do not compete in this respect, there is the prospect that Constitution can complement standard cognitive science and, indeed, this is how its more temperate spokespersons present it. That the constituents of cognition extend beyond the brain is, if true, revelatory. If I'm right that pursuit of Constitution comes without a cost to standard cognitive science, then there's no harm in trying, and, perhaps, tremendous benefit.

7.5 The Final(?) Score

The score card for the three areas of research that comprise embodied cognition goes like this. Conceptualization competes with standard cognitive science and loses. Replacement competes with standard cognitive science and wins in some domains, but likely loses in others. Constitution does not compete with standard cognitive science, but pushes it to extend its boundaries further than many of its practitioners would have anticipated.

However, there is ample reason to wonder whether the score card might change. Work on Conceptualization is ongoing, and neuroscientific findings promise to energize some of its basic assumptions. Replacement too remains an active area of research, and, as happened with the development of connectionism, time may reveal that far more of cognition lends itself to Replacement-style explanations than one could originally have foreseen. Finally, critics continue to assail Constitution, and perhaps various of its metaphysical consequences for personal identity will prove to be unacceptable. The foregoing investigation of embodied cognition is clearly only a starting point for its further examination.

GLOSSARY

a priori: one knows a proposition a priori when experience with the world is not necessary for knowledge. For instance, one knows a priori that squares have four sides.

action-sentence compatibility effect: in experimental psychology, subjects are faster to respond to a stimulus sentence when the response is compatible with the action the sentence describes (e.g. pulling a lever in response to a sentence that describes a "toward oneself action").

affordance: J. J. Gibson's term for a property of an object that invites opportunities for particular sorts of action. A branch affords perching for a bird, but not a pig.

algorithm: a finite sequence of steps that transforms an input, e.g., information about shading, into an output, e.g., information about depth.

ambient optic array: the convergence of light on a point, e.g., an observer, that has a structure as a result of its reflectance from surfaces in the environment.

amodal symbol: see *symbol (modal v. amodal)*.

A-not-B errors: infants at a particular age (roughly 7–12 months old) will continue to reach for an object in one location even after observing that it has been moved to a new location.

Argument Against Colors in the World: an argument that colors do not exist in the world, but only in a perceiver's mind.

Argument for Representational Skepticism: an argument that organisms in dynamical relationships with their environments have no need for representations.

Argument for Wide Computationalism: an argument for conceiving of the computational relations that constitute cognitive processes as extending beyond the brain.

Argument from Envatment: an argument against extended cognition that depends on imagining a brain in a vat that has normal experiences.

basic concepts: in Lakoff and Johnson's theory of metaphor, basic concepts are those that are tied directly to properties of the body, and hence do not require understanding through other concepts.

behavior-based robot: a robot built upon simple mechanisms that connect perception directly with action, with no representational intermediaries.

behaviorism: a school of psychology prominent in the early and middle decades of the twentieth century that was averse to explanations of behavior that posited internal representational states. The proper subject matter of psychology was conceived as limited to observable behavior and its observable causes.

bimodal: canonical and mirror neurons are bimodal in the sense that they correlate with two distinct sorts of properties, e.g. the observation of a tennis ball and the activity of grasping a tennis ball.

canonical neuron: a neuron in the premotor cortex that triggers when seeing an object or when acting on that object.

categorical perception: the perception of objects or properties as belonging to a particular category, as when, e.g., a sound is perceived as a phoneme.

Chinese Room Thought Experiment: John Searle's thought experiment in which an agent's computational operations produce intelligent conversation without the agent understanding what he says.

cognitive psychology: the currently reigning school of psychology that conceives of psychological processes as involving the manipulation of symbolic representations.

collective variable: a variable in a dynamical system that expresses the behavior ensuing from the interaction of parts. Also called an *order parameter* (q.v.).

color conceptualization: the thesis that color experience is created through interactions between body and world and does not reflect any objective property in a pregiven world.

computational theory of mind: the view of mind according to which cognition consists in computational operations on symbolic representations, where these symbols are discrete entities, and where the operations begin on representations of sensory input and end with thoughts or instructions to the motor system.

Conceptualization: a hypothesis within embodied cognition according to which properties of an organism's body determine which concepts about the world an organism can acquire.

cone cells: cells in the retina that are responsible for color vision.

connection weights: within a connectionist net, the signal that one node transmits to others is modulated, or weighted, so that it expresses a function of its own level of excitation.

connectionism: an approach to cognition that seeks to explain cognitive phenomena by appeal to vast networks of nodes and the connections between them.

Constitution: a hypothesis within embodied cognition according to which the constituents of cognitive processes may extend beyond the brain, to include features of the body or world.

contingent intracranialism: Adams and Aizawa's view that cognitive processing in fact occurs wholly within the brain, although it does not necessarily do so.

control parameter: within a dynamical system, the control parameter determines the behavior of other parts of the system, as when, e.g., heat determines the formation of convection rolls in a volume of oil.

coupling: a relationship between two parts of a system. Within dynamical systems, parts are coupled when the equation describing the behavior of one must contain a term that describes the behavior of the other, and vice versa.

coupling-constitution fallacy: Adams and Aizawa's name for a fallacy they attribute to proponents of Constitution. It is the fallacy of concluding from the fact that X is coupled to process Y that X is a constituent of process Y.

derived content: content of representational states that is a result of convention or stipulation, as would be the content of words or arrows. Contrasts with *intrinsic content* (q.v.).

descriptive framework: a stance or perspective toward some system, e.g., that it is performing computations.

dishabituation: within experimental psychology, dishabituation is a reaction of surprise that suggests the perception of novelty.

disparity (degree of): the amount of difference in location between points on two retinas caused by a single object.

Dynamical Hypothesis: van Gelder's claim that cognitive systems are dynamical systems and should be investigated from the perspective of dynamical systems theory.

dynamical system: any system that undergoes change.

dynamical systems theory: the mathematical apparatus used to study the behavior of dynamical systems.

ecological psychology: a school of psychology closely associated with J. J. Gibson that understands cognition as emerging from continuous interactions between an organism and its environment.

embodied action: Varela, Thompson, and Rosch's term for their view that cognition depends on bodily experiences that are embedded within a broader biological, psychological, and cultural context.

emergence: a phenomenon is emergent when it is the product of distinct processes in interaction with each other.

enactive approach: Varela, Thompson, and Rosch's approach to understanding cognition that emphasizes a perceiver's actions within its niche.

exhaustive search: a matching strategy in which a test stimulus is compared to every item on a list.

extended cognition: the view that the constituents of cognitive processes extend beyond the brain.

General Problem Solver: a program designed by Newell, Simon, and Shaw that sought to simulate human reasoning.

hidden layer: the layer of nodes within a connectionist net that receive signals from input nodes and transmit signals to output nodes.

horizon cuts: an example of an perceptual invariant. The proportion of an object below and above the horizon carries information about its height.

Hypothesis of Embedded Cognition (HEMC): the hypothesis that cognition is more thoroughly dependent on the environment than cognitive science has typically supposed, but does not actually extend into the environment.

Hypothesis of Extended Cognition (HEC): the hypothesis that cognitive processes extend beyond the brain and into the world.

idealism: the view that there is no world external to the mind.

Indexical Hypothesis: Glenberg offers this hypothesis to explain how language becomes meaningful. Language comprehension involves extracting and meshing affordances from perceptual symbols.

information in light: the properties of light are such that it is capable of specifying features of the surfaces in the environment that reflect it. Thus, light is said to carry or contain information about the environment.

information self-structuring: Clark's term for describing systems that structure their environment for the purpose of simplifying cognitive tasks.

input layer: the first layer of nodes in a connectionist net. They represent stimulus features.

interaural time difference: the difference in the time that sound reaches the ears on either side of the head.

intrinsic content: the content that representational states have naturally, without recourse to conventions or stipulations. Also called *non-derived* or *original content*. Contrasts with *derived content* (q.v.).

invariant: Gibson's term for feature in light that remains unchanged as other features of light change. An invariant thus carries information about the world.

inverse optics: the problem of deriving information about the world from a static image on the retina.

linguistic determinism: Whorf's thesis that the language one speaks determines how one thinks about the world.

linguistic v. nonlinguistic thought: a distinction between thought processes necessary to speak a particular language, e.g., Spanish, and thought processes that language might influence, e.g., category judgments.

marks of the mental: Adams and Aizawa's term for criteria by which to judge a process to be cognitive. Cognitive processes must (i) have intrinsic content, and (ii) observe various causal regularities.

meshing: Glenberg's term for the process by which a language comprehender attempts to fit together the affordances he has derived from perceptual symbols.

metaphor: for Lakoff and Johnson, metaphor is the means by which one comes to understand more abstract concepts through their explication in simpler, already understood, concepts.

mirror neuron: a neuron in the premotor system that becomes active when observing an action or performing that action.

modal symbol: see *symbol (modal v. amodal)*.

monocular depth perception: depth perception that proceeds without disparity information (that is available to one eye).

motion parallax: a monocular depth cue, obtained through movement that causes the foreground to appear to move against the background.

Motley Crew Argument: an argument against extended cognition that rests on assumptions about the nature of scientific kinds.

motor cortex: the part of the brain involved in organizing muscular movement.

niche: an environment defined relative to an organism's adaptations.

nomic relationship: a relationship that obeys some law, as with smoke and fire.

noncognitive computationalism: Hatfield's term for an approach to psychology that conceives of psychological processes as noninferential but involving transformations of representations.

non-occurrent belief: a belief of which one is not presently aware. Also called *standing belief*.

nontrivial causal spread: Clark's term for the manner in which some systems avail themselves of a diversity of factors to achieve what might have been thought to be the product of a control system.

object concept: Piaget's term for the concept of an object that (he argued) undergoes various stages of development through infancy into childhood.

occurrent belief: a belief of which one is presently aware.

ontological commitment: different theories will assume the existence of different objects or processes. These are the theories' ontological commitments.

open channel perception: Clark's term for perception that depends on a constant connection between the perceiver and the world.

opponency system: cells in the visual color system are wired so that their excitation in response to one color, e.g., blue, causes inhibition to another, e.g., yellow, thus preventing a bluish yellow experience.

optic flow: as an observer moves, the pattern of light on his retina will flow. This flow carries information, e.g., when the flow is expanding, one is moving toward an object; when contracting, one is moving away. The point of zero flow is always straight ahead.

orbit: the path an initial state takes through the space of all possible states within a dynamical system.

order parameter: in a dynamical system the term that expresses the behavior ensuing from the interaction of parts. Also called the *collective variable* (q.v.).

organism-bounded process: Clark's term for a process that takes place within the bounds of an organism. Contrasts with *organism-centered process* (q.v.).

organism-centered process: Clark's term for a process that extends beyond an organism, but in which the organism is a central component. Contrasts with *organism-bounded process* (q.v.).

output layer: the final layer of a connectionist network, which receives signals from the hidden layer.

parameter: a term in a dynamical system that stands for one of the forces acting on or within the system.

parity principle: Clark and Chalmers' label for the idea that processes should be considered cognitive if they would be judged so were they to occur in the brain.

perception-action cycle: a cycle in which perception leads to particular actions, which in turn create new perceptions, which then lead to new actions, and so on.

perceptual symbol: Barsalou's term for a symbol in a cognitive system that is coded in the language of the sensory system that initially caused its presence in a cognitive system. See *symbol (modal v. amodal)*.

perseverative behavior: behavior that perseveres despite no longer being appropriate.

phenomenological tradition: a philosophical tradition with historical roots in France and Germany that emphasizes the close inspection and analysis of experience.

pregiven world: Varela, Thompson, and Rosch's term for the world apart from our experiences of it.

premotor cortex: the part of the brain responsible for planning action.

priming: within experimental psychology, priming experiments expose the subject to an initial stimulus (a prime) and measure the effect of this exposure on the subject's later performance in some task.

principle of ecological assembly: Clark's term for the idea that organisms will exploit the environment in different ways depending on their own internal resources.

process-constituent fallacy: the assumption that those who defend X as a constituent of process Y must believe that process Y occurs in X.

reaction time experiment: an experiment in which the crucial variable is the time it takes a subject to respond to a stimulus.

realism: the view that there is an observer-independent world to which our perceptual systems give us access.

Replacement: a hypothesis within embodied cognition according to which computational and representational explanations of behavior should be abandoned in favor of explanations that emphasize self-organizing behavior or dynamic interactions between an organism's brain, body, and environment.

representation: most basically, something that is used to stand-in for something else. Theories of representation seek to explain in virtue of what something, like a thoughts or perceptual state, comes to stand-in for objects or properties.

representational content: that which a representation is about is its content.

representational vehicle: the physical state or object that bears the representational content. The red road sign is the vehicle that carries the content *stop.*

representation-hungry problem: Clark and Toribio's term for a problem whose solution requires the presence of representations.

research program: in contrast to a well-defined theory with clearly stated ontological commitments and methods of investigation, a research program is a collection of thematically related ideas that suggest lines of research that might eventually coalesce into a theory.

resonate: Gibson's term for the process by which the brain picks up information in light.

second-generation cognitive science: Lakoff and Johnson's term for cognitive science in the post-embodied cognition era.

secondary quality: a quality, like color, that is taken not to resemble any real property in the world.

self-organizing: a system is self-organizing when it produces a complex behavior through the unguided interactions of its parts.

self-terminating search: a matching strategy in which a test stimulus is compared to each member of a list until a match is found.

sense-model-plan-act framework: a framework within traditional AI that describes a sequence of steps necessary for action.

sensorimotor skills: skills that grow from the association of particular sensations with particular action.

sensorimotor theory of perceptual experience: a theory that identifies perceptual experience with sensorimotor skills.

Shakey: an early robot that adopted the sense-model-plan-act framework.

situatedness: the cognitive-enriching relationship between an organism and its environment.

solipsism: the view that an explanation of cognition can begin and end with events in the nervous system so that no mention of the world is necessary.

standard cognitive science: a solipsistic approach to cognition that sees cognitive processes as computational, ranging over symbolic representations.

state space: within dynamical system theory, the space of all possible states of a dynamical system.

steady-state horizontal velocity field (SSHVS): a map of all steady-state velocities an agent would adopt at every possible location for a falling object.

stereopsis: depth vision that comes about through the detection of disparity information.

stereovision: see *stereopsis*.

strong internal representation: Clark's term for representations of the sort necessary for counterfactual reasoning or abstract reasoning. Contrasts with *weak internal representation*.

subsumption architecture: the architecture Brooks implemented in his robots, consisting of simple layers of sense-act mechanisms that are capable of inhibiting each other.

surface spectral reflectance: the spectrum of light a surface reflects in a given lighting condition.

symbol (modal v. amodal): a modal symbol is a representation that bears the signature of the sensory system that created it. An amodal symbol carries no information about its perceptual origin, and is, in this sense, arbitrarily connected with its content.

symbol grounding problem: the problem of how symbols acquire their meaning.

testability: a hypothesis is testable when contrasted with another that predicts different observations.

trajectory: see *orbit*.

transduction: the process by which stimuli are encoded into representations that can then be processed further.

Turing machine: a simple computer consisting of a head that reads and then performs operations on symbols on a tape.

underdetermination: evidence is said to underdetermine theories or hypotheses in the sense that more than one theory or hypothesis can explain the evidence.

using the world as its own best model: Brooks's slogan to capture the idea that when creatures are in continuous contact with the world they have no need to build representations of the world.

von Neumann computer: a computer architecture in which a central processing unit organizes operations on symbolic expressions stored in memory.

Watt's centrifugal governor: an example of a dynamical system for controlling the speed of an engine.

weak internal representation: Clark's term for a representation that has the function of correlating with a feature in the world and that persists for only as long as the organism is in contact with the world. Contrasts with *strong internal representation*.

wide computationalism: Wilson's term for the view that computational systems can extend beyond the confines of the brain.

NOTES

Introduction

1   In the following chapter I will present in detail what I take to be the hallmarks of "standard" cognitive science.

2   Indeed, the rise of connectionism in the 1980s was taken by many to present a serious threat to cognitive science because it promised to explain traditionally cognitive phenomena like language learning in terms that appeared at odds with the rules and representation framework of standard cognitive science (Rumelhart and McClelland 1986; Fodor and Pylyshyn 1981).

3   I introduced this way of breaking down embodied cognition in Shapiro (2004) and expanded on it in Shapiro (2007) and Shapiro (forthcoming).

4   For instance, Margaret Wilson (2002) mentions six. Her larger number in part reflects her desire to separate ideas that I am happy to leave together.

Chapter 1

1   For the reader interested in an extensive appraisal of the important developmental stages of cognitive science, see von Eckardt (1995).

2   I do not claim that each project displays commitment to all the same aspects of computationalism (the view, roughly, that the mind is like a computer program that is run on the hardware of the brain) but I would claim that each shows a commitment to some aspects of computationalism.

3   Also collaborating in the design of GPS was J. C. Shaw.

4   The qualifier "some" is necessary because not all symbols are combinatorial. Wedding rings, for instance, despite being symbolic, do not combine with other symbols in rule-defined ways.

5 For a very clear and more precise discussion of these matters, see Haugeland (1981).

6 It is worth noting that the CPU responds to a symbol in virtue of its syntax, or physical properties, rather than its semantics, or meaning. Thus, although symbols typically do stand for things, something may be recognized as a symbol without attending to its representational function.

7 This question about how symbols come to represent is part of what philosophers call the problem of intentionality, where "intentionality" is a technical term meaning, roughly, *aboutness*. I will have more to say in later chapters (especially chapter 5) about theories of representation.

8 Newell and Simon seem too complacent in their assumption that "thinking out loud" reflects the actual operations of nonverbal (unconscious) thought. If the solution of logic problems relies on unconscious cognitive processes, and if the "translation" of these processes into verbal responses does not preserve the structure of the unconscious processes, then the subject's out-loud thinking is of little value in testing the veracity of GPS as a model of human problem-solving capacities. Still, thinking out loud may find use in investigations of conscious thought.

9 Certainly there is a causal story to tell about why a particular kind of symbol ends up representing that which it does, so the connection between symbol and content is not arbitrary in the sense of indeterminate, or uncaused. I mean "arbitrary" in the sense I described above: there is nothing about the structure of the symbol that makes it, rather than some other symbol, represent what it does.

10 These tasks correspond to what Marr (1982) called research at the computational and algorithmic levels. At the third, implementational, level, attention would turn toward understanding how a given algorithm might be realized in the brain.

11 Figure 1.5 illustrates a case in which there are literally an infinite number of possible solutions, i.e. answers, to the question "What is the shape of the surface that produced this retinal image?" But not all problems the visual system must solve have an infinite number of solutions. The number of solutions to the correspondence problem I describe below will depend on the number of points to be matched.

12 Some would. There is a region known as the horoptor which marks an imaginary surface drawn through the point of fixation on which any object will project to the same points on each retina.

13 Goldstein (1989).

14 See Pinker (1997: 233–3) for a very clear and accessible discussion of this algorithm.

15 The need for the explicit representation of the rules is questionable. For discussion, see Shapiro (1997a) and Wilson (2004).

16 There is actually a fair bit of controversy over what the elements in computational theories of vision represent (or even if they do represent), and my use of "feature" in this context is an attempt at neutrality. See, for instance, Burge (1986), Segal (1989), Egan (1991; 1992), Shapiro (1993; 1997a), Wilson (2004).

17 Hurley is not an advocate of this view, but presents it only to criticize it. Also critical of this view is Rowlands (1999).

Chapter 2

1 If the eye were immobilized completely, preventing even the microtremors that keep the eye in constant motion, perception would fade away.

2   Gibson is surely overstating matters when he claims that motion constrains the possible solutions to just one. One can imagine a very clever experimenter manipulating the environment so that objects arrange themselves to compensate for the subject's motions, thus appearing *as if* they were "normal" when they were not. Still, Gibson would be safe in claiming that motion provides a much richer source of information than would stationary observation.

3   See Rowlands (1995) for further discussion of this point.

4   Feldman and Ballard (1982) call this the hundred-step constraint.

5   See Dretske (1981; 1988; 1994) and Stampe (1977) for efforts to analyze representation along these lines.

6   See Hatfield (2009: ch. 2; ch. 3, intro) and Shapiro (1992).

7   We'll see in chapter 6 that some, like Rob Wilson, would reject this contrast, finding the ideas of brain as controller and as part of a computational system as consistent with each other.

Chapter 3

1   Prior to this list, Margaret Wilson (2002) composed her own list of six claims that capture the various research programs within embodied cognition. Her list is similar to the list of Clark's I present here, and is indeed indebted to Clark (1997a).

2   In fact, because the visual fields of pigeons' eyes do not overlap, they are completely dependent on monocular cues for depth perception.

3   Lindblom and Ziemke (2005).

Chapter 4

1   On occasion, English speakers might use vertical spatial terms to describe time (the past is "water *under* the bridge," and the future is "*down* the road." However, first, some of these expressions seem not to express vertical alignment (down the road is a point in front of you, not below you), and second, the frequency of such terms to describe time is much less than one finds in Mandarin.

2   Although attentive to this distinction, whether Boroditsky's experiments *in fact* succeed in disambiguating the two kinds of thinking remains controversial.

3   I am ignoring the sort of difficulties that led Duhem (1914/1954) to insist on the importance of auxiliary assumptions.

4   Hilbert (1998) holds such a view.

5   Might one compare populations of, say, tall human beings to short human beings, or bipedal human beings to wheelchair-bound human beings? I take up this question at the end of §4.9.2.

6   Lakoff's list of first-generation features is not identical to the list he and Johnson offer in their (1999). However, it is close, and spares us the need for exposition of some philosophical jargon.

7   For a discussion of how neuroscience and psychology might inform each other, see Hatfield (2009: ch. 15), and Shapiro (2004: ch. 4).

8   This is generally true, but fails for high frequency sounds that may be absorbed by the head, thereby preventing detection by the ear that is on the side of the head away from the source of the sound.

9 I'm grateful to an anonymous reviewer for helping me to appreciate this point.

10 See Shapiro (2008a) for further discussion.

11 Perhaps "cardinal" is not an arbitrary choice for cardinals because it also names the color of cardinals. Likewise, the word "chickadee," when pronounced, mimics part of the song of the chickadee.

12 At issue is not the grammatical sensibility of the sentence, but the sensibility of its meaning. One might wonder whether judgments of sensibility are relevant to whether a subject understands the meaning of a sentence. We will take up this issue below.

13 Not all the sentences were imperatives. Glenberg and Kaschak (2002) also used sentences with two objects (e.g., "X gave S the P") or an indirect object (e.g. "X gave the P to S").

14 Buttons two and four served no purpose except to create greater space between the center button and buttons one and five.

15 And surely more needs to be said in its defense. Why should associations between symbols and their representational contents suffice for understanding? If they did, then philosophers' theories of content might as well be theories of how content is understood.

16 This possibility is not so far-fetched. Synaesthesia is a not uncommon condition in which people combine sensory experiences from different perceptual modalities, thus experiencing the sound of a pitch, e.g. middle-C, as blue, or experiencing the number "3" as yellow and "4" as orange.

17 See Shapiro (2008b) for an argument that mirror neurons are part of a sixth sense – a sense for the perception of action.

18 Scant, but not altogether absent. See Iacaboni (2009)

Chapter 5

1 Van Gelder actually defines dynamical systems in a fairly narrow way, perhaps hoping to avoid concerns like these. However, in doing so, he seems to be swimming upstream against standard views of dynamical systems. See Beer (1998: 630; and forthcoming) for discussion.

2 This is a gross simplification. The relationship between connectionism and dynamical systems approaches to cognition is a matter of controversy. For a number of perspectives, see *Developmental Science* 6:4 (2003), Spencer, Thomas, and McClelland (2009), and commentary on van Gelder (1998).

3 Watt, in fact, did not invent centrifugal governors, which had been in use for at least one hundred years in grain mills and windmills. He did, however, make important improvements to steam engines.

4 More precisely, the equations describe how changes in the state of one part of the system change how the states of the other parts *change*.

5 Van Gelder (1998) provides several more reasons, but they are of a more technical nature and seem secondary to the two I present here.

6 The difficulty of reconciling these remarks with van Gelder's suggestion that the centrifugal governor might be a better model for cognition than the Turing machine is probably what leads Daniel Dennett to claim that "[t]here seem to be two van Gelders:" "Hardline van Gelder" and "Soft line van Gelder" (Dennett 1998: 636).

7 See Beer (forthcoming) for some discussion of Gibson's influence on dynamical systems approaches.

8 I have been so far silent about how systems might be individuated, i.e. about what makes something a system. I doubt that any proposal of necessary and sufficient conditions would be impervious to counter examples. Thus, I count on the reader's good graces to allow the existence of systems that have bodies, brains, and environments as parts.

9 Beer selected these variables from the sixteen state variables that characterize the entire system because they provided an especially clear visualization of the dynamics involved in the system (personal communication).

10 For the possibility of "userless" representations, see Shapiro (1997b).

11 See, for example, Cummins 1996; Fodor 1990; Millikan 1984; Stampe 1977.

12 Some might insist that properties, rather than objects, are the contents of representations. Nothing that follows hangs on these issues.

13 See Shapiro (1999) for further discussion of these issues.

14 For a similar argument, see Chemero (2001).

Chapter 6

1 The modality of "must" is very narrow, perhaps limited to how things must be in the actual world. My hope is to avoid worries that claims about the necessity of given constituents might raise, talking instead of the importance or centrality of some constituents relative to others.

2 I am here using "body" and "world" to refer to those parts or processes in or within the body and world that are reasonable candidates to be constituents of cognition. I do not mean to imply that the *entire* body or *entire* world might be constituents of cognition.

3 I am altering Clark's argument to fit this particular example, but I trust that I have kept true to his reasoning.

4 For those familiar with the issue of externalism regarding representational content, forget about it. O'Regan and Noë's claims are not about the individuation of content, but about what I earlier (§5.9.3) called the *vehicles* of content or experience, the physical stuff that realizes the experience (see also Block 2005).

5 This was suggested to me by an anonymous reviewer.

6 This article is expanded in Adams and Aizawa (2008).

7 There is little doubt that Noë does subscribe to COH. In addition to the quotations I cited above (pp. 164–5), he also says, "The basic claim of the enactive approach is that the perceiver's ability to perceive is constituted (in part) by sensorimotor knowledge (i.e., by practical grasp of the way sensory stimulation varies as the perceiver moves)" (2004: 12).

8 As another example of this sort of inattentiveness, consider this claim: "Some cognitive states – for example, states of thinking, calculating, navigating – may be partially external because, at least sometimes, these states depend on the use of symbols and artifacts that are outside the body" (2004: 220). Noë's suggestion seems to be that because cognitive states may *depend* on the use of symbols and artifacts, these symbols and artifacts are constituents of cognitive states. This reasoning would give new meaning to the expression "You are what you eat."

9 In their (2008), this is the hypothesis of extended cognition, in contrast to the hypothesis of extended cognitive systems, which is (in my view) the more likely hypothesis that cognitive systems, rather than cognitive processes themselves, extend beyond the brain.

10 I am being cautious here, because, as we saw in Noë's case, Adams and Aizawa's charge can be made to stick. Perhaps starting from cases that do commit the coupling-constitution fallacy primes one to see the fallacy in cases that are open to other interpretations.

11 Clark and Chalmers are less certain of the importance of this final condition. Perhaps, they suggest, some memories are present as a result of subliminal processes, or other events that bypass the procedures that normally leave memories.

12 I do not understand why Clark and Chalmers include the phrase "as we confront some task." The principle seems as true, or false, without this phrase, and is in either event more concise.

13 Of course, one can ask this second question as well, but, as far as the concerns of Constitution go, it is not a question that needs an answer. Perhaps work like Hutchins (1995) addresses this second question.

14 As I've noted several times, Adams and Aizawa are proponents of *contingent intracranialism*. In the present context, this means that they believe *as a matter of fact* only neural states have intrinsic content. This leaves open the logical or nomological *possibility* of non-neural states with intrinsic content.

15 Another interesting issue that I will not take up concerns the distinction between intrinsic and extrinsic content. Consider, for instance, the gestures that people use to represent spatial relations. These gestures seem to represent aspects of space. Is their content intrinsic or extrinsic?

16 One might ask why the sentence is a *constituent* of this process rather than having an *effect* on this process. This question returns us to earlier issues involving causes and constituents. The present controversy concerns whether Constitution can meet the demand for intrinsic content.

17 Rupert (2004) discusses a number of fascinating ways in which a cognitive psychologist would distinguish Otto's memory processes from Inga's.

18 I base this argument on Wilson and Clark (2009: 61).

19 Your friend is aware that she should be saying "the same as *I*," but chooses the accusative case over the nominative for colloquial congeniality.

20 Gertler actually raises two objections, the first of which, concerning introspection, I shall not discuss here.

21 I'm changing Gertler's story a bit, but not in a way that affects its point.

22 Gertler is of course aware of this consequence of her view. She offers an account of psychological unity that looks to a common origin of mental states to justify their unity.

23 See, for instance, Dennett (1978).

Chapter 7

1 My thanks to Andy Clark for clarifying this point in a personal communication. Clark was responding to a remark in Shapiro and Spaulding (2009) that questioned the novelty of his project, given its apparent consistency with a standard functionalist conception of the mind.

REFERENCES

Adams, F. (forthcoming). "Embodied Cognition," *Phenomenology and the Cognitive Sciences*.

Adams, F. and Aizawa, K. (2001). "The Bounds of Cognition," *Philosophical Psychology* 14: 43–64.

—— (2008). *The Bounds of Cognition* (Malden: Blackwell Publishing).

—— (2009). "Why the Mind is Still in the Head," in P. Robbins and M. Aydede (eds.) *Cambridge Handbook of Situated Cognition* (Cambridge: Cambridge University Press, pp. 78–95).

—— (forthcoming). "Defending the Bounds of Cognition," in R. Menary (ed.) *The Extended Mind* (Cambridge: MIT Press).

Ahmed, A. and Ruffman, T. (1998). "Why Do Infants Make A Not B Errors in a Search Task, Yet Show Memory for the Location of Hidden Objects in a Nonsearch Task?," *Developmental Psychology* 34: 441–53.

Aizawa, K. (2007). "Understanding the Embodiment of Perception," *Journal of Philosophy* 104: 5–25.

Barnard, K., Finlayson, G., and Funt, B. (1997). "Color Constancy for Scenes with Varying Illumination," *Computer Vision and Image Understanding* 65: 311–21.

Barsalou, L. (1999). "Perceptual Symbol Systems," *Behavioral and Brain Sciences* 22: 577–609.

Barsalou, L., Simmons, W., Barbey, A., and Wilson, C. (2003). "Grounding Conceptual Knowledge in Modality-Specific Systems," *Trends in Cognitive Sciences* 7: 84–91.

Bechtel, W. (1998). "Representations and Cognitive Explanations: Assessing the Dynamicist's Challenge in Cognitive Science," *Cognitive Science* 22: 295–318.

Beer, R. D. (1998). "Framing the Debate between Computational and Dynamical Approaches to Cognitive Science," *Behavioral and Brain Sciences* 21: 630.

Beer, R. D. (2000). "Dynamical Approaches to Cognitive Science," Trends in Cognitive Science 4: 91–99.

Beer, R. (2003). "The Dynamics of Active Categorical Perception in an Evolved Model Agent," *Adaptive Behavior* 11: 209–43.

—— (forthcoming). "Dynamical Systems and Embedded Cognition," in K. Frankish and W. Ramsey (eds.), *The Cambridge Handbook of Artificial Intelligence* (Cambridge: Cambridge University Press).

Block, N. (2005). "Review of Alva Noë," *Journal of Philosophy* 102: 259–72.

Boroditsky, L. (2001). "Does Language Shape Thought? Mandarin and English Speakers' Conceptions of Time,' *Cognitive Psychology* 43: 1–22.

Boroditsky, L., Schmidt, L., and Phillips, W. (2003). "Sex, Syntax, and Semantics," in D. Gentner and S. Goldin-Meadow (eds.) *Advances in the Study of Language and Thought* (Cambridge: MIT Press, pp. 61–80).

Brooks, R. (1991a). "New Approaches to Robotics," *Science* 253: 1227–32.

—— (1991b). "Intelligence Without Representation," *Artificial Intelligence* 47: 139–59.

Brooks, R., Breazeal, C., Marjanovic, M., Scassellati, B., and Williamson M. (1999) "The Cog Project: Building a Humanoid Robot," in C. Nehaniv (ed.) *Computation for Metaphors, Analogy, and Agents. Lecture Notes in Artificial Intelligence* 1562 (New York: Springer, pp. 52–87).

Burge, T. (1986). "Individualism and Psychology," *Philosophical Review* 95: 3–45.

Chalmers, D. (1990). "Syntactic Transformations on Distributed Representations," *Connection Science* 2: 53–62.

—— (1993). "Connectionism and Compositionality: Why Fodor and Pylyshyn Were Wrong," *Philosophical Psychology* 6: 305–19.

Chemero, A. (2001). "Dynamical Explanation and Mental Representations," *Trends in Cognitive Sciences* 5: 141–2.

Clark, A. (1997a). *Being There: Putting Brain, Body and World Together Again* (Cambridge: MIT Press).

—— (1997b). "The Dynamical Challenge," *Cognitive Science* 21: 461–81.

—— (2008). *Supersizing the Mind: Embodiment, Action, and Cognitive Extension* (Oxford: Oxford University Press).

Clark, A. and Chalmers, D. (1998). "The Extended Mind," *Analysis* 58: 7–19.

Clark, A. and Toribio, J. (1994). "Doing Without Representing?" *Synthese* 101: 401–31.

Clearfield, M., Diedrich, F., Smith, L., and Thelen, E. (2006). "Young Infants Reach Correctly in A-not-B Tasks: On the Development of Stability and Perseveration," *Infant Behavior and Development* 29: 435–44.

Collins, S., Ruina, A., Tedrake R., and Wisse, M. (2005). "Efficient Bipedal Robots Based on Passive-Dyamic Walkers," *Science* 307: 1082–5.

Cummins, R. (1996). *Representations, Targets, and Attitudes* (Cambridge: MIT Press).

Dawson, M. (1998). *Understanding Cognitive Science* (Malden: Blackwell Publishers, Inc.).

—— (2004). *Minds and Machines: Connectionism and Psychological Modeling* (Malden: Blackwell).

Dennett, D. (1978). "Where Am I?" as reprinted in *Brainstorms* (Montgomery, VT: Bradford Books and Hassocks, pp. 310–23).

—— (1998). "Revolution, No! Reform, Si!" *Behavioral and Brain Sciences* 21: 636–7.

Dretske, F. (1981). *Knowledge and the Flow of Information* (Cambridge: MIT Press).

—— (1988). *Explaining Behavior: Reasons in a World of Causes* (Cambridge: MIT Press).

—— (1994). "If You Can't Make One, You Don't Know How It Works," *Midwest Studies in Philosophy*, 19: 468–82.

Duhem, P. (1914/1954). *The Aim and Structure of Physical Theory* (Princeton: Princeton University Press).

Egan, F. (1991). "Must Psychology Be Individualistic?" *The Philosophical Review* 100: 179–203.

—— (1992). "Individualism, Computationalism, and Perceptual Content," *Mind* 101: 443–59.

Ehrlich, S., Levine, S., and Goldin-Meadow, S. (2006). "The Importance of Gesture in Children's Spatial Reasoning," *Developmental Psychology* 42: 1259–68.

Elman, J. (1995). "Language as a Dynamical System.," in R. Port and T. van Gelder (eds.) *Mind as Motion: Explorations in the Dynamics of Cognition* (Cambridge: MIT Press: pp. 195–225).

—— (1998). "Connectionism, Artificial Life, and Dynamical Systems," in W. Bechtel and G. Graham (eds.) *A Companion to Cognitive Science* (Oxford: Basil Blackwell, pp. 488–505).

Feldman, J. and Ballard, D. (1982). "Connectionist Models and Their Properties," *Cognitive Science* 6: 205–54.

Ferrari, P., Rozzi, S., and Fogassi, L. (2005). "Mirror Neurons Responding to Observation of Actions Made with Tools in Monkey Ventral Premotor Cortex," *Journal of Cognitive Neuroscience* 17: 212–26.

Fitzpatrick, P., Metta, G., Natale, L., Rao, S., and Sandini, G. (2003). "Learning About Objects Through Action: Initial Steps Towards Artificial Cognition," in 2003 IEEE *International Conference on Robotics and Automation (ICRA)*.

Fodor, J. (1975). *The Language of Thought* (Cambridge: Harvard University Press).

—— (1980). "Methodological Solipsism as a Research Strategy in Cognitive Psychology," *Behavioral and Brain Sciences* 3: 63–73.

—— (1990). *A Theory of Content and Other Essays* (Cambridge: MIT Press).

Fodor, J. and Pylyshyn, Z. (1981). "How Direct is Visual Perception? Some Reflections on Gibson's 'Ecological Approach'," *Cognition* 9: 139–96.

—— (1998). "Connectionism and Cognitive Architecture," *Cognition* 28: 3–71.

Gabarini, F. and Adenzato, M. (2004). "At the Root of Embodied Cognition: Cognitive Science Meets Neurophysiology," *Brain and Cognition* 56: 100–6.

Gallese, V., and Lakoff, G. (2005). "The Brain's Concepts: The Role of the Sensory-Motor System in Reason and Language," *Cognitive Neuropsychology* 22: 455–79.

Gertler, B. (2007). "Overextending the Mind?" in B. Gertler and L. Shapiro (eds.) *Arguing about the Mind* (New York: Routledge, pp. 192–206).

Gibson, J. J. (1966). *The Senses Considered as Perceptual Systems* (Prospect Heights: Waveland Press, Inc.).

—— (1979). *The Ecological Approach to Visual Perception* (Boston: Houghton-Mifflin).

Gigerenzer, G. and Hoffrage, U. (1995). "How to Improve Bayesian Reasoning Without Instruction: Frequency Formats," *Psychological Review* 102: 684–704.

Glenberg, A. (1997). "What Memory is For," *Behavioral and Brain Sciences* 20: 1–55.

Glenberg, A. and Kaschak, M. (2002). "Grounding Language in Action," *Psychonomic Bulletin & Review* 9: 558–65.

Glenberg, A. and Robertson, D. (2000). "Symbol Grounding and Meaning: A Comparison of High-Dimensional and Embodied Theories of Meaning," *Journal of Memory and Language* 43: 379–401.

Glenberg, A., Havas, D., Becker, R., and Rinck, M. (2005). "Grounding Language in Bodily States: The Case for Emotion," in R. Zwaan and D. Pecher (eds.) *The Grounding of Cognition: The Role of Perception and Action in Memory, Language, and Thinking* (Cambridge: Cambridge University Press, pp. 115–28).

Goldin-Meadow, S. (2003). *Hearing Gesture: How Our Hands Help Us Think* (Cambridge: Harvard University Press).

Goldstein, E. (1981). "The Ecology of J. J. Gibson's Perception," *Leonardo* 14: 191–5.

—— (1989). *Sensation and Perception*, 3rd ed. (Belmont: Wadsworth, Inc.).

Gregory, R. (1972). "Seeing as Thinking: An Active Theory of Perception," *London Times Literary Supplement*, 23 June: 707–8.

Harnad, S. (1990). "The Symbol Grounding Problem," *Physica D* 42: 335–46.

Hatfield, G. (1988). "Representation and Content in Some (Actual) Theories of Perception," as reprinted in Hatfield (2009, pp. 50–87).

—— (2009). *Perception and Cognition* (New York: Oxford University Press).

Haugeland, J. (1981). "Semantic Engines: An Introduction to Mind Design," in J. Haugeland (ed.) *Mind Design*, 1st ed. (Cambridge: MIT Press, pp. 1–34).

Held, R. and Hein, A. (1963). "Movement-Produced Stimulation in the Development of Visually Guided Behaviour," *Journal of Comparative and Physiological Psychology* 56: 872–6.

Hilbert, D. (1998). "Colours, Theories of," in E. Craig (ed.) *The Encyclopedia of Philosophy* (London: Routledge).

Holyoak, K. (1999). "Psychology," in R. Wilson and F. Keil (eds.) *The MIT Encyclopedia of the Cognitive Sciences* (Cambridge: MIT Press, pp. xxxix–xlix).

Hurley, S. (1998). *Consciousness in Action* (Cambridge: Harvard University Press).

Hutchins, E. (1995). *Cognition in the Wild* (Cambridge: MIT Press).

Iacaboni, M. (2009). *Mirroring People: The Science of Empathy and How We Connect with Others* (London: Picador).

Kelso, S. (1995). *Dynamic Patterns* (Cambridge: MIT Press).

Lakoff, G. (2003). "How the Body Shapes Thought: Thinking with an All Too Human Brain," in A. Sanford and P. Johnson-Laird (eds.) *The Nature and Limits of Human Understanding: The 2001 Gifford Lectures at the University of Glasgow* (Edinburgh: T. & T. Clark Publishers, Ltd., pp. 49–74).

Lakoff, G. and Johnson, M. (1980). *Metaphors We Live By* (Chicago: University of Chicago Press).

—— (1999). *Philosophy in the Flesh: The Embodied Mind and its Challenge to Western Thought* (New York: Basic Books).

Lindblom, J. and Ziemke, T. (2005). "The Body-in-Motion and Social Scaffolding: Implications for Human and Android Cognitive Development," *Cognitive Science Society*: 87–95.

Lungarella, M. and Sporns, O. (2005). "Information Self-Structuring: Key Principles for Learning and Development," *Proceedings 2005 IEEE International Conference on Development and Learning*: 25–30.

MacKay, D. (1967). "Ways of Looking at Perception," in W. Wathen-Dunn (ed.) *Models for the Perception of Speech and Visual Form* (Cambridge: MIT Press, pp. 25–43).

Marr, D. (1982). *Vision* (San Francisco: Freeman).

Marr, D. and Poggio, T. (1976). "Cooperative Computation of Stereo Disparity," *Science* 194: 283–7.

Martin, J. (1990). *A Computational Model of Metaphor Interpretation* (San Diego: Academic Press Professional, Inc).

McNeill, D. (2005). *Gesture and Thought* (Chicago: University of Chicago Press).

Millikan, R. (1984). *Language, Thought, and Other Biological Categories* (Cambridge: MIT Press).

Myin, E. and O'Regan, J. (2009). "Situated Perception and Sensation in Vision and Other Modalities: A Sensorimotor Approach," in P. Robbins and M. Aydede (eds.) *Cambridge Handbook of Situated Cognition* (Cambridge: Cambridge University Press, pp. 185–200).

Newell, A. and Simon, H. (1961). "Computer Simulation of Human Thinking," *Science* 134: 2011–17.

—— (1976). "Computer Science as Empirical Inquiry: Symbols and Search," *Communications of the Association for Computing Machinery* 19: 113–26.

Noë, A. (2004). *Action in Perception* (Cambridge: MIT Press).

Oaksford, M. and Chater, N. (1994). "A Rational Analysis of the Selection Task as Optimal Data Selection," *Psychological Review* 101: 608–31.

O'Regan, J. and Noë, A. (2001). "A Sensorimotor Account of Vision and Visual Consciousness," *Behavioral and Brain Sciences* 24: 939–1031.

Piaget, J. (1954). *The Construction of Reality in the Child* (New York: Basic Books).

Pinker, S. (1997). *How the Mind Works* (New York: W. W. Norton & Company, Inc.).

Prinz, J. and Barsalou, L. (2000). "Steering a Course for Embodied Representation," in E. Dietrich and A. Markman (eds.) *Cognitive Dynamics: Conceptual Change in Humans and Machines* (Cambridge: MIT Press, pp. 51–77).

Quine, W. (1951). "The Two Dogmas of Empiricism," *Philosophical Review* 60: 20–43.

Ramsey, W., Stich, S., and Rumelhart, D. (eds.) (1991). *Philosophy and Connectionist Theory* (Hillsdale: Lawrence Erlbaum Associates).

Rauscher, F., Krauss, R., and Chen, Y. (1996). "Gesture, Speech, and Lexical Access: The Role of Lexical Movements in Speech Perception," *Psychological Science* 7: 226–31.

Richardson, D., Spivey, M. and Cheung, J. (2001). "Motor Representations in Memory and Mental Models: Embodiment in Cognition," *Proceedings of the Twenty-third Annual Meeting of the Cognitive Science Society*: 867–72.

Rizzolatti, G. and Craighero, L. (2004). "The Mirror-Neuron System," *Annual Review of Neuroscience* 27: 169–92.

Rosenfeld, A. (1988). "Computer Vison: Basic Principles," *Proceedings of the IEEE* 76: 863–8.

Rowlands, M. (1995). "Against Methodological Solipsism: The Ecological Approach," *Philosophical Psychology* 8: 5–24.

—— (1999). *The Body in Mind: Understanding Cognitive Processes* (Cambridge: Cambridge University Press).

Rumelhart, D. and McClelland, J. (1986). "On Learning the Past Tenses of English Verbs," in J. McClelland, D. Rumelhart, and the PDP Research Group (eds.) *Parallel Distributed Processing: Explorations in the Microstructure of Cognition, Vol. II* (Cambridge: MIT Press, pp. 216–71).

Rupert, R. (2004). "Challenges to the Hypothesis of Extended Cognition," *Journal of Philosophy* 101: 1–40.

Searle, J. (1980). "Minds, Brains, and Programs," *Behavioral and Brain Sciences* 3: 417–24.

Segal, G. (1989). "Seeing What is Not There," *Philosophical Review* 98: 189–214.

Shapiro, L. (1992). "Darwin and Disjunction: Foraging Theory and Univocal Assignments of Content," in D. Hull, M. Forbes and K. Okruhlik (eds.), *PSA 1992*, vol. 1 (East Lansing, MI: Philosophy of Science Association: 469–80).

—— (1993). "Content, Kinds, and Individuation in Marr's Theory of Vision," *The Philosophical Review* 102: 489–514.

—— (1997a). "A Clearer Vision," *Philosophy of Science* 64: 131–53.

—— (1997b). "Junk Representations," *The British Journal for the Philosophy of Science* 48: 345–61.

—— (1999). "Presence of Mind," in V. Hardcastle (ed.), *Biology Meets Psychology: Constraints, Connections, Conjectures* (Cambridge: MIT Press, pp. 83–98).

—— (2004). *The Mind Incarnate* (Cambridge: MIT Press).

—— (2007). "The Embodied Cognition Research Programme," *Philosophy Compass* 2: 338–46.

—— (2008a). "Symbolism, Embodiment, and the Broader Debate," in M. de Vega, A. Glenberg, and A. Graesser (eds.) *Symbols and Embodiment: Debates on Meaning and Cognition* (Oxford: Oxford University Press, pp. 57–74).

—— (2008b). "Making Sense of Mirror Neurons," *Synthese* 167: 439–56.

—— (2009). "A Review of Frederick Adams and Kenneth Aizawa: *The Bounds of Cognition*," *Phenomenology and the Cognitive Sciences* 8: 267–73.

—— (forthcoming). "Embodied Cognition," in E. Margolis, R. Samuels, and S. Stich (eds.) *Oxford Handbook of Philosophy and Cognitive Science* (Oxford: Oxford University Press).

Shapiro, L. and Spaulding, S. (2009). "Review of Andy Clark: *Supersizing the Mind: Embodiment, Action, and Cognitive Extension*," *Notre Dame Philosophical Reviews*, available at http://ndpr.nd.edu/.

Slobin, D. (1996). "From 'Thought and Language' to 'Thinking for Speaking'," in J. Gumperz and S. Levinson (eds.) *Rethinking Linguistic Relativity* (Cambridge: Cambridge University Press, pp. 70–96).

Smith, E. and Medin, D. (1981). *Categories and Concepts* (Cambridge: Harvard University Press).

Smith, L. and Samuelson, L. (2003). "Different is Good: Connectionism and Dynamic Systems Theory Are Complementary Emergentist Approaches to Development," *Developmental Science* 6: 434–9.

Smith, L. and Thelen, E. (2003). "Development as a Dynamic System," *Trends in Cognitive Sciences* 7: 343–8.

Sober, E. (1999). "Testability," *Proceedings and Addresses of the APA* 73: 47–76.

Spencer, J., Thomas, M., and McClelland, J. (eds.) (2009). *Toward a Unified Theory of Development: Connectionism and Dynamic Systems Theory Re-Considered* (New York: Oxford University Press).

Stampe, D. (1977). "Toward a Causal Theory of Linguistic Representation," in P. French, T. Uehling, and H. Wettstein (eds.) *Midwest Studies in Philosophy 2* (Minneapolis: Minnesota University Press, pp. 42–63).

Stanley, J. and Williamson, T. (2001). "Knowing How," *Journal of Philosophy* 98: 411–44.

Sternberg, S. (1969). "Memory Scanning: Mental Processes Revealed by Reaction-Time Experiments," *American Scientist* 57: 421–57.

Stich, S. (1983). *From Folk Psychology to Cognitive Science* (Cambridge: MIT Press).

Thelen, E. and Smith, L. (1994). *A Dynamic Systems Approach to the Development of Cognition and Action* (Cambridge: MIT Press).

Thelen, E., Schöner, G., Scheier, C., and Smith, L. (2001). "The Dynamics of Embodiment: A Field Theory of Infant Perseverative Reaching," *Behavioral and Brain Sciences* 24: 1–86.

Tversky, B. (2009). "Spatial Cognition: Embodied and Situated," in P. Robbins and M. Aydede (eds.), *Cambridge Handbook of Situated Cognition* (Cambridge: Cambridge University Press, pp. 201–16).

Van Gelder, T. (1995). "What Might Cognition Be, If Not Computation," *Journal of Philosophy* 92: 345–81.

—— (1998). "The Dynamical Hypothesis in Cognitive Science," *Behavioral and Brain Sciences* 21: 615–65.

Varela, F., Thompson, E., and Rosch, E. (1991). *The Embodied Mind: Cognitive Science and Human Experience* (Cambridge: MIT Press).

Von Eckardt, B. (1995). *What is Cognitive Science?* (Cambridge: MIT Press).

Whorf, B. (1956). *Language, Thought and Reality: Selected Writings of Benjamin Lee Whorf*, J. Carroll (ed.) (Cambridge: MIT Press).

Wilson, M. (2002). "Six Views of Embodied Cognition," *Psychological Bulletin and Review* 9: 625–36.

Wilson, R. (1994). "Wide Computationalism," *Mind* 103: 351–72.

—— (2004). *Boundaries of the Mind. The Individual in the Fragile Sciences: Cognition* (Cambridge: Cambridge University Press).

Wilson, R. and Clark, A. (2009). "How to Situate Cognition: Letting Nature Take its Course," in P. Robbins and M. Aydede (eds.) *Cambridge Handbook of Situated Cognition* (Cambridge: Cambridge University Press, pp. 55–77).

Wittgenstein, L. (1953/1958). *Philosophical Investigations*, 3rd ed., E. Anscombe (tr.) (Oxford: Blackwell).

Zwaan, R. and Madden, C. (2005). "Embodied Sentence Comprehension," in D. Pecher and R. A. Zwaan (eds.) *The Grounding of Cognition: The Role of Perception and Action in Memory, Language, and Thinking* (Cambridge: Cambridge University Press, pp. 224–45).

INDEX

A-not-B error 57–9, 61, 114, 126–7
action-sentence compatibility effect
102–4, 106–8, 111, 203
Adams, F. 106–7, 163, 176, 178–82,
184–91, 193, 199–200, 208–9
affordance 98, 100–3, 106, 112, 203,
206
Aizawa, K. 163, 169–72, 176, 178–82,
184–91, 193, 199–200, 208–9
ambient optic array 31–3
Argument against colors in the world
84
Argument for wide computationalism
192
Argument from envatment 161–3,
165, 169, 175, 177–8, 181
Barsalou, L. 95, 98–9, 101, 104–5,
108, 145–8
basic concepts 87–90, 112, 206
Bechtel, W. 145–7
Beer, R. 115, 124–30, 133, 135–9,
142, 144, 149–52, 154–7, 196, 207
behavior-based robotics 139
behaviorism 38
bimodal neurons 109
Block, N. 170–72

Boroditsky, L. 72–8, 80–1, 85–6,
89–90, 108
Brooks, R. 68, 137–42, 144, 150–7,
207
canonical neurons 109–11, 113, 206
categorical perception 127–9, 133,
207
Chalmers, D. 48, 179, 182–3, 185–6,
188, 194, 197–8, 200
Chinese Room 95–8, 101
Clark, A. 61–3, 65–9, 123, 152–4,
157, 162–3, 174–86, 188, 191,
193–200, 207–9
color 81–6, 92, 112–13, 202–3, 205
color conception 82–5
computational vision 20–1, 35, 53, 58,
120, 191
concept 70–2, 74–8
conception 72, 77–8
connectionism: as challenge to standard
cognitive science 5, 29, 41–8, 50,
52, 91, 113, 115, 118–19, 128,
155, 207, 209–10; and dynamical
systems 125–6;
constitution v. causation 65–6, 159–61,
170–2, 174–5

contingent intracranialism 163, 178, 185
coupling 81–3, 117, 122–4, 139, 146–7, 175–6, 179–182, 193, 203
coupling-constitution fallacy 179–82
Dawson, M. 27, 44–5, 50
derived content 187
descriptive framework 9
disparity 21–2, 24–5, 29, 41, 64, 90, 93, 204
Dretske, F. 97, 143–5, 147–8, 151, 186–7
dynamical explanation 133
Dynamical hypothesis 118–19, 123–4, 126, 157
dynamical systems theory 56, 67–8, 115–16, 118–19, 122, 124, 126–8, 135–7, 149, 156, 207, 209
ecological psychology 5, 29, 38, 100, 207
embodied action 52, 54–5
emergence 59, 61, 117
enactive approach 55
explanation 133–7
first-generation cognitive science 91, 93
Fodor, J. 11, 26–7, 38, 41, 47, 92, 187
Gallese, V. 109–10, 113
General Problem Solver 7, 12, 120, 140–1
Gertler, B. 197–9
gesture 173–8, 180, 182, 185, 199
Gibson, J. J. 5, 29–41, 49–50, 52, 63–4, 100–1, 113, 115, 124, 139, 164–6
Glenberg, A. 95–108, 111–13, 203–5
Goldin-Meadow, S. 173–4
Gregory, R. 20, 39
Hatfield, G. 37, 39–41, 45–6, 49–50, 113, 115, 207
Haugeland, J. 27
Hein, A. 171
Held, R. 171
Holyoak, K. 26
horizon cuts 34, 38
Hurley, S. 26
Huygens, C. 118
Hypothesis of embedded cognition (HEMC) 194–7

Hypothesis of extended cognition (HEC) 194–7
Indexical hypothesis 98, 100–2, 104, 107, 112, 203
intentionality 222
interaural time difference 93, 205
intrinsic content 186, 188–9
invariant 30, 32–6, 38–9, 49, 63–5, 165–6
inverse optics 21, 29, 33, 49
Johnson, M. 86–94, 110–13, 203–6
Kelso, S. 117, 126
Lakoff, G. 86–94, 109–13, 203–6
language of thought 11, 47, 50, 97, 99, 154
likelihood 79–80
linguistic determinism 71–2, 75–6, 78, 81, 85–6, 89
MacKay, D. 166
marks of the cognitive 184–6, 200, 208
Marr, D. 21–2, 24, 58, 77–8, 204
meshing 98, 101, 103, 106, 112, 203, 206
metaphor 86–8, 92, 94, 112–13
mirror neurons 94, 109–11, 113, 206
motion parallax 64
Motley crew argument 189–90, 193
Myin, E. 167–168
Newell, A., 7–9, 11–13, 18–19, 119, 140
Noë, A. 65–6, 164–72, 179, 200, 208
noncognitive computationalism 37, 39, 40, 49, 207
O'Regan, J. 65, 66, 164–70, 208
optical flow 63
organism-bounded process 195, 197
organism-centered process 195, 197
parity principle 179, 184, 186
perception-action cycle 53, 55
perceptual symbol 98–105, 112
perseverative behavior 57–8, 60, 207
Piaget, J. 57–9
Pinker, S. 27
Poggio, T. 21–2, 24, 204
Prinz, J. 145–8
process-constituent fallacy 181
Pylyshyn, Z. 38, 41, 47

representation 143–9
representation-hungry problems, 152–3, 155, 207–8
representational skepticism 137, 141, 149–51, 153
representational vehicle 154–5
resonate 30, 35–9, 42
robotics 64, 116, 133, 136–7, 139, 156
Rosch, E. 52, 67–9, 81, 112–13, 202–5
Rowlands, M. 50
Rupert, R. 190–1, 193–6, 208
Searle, J., 95–7, 101
second-generation cognitive science 91–94
secondary quality 55
sensibility judgments 103–4, 106
sensorimotor contingency 165–166: see also sensory motor dependency
sensorimotor dependency 65, 165: see also sensory motor contingency
sensorimotor theory 165, 169, 172
Shakey 138–41
Shapiro, Lawrence, 6, 69, 181
Simon, H. 7–9, 11–13, 18–19, 120, 140
situatedness 116, 124–7, 139, 141–2, 155–6
Slobin, D. 75
Smith, L. 3, 56–60, 69, 78, 115, 126, 142
Sober, E. 79
solipsism 26–7, 35, 50

stereo vision 21, 29, 64
stereopsis see stereo vision
Sternberg, S. 7, 14–19, 91
strong internal representation 152–3
structure in light 30
subsumption architecture 68, 139–41, 156
symbol 9–12; amodal, 98–9, 104–6, 108, 204–5; modal, 98–9, 101–2, 104–6, 108, 204–5
symbol grounding problem 95–7, 101, 105, 113
testability 79–81, 110, 204, 206
Thelen, E. 3, 56–60, 66–9, 114–15, 126, 142, 156
Thompson, E. 52, 67–9, 81, 112–13, 202–5
Toribio, J. 123, 152–3, 157, 207
Tversky, B. 174
Van Gelder, T. 115, 118–20, 122–5, 127, 133, 141, 144, 146, 149–50, 157
Varela, F. 52, 67–9, 81, 112–13, 202–5
Von Eckardt, B. 27
Watt governor 37, 119, 121, 123, 141–9, 176
weak internal representation 152–3
Whorf, B. 71–2, 74, 86
wide computationalism 179, 191–3, 196, 200, 209
Wilson, M. 69
Wilson, R. 179, 181–2, 191–3, 196, 199–200, 208–9
Wittgenstein, L. 78